Lake Superior to Manitoba by Canoe

Lake Superior to Manitoba by Canoe

Hap Wilson

Mapping the Route into the Heart of the Continent

Firefly Books

A FIREFLY BOOK

Published by Firefly Books Ltd. 2017

First printing

Publisher Cataloging-in-Publication Data (U.S.)
A CIP record for this title is available from Library of Congress

Library and Archives Canada Cataloguing in Publication
A CIP record for this title is available from Library and Archives Canada

Published in the United States by
Firefly Books (U.S.) Inc.
P.O. Box 1338, Ellicott Station
Buffalo, New York 14205

Published in Canada by
Firefly Books Ltd.
50 Staples Avenue, Unit 1
Richmond Hill, Ontario L4B 0A7

Cover and interior design: Hartley Millson
Copy editor: Gillian Watts

Printed in China

Canada We acknowledge the financial support of the Government of Canada.

The author, publisher and sponsors accept no responsibility for injury or loss of life while using the information in this publication. *Lake Superior to Manitoba by Canoe* is intended for use as a reference only. It is the sole responsibility of paddlers and kayakers to determine whether they are qualified to safely handle fast or rough waters and difficult trails and road conditions, and to accurately assess travel conditions in relation to the material in this book. Before choosing to navigate rapids or large open waters, the users of this guidebook must first evaluate water volumes, water and air temperatures, the skill levels of all participants, the amount of freeboard (load weight), the value and waterproofing of the load, the degree of isolation, the feasibility of rescue and the level of risk.

The opinions expressed in this publication are those of the author and in no way reflect the views of the publisher, the Trans Canada Trail, sponsors or other contributors.

DEDICATION

Bruises, cuts, mud, bug bites, sweat, tears . . . and still beautiful despite what I put her through. To my wife, Andrea, in appreciation for her love and support.

Contents

Foreword

Path of the Paddle and the Politics of Wilderness

Great ideas often come from grassroots simplicity — there resides an enthusiastic energy and a singular, unblemished purpose. Add to this excitement an ulterior motive, a time constraint, bureaucratic complexities and political objectives, and the initial fervor and purity of the idea quickly wane. This is what happened to the Trans Canada Trail initiative to create a Canadian water trail, aptly named "Path of the Paddle."

In 2009 the Ontario section of the Trans Canada Trail approached me to design and map out a linear canoe route from Thunder Bay to the Manitoba border. Before that I had felt cautious appreciation for the national trail system, as it seemed focused primarily on repurposing defunct rail lines and eventually, in many instances, encouraged mechanized travel — a far cry, it seemed, from the sanctity and soul-touching imminence of the ideal woodland trail. But a water trail certainly piqued my interest.

The Trans Canada Trail (TCT) was born in 1992, during Canada's 125th anniversary. Officials want it completed by 2017, the country's 150th birthday — a monumental task to be sure. The "Great Trail," as it is promoted today, is planned to connect all three oceans, a distance of 24,000 kilometers (15,000 miles), making it the world's longest single trail. But on paper anything can look good, or easy. The mélange of lakes, rivers and muskeg that defines Northwest Ontario, according to railroad historians, stalled the construction of the Canadian Pacific Railway a century and a half ago. "Construction through the rock and muskeg of the Canadian Shield almost equaled in difficulty the engineering feats of construction through the mountains of British Columbia."[1] The administrators of the TCT shared the same complex challenges as their predecessors. A land-based trail from Thunder Bay to Manitoba would take too long to construct, be extraordinarily expensive to build and cost too much to maintain over time. The notion of "building" a water trail was brilliant and entirely feasible. I accepted the offer to chart a truly Canadian water trail, on the assumption that politics and the bureaucracy would be, perhaps, silent partners at best. That did not happen.

Why a Water Trail?

Canada has the largest still mostly intact aboriginal trail system in the world, chiefly canoe routes. That's quite an achievement, considering how devastating today's industrial intrusion into wilderness areas worldwide has been. First Nations call summer canoe routes *nastawgan*; in Northwest Ontario they are known as *onigum*. Winter trails, or *bon ka naw*, often follow natural geological formations, while summer portage routes allow free movement to and from traditional hunting and trade territories, following prescribed water trails. These were Canada's first trails. In this context, then, it was a wise decision by the TCT to include the canoe route as part of the national trail system. The water trails are several thousand years old; they existed long before the European invasion and the fervor of colonial exploration, trade and settlement.

When we think of the word *trails*, we often don't think about canoe routes as such. In so doing, we omit an integral part of Canadian history and cultural significance — the romantic history of voyageur, coureur de bois and Oblate priest; canoes laden with furs, supplies and settlers heading for points east or west; and life on the trail as depicted in the poignant paintings of Paul Kane and Frances Hopkins. Trails traveled for centuries by our first peoples should naturally be a respected component of the Great Trail.

It would be a water trail from Thunder Bay to Manitoba to connect the existing land-based trails at either end — a less than modest distance

---

1 Omer Lavallée, "Canadian Pacific Railway," The Canadian Encyclopedia, revised April 3, 2015, http://thecanadianencyclopedia. com/en/article/canadian-pacific-railway/.

Author Hap Wilson at White Otter Castle.

BILL MASON - Born 1929 in Winnipeg; Died 1988 at Meech Lake Quebec.
The "patron saint of canoeing", Bill Mason was a Canadian naturalist, artist, author, conservationist and filmmaker. Noted primarily for his popular "Path of the Paddle" canoeing books and films, Bill developed particular techniques for serious paddling and a traditional camping lifestyle. Bill's films can be viewed for free on the internet through the National Film Board of Canada website.

of 500 kilometers. However, that distance was calculated as the crow flies. The end product would soon unfold over a thousand kilometers, given that no water trail can be knitted together in a straight line. It was a daunting challenge, to be sure, and one that would go through many phases both frustrating and enlightening. As a pathfinder, cartographer and wilderness explorer, I knew that this type of project, although somewhat formidable, had to adhere to a workable formula in order to maintain continuity and integrity — nothing new to me, as I had been doing this type of exploration for half a century. But this was different.

The Trans Canada Trail system operated on a whole different level, a level that worked on a local scale and through the recruitment of volunteers. The TCT at the time was made up of more than 400 community trails, each developed and managed locally by a trail group. This model worked well on a small scale, but the proposed water trail from Lake Superior to Manitoba would comprise 5 percent of the entire national trail — a very significant link spanning several administrative jurisdictions. The first two years went rather well; it was all coming together neatly and a route had been selected after intense field investigation.

And we now had a name for the trail. I was sitting in the lounge of the Riverview Inn in Dryden with local canoe guru Garth Gillis and Vicky Kurz, from the economic development office, pondering what to call it. It was Garth who came up with the name "Path of the Paddle," in honor of canoeing icon Bill Mason, who had coined the phrase in his own works. It was brilliant, and fitting, because Bill grew up canoeing part of the very route selected for the national water trail. I contacted the Mason family immediately, and with their blessing, the name was approved.

Then things changed. New TCT officials took over and Path of the Paddle became an incorporated entity; it was caught up in the political objective of completing the Great Trail by the 2017 deadline. First Nations were not appropriately or fairly consulted, selected routes were arbitrarily changed (several times), and too many opinions and boardroom discussions left Path of the Paddle gridlocked. What transpired next would be a convenient quick fix and an easy solution to the stalemate, with little regard for the quality of the experience — simply drawing a line on the map. At the time of writing, Path of the Paddle is entangled in a complex web of land issues. The "quick fix" route simply was intended to follow Lake of the Woods south to Rainy Lake and then east to join up with the Pigeon River.[2] But that route had been initially avoided for many good reasons, in particular because Path of the Paddle was supposed to connect all the main towns between Thunder Bay and the Manitoba border. Instead of ending the water trail on the Canadian side of the border to join up with the TCT land trail at Pigeon River Provincial Park, the route now ended[3] at the Grand Portage on the American side, in Minnesota: a 14-kilometer historic trail that few people would entertain the thought of lugging canoes and gear over. The Trans Canada Trail was no longer an all-Canadian trail.

To its credit, the TCT has orchestrated a symbolic effort at uniting the people of Canada with a singular linear trail. There are many unique trail sections constructed by dedicated groups and individuals. But the canoe trail — the *onigum* — is a sacred entity that served our first peoples well, long before the notion of the trail became politicized, during a time when there were no boundaries, private property or administrative districts. To paddle its waters is a privilege, not a right, as some may believe.

Lake Superior to Manitoba by Canoe is a grassroots version of Path of the Paddle as it was initially intended — the very best Canada has to offer. It is a merger of landscapes, people and history. It describes a trail that all people can wander whether they ply its waters or not. Perhaps this journey will help us understand a little more about the Canadian wilderness. It is also an epic six-year adventure story, a graphic depiction of life on the wilderness trail as it unfolded. The cartography embraces a lost art form, with maps hand-drawn from field notes and calculations, much like those drawn by the early surveyors David Thompson and Joseph Tyrrell. Journal entries portray the trials and tribulations and the beauty of exploration and mapping. Most of all, this book aspires to impress upon its readers the importance of protecting and cherishing the magnificence at the heart of the Canadian landscape — a soulful place like no other on the face of this earth.

The Art of Pathfinding

Pathfinding, a skill attributed to early explorers, is all but a lost art. GPS (the Global Positioning System) has replaced our need to depend on basic, once inherent navigational abilities. Even the term *pathfinding* now refers to solving mazes and algorithms, tracing trails through computer games or exploring last-resort techniques to reduce the thermal noise of mirrors and suspensions in cryogenic gravitational wave detectors. It no longer has anyhing to do with finding your way through the woods.

Less than a century ago, the network of canoe routes across northern Ontario was utilized by canoe brigades of rangers stationed at the various fire-lookout towers. Prospectors, trappers and sportsmen plied the waters for their own purposes. Before them, the trails were well traveled by First Nations. Since then, many of these routes have been lost to neglect; portages have been logged over, razed by fire, damaged by storms or just allowed to revert back to nature. Locating these centuries-old trails is something of a lost art, and something I take great pride in as part of a route survey. The telltale signs may be elusive: an old axe blaze grown over; perhaps a cairn of small rocks denoting the trail entrance; sometimes an old tin can or a boot no longer serviceable nailed to a tree. Often there's nothing at all — nothing until you walk in a short distance from shore and discover a trodden path, kept partially open by moose or other animals, mostly obscured by fallen logs and other forest detritus, barely discernable, but there all the same.

There is no money in the Ontario coffers for maintaining these canoe routes on Crown land. Even in established provincial parks such as La Verendrye — an integral component of the Boundary Waters

---

2 Conversations with Garth Gillis (October 2016) who had been conscripted by Ontario TCT to help work out route changes.
3 See note about final route changes to Omimi Trail.

Heritage Waterway — portages and campsites have not been serviced in decades. Whatever maintenance happens is purely incidental. Many of the routes illustrated in this book have been out of use for a long time. Canoe route information obtained from the Ministry of Natural Resources was long out of date, inaccurate and poorly scripted. I relied on topographical charts (1:50,000, as well as the 1:100,000 series maps), a Garmin GPS and hours of scanning Google Earth.

In the past, scouting routes along small creeks or rivers was a hit-or-miss operation. Sometimes there wouldn't be enough water to float a canoe, or the waterway would be jammed with fallen timber, clogged with floating bog material or even non-existent. This could take up a lot of exploration time, not to mention the effort involved in dragging a canoe through rough terrain, then having to retrace your steps for several hours or even days. Google Maps allowed me to analyze the breadth and volume of a creek, note any elevation changes and make alternative choices before actually physically going there. This information, paired with known routes (new or suspected), allowed me to organize the many field explorations it took to complete the entire route system.

I did take it upon myself to clear portages and campsites that required identification. In many cases this had to be done so that others could find them in the following years. With only simple tools — an axe, a saw and brush loppers — the work was slow and tedious, aided in several cases by my wife, Andrea, and my children, Alexa and Christopher. The routes selected best fit the established criteria in terms of variety, stunning landscapes, cultural and historic curiosity, and level of adventure. It was also paramount, as prescribed by Trans Canada Trail protocol, to design a route that would include the towns of Atikokan, Ignace, Dryden and Kenora, along with First Nations communities.

The overall route was not mapped out from one end to the other but rather in segments, depending on the season and when I could get away from our busy expedition and trail-building schedules. The reader will notice that the journal dates bound back and forth from season to season and year to year. The journal notes are not meant to form an unbroken daily diary but are an intermittent account of some notable events that define the challenges of pathfinding.

Charting the Route: The Process

By the time I climb into the canoe I've exhausted the search for helpful written material. I've even relied on 300-year-old maps for traditional routes or to glean possible helpful information. The next step is to map out a route that avoids things such as logging clearcuts, mine tailings and developments.

Once on the water, I keep both camera and journal handy for note-taking and referencing points of interest. Campsite locations are also explored — they have to fit sustainability criteria — and portages are paced for distance (GPS and mechanical wheels are not reliable in such cases). New portages take time to explore, and rock cairns, dolmen markers and old tree blazes sometimes indicate earlier use by trappers or First Nations. Charting and grading whitewater rapids using the International River Grading System (IRGS) requires an eye for water-level vagaries and finding early takeout points during high water. Rapids are sometimes run several times, in both high and low water, so that safe navigation channels can be mapped.

It's a lot of work on top of the normal canoe-trip stuff. I often find myself zigzagging down a lake as I explore potential campsites, climb ridges that might offer a viewpoint, or meander off on side routes or through fens, hoping for some classic wildlife shots. I'll GPS specific reference points such as the start and end of a portage trail, but for the most part I still rely on 1:50,000 topographical charts for navigation. The information collected is guarded in a waterproof Pelican case. I fine-tune my notes or redraw rapids diagrams at night by candle-lantern while sipping good Scotch from a brass pannikin.

Introduction

"Heart of the Continent" refers to the geographic landscape that begins at Lake Superior in the east, rises abruptly in a series of dolomite-capped mesas, and then gradually descends westward to the Great Plains, beyond the Manitoba border. Jointly promoted as a tourist attraction by Ontario and Minnesota, it is considered one of the most challenging destinations for the adventurer. Aside from Quetico Provincial Park in Ontario, however, most of the destinations have been promoted on the American side of the border. Minnesota has long acknowledged the benefits of non-mechanized tourism, specifically through its history of wilderness protection; the Boundary Waters Canoe Area Wilderness and Superior National Forest are prime examples. Ontario, conversely, has preferred to privilege corporate interests and traditional consumption-based tourism.

The challenge for this author was to chart a single path that opened up old canoe routes (or created new ones) for the Trans Canada Trail (TCT). The Path of the Paddle would effectively close the gap between the TCT's land trails, which are separated by 1,000 kilometers (620 miles). The criteria I established for the route were somewhat daunting: (1) to avoid long portages and big lakes and bypass logging and mining operations, roads and other developments; (2) to highlight cultural sites and scenic areas, vistas and hiking opportunities, the best places for wildlife viewing, waterfalls, some hair-raising (but not too dangerous) whitewater and maybe a couple of token ghost stories; and (3) to connect with the communities along the way. After six years in the field, I can honestly claim to have met all those goals and more. The emphasis is on uniqueness. What makes a route special, perhaps more so than any other in Canada? What are its alluring qualities for the modern-day explorer?

In a region that has thrived for nearly three centuries on resource development and extraction, from the quest for furs to modern-day clearcut logging, mining, river diversions and coal-fired power plants, you might assume that finding any wilderness at all would be an elusive quest. Quite the contrary. Although Path of the Paddle occasionally edges close to developed areas, the wilderness portions are outstanding. Places such as Quetico attained protected status in 1913, the same year that Minnesota's Superior National Forest and Boundary Waters Canoe Area gained national prominence as wilderness preserves.

Having traveled extensively in remote places across the country, I was surprised at the actual untrammeled nature of the region. It offers the best of everything. Even though this singular linear water trail can be paddled in its entirety in either direction, it is not one route. It is a collection of many routes, and therefore I recommend that it be approached selectively. Within the seven route sections there are wind and waterflow patterns that affect which direction to travel. Even the mode of travel may differ, from traditional stock recreational canoes to touring kayaks or standup paddleboards. Whatever you may be looking for, you will find it along the Path of the Paddle and its adjoining spur routes.

There are two dozen rivers and creeks, both grand and unassertive. Some are challenging while others charm and relax with their air of secrecy. You will find mystic paintings on rock walls, towering cliffs and eagle nests; boulders the size of houses dropped by retreating glaciers, like pieces of some terrestrial board game played by giants; emerald lakes of pure, clear water and untrammeled forests; ocean-like vistas and ragged coastlines; shipwrecks and old fur-trading posts, campsites centuries old, a log castle, an abandoned mine, lakes choked with wild rice, waterfalls that rival the height and majesty of Niagara, a borderless path into another country. Countless ghosts (true!). They're all here in this compendium of Canadian treasures. Within the wild landscapes, the folds of gray granite and indigo lakes, the old-growth pine forests and portage trails, you will find adventure here.

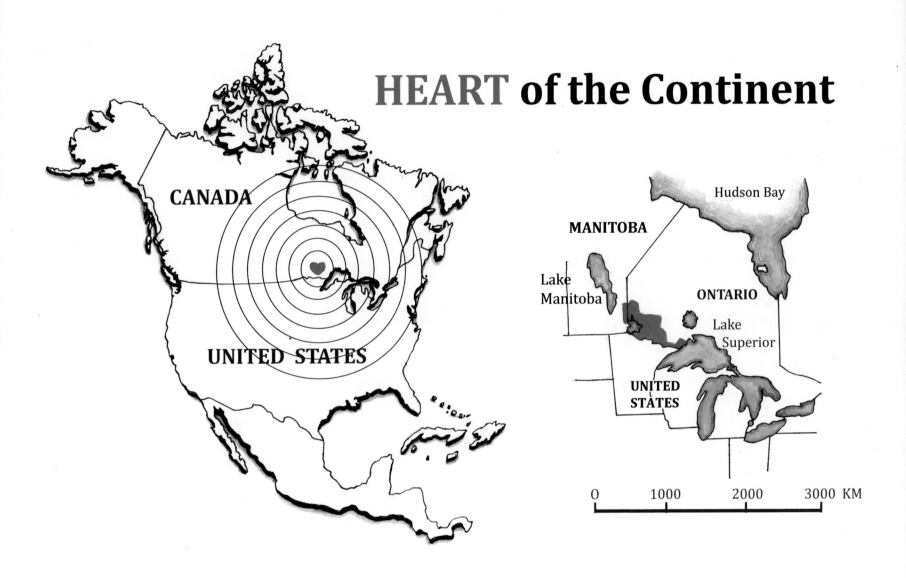

HEART of the Continent

Hudson Bay

MANITOBA

Lake Manitoba

ONTARIO

Lake Superior

CANADA

UNITED STATES

UNITED STATES

| 0 | 1000 | 2000 | 3000 KM |

Do not follow where the path may lead. Go instead where there is no path and leave a trail.
— Ralph Waldo Emerson

Chapter 1

The Heart of Canada

Geographically, Path of the Paddle territory lies in the center of Canada. For the First Nations it can be celebrated as land created on the turtle's back after the great flood; for the fur-trade empires it was the pulsing heartbeat of a new nation, with trade routes branching out in all directions. Lake Superior was the stepping-off place for lands to the west and northwest, the canoe a ubiquitous component of trade and the lifestyle of the voyageurs. These heroes, much celebrated in music, folklore and story, led a colorful life full of adventure, freedom and revelry.

> *I could carry, paddle, walk and sing with any man I ever saw.*
> *I have been twenty-four years a canoe man, and forty-one years*
> *in service; no portage was ever too long for me, fifty songs I could*
> *sing. I have saved the lives of ten voyageurs, have had twelve wives*
> *and six running dogs. I spent all my money in pleasure. Were I*
> *young again I would spend my life the same way over. There is no*
> *life so happy as a voyageur's life!*[4]

The carefree, adventurous slant we give to the life of the voyageur, of the early explorers, the traders and the Oblate priests, is largely romanticizing. The voyageur life depicted in the paintings of Frances Hopkins and the sketches of C.W. Jefferies prompts us to believe that Canada back then was almost boringly light-hearted and easy, albeit colorful. But the heart of the nation beat furiously, primed by centuries of conflict, murder and deceit. The Ojibwe fought constantly with their western enemies the Sioux, and the skirmishes — battles fought on the turtle's back — were brutally deadly on both sides.

What Canada was to become would play out here: resolution of border disputes, rivalry between fur-trade companies, exploration of new territory and exploitation of resources, all between the plains of Manitoba and the Great Inland Sea. Far from the comforts of Montreal's trading houses, markets and women, life on the trail — and the opportunity to be a distinguished voyageur, to work for the Company — attracted young French-Canadian men, many of whom would perish in the wilderness.

Le Petit Nord

The land beyond the Grand Portage, known as *le petit nord* (the little north), was traversed by the burgeoning trade routes of the North West Company. It was a challenging but coveted occupation to be

---

4 Retired voyageur, quoted in James H. Baker, "Lake Superior," lecture to the Minnesota Historical Society, 1879, in Collections of the Minnesota Historical Society, vol. 3 (MHS, 1880).

a *voyageur*, a "traveler" who moved furs and supplies over long distances between Montreal and Grand Portage, and later to Fort William on the Kaministiquia. Some voyageurs overwintered and often worked alongside the *coureurs des bois* (runners of the woods), *hivernants* who aspired to make new deals for the Company.

One-third of the voyageurs would become *hommes du nord* (northern men) who would go on to take supplies into the interior of the Little North. In the fall, inbound canoe brigades would haul trade goods and winter supplies to remote posts on Lake of the Woods and as far as Red River (Winnipeg), an arduous canoe trek from Fort William that would take 20 days to complete. Outbound canoe brigades laden with 90-pound bales of furs would take advantage of the spring high water to deliver their bounty to the depot, a trip of no more than 18 days over a distance of more than 1,000 kilometers. The average paddler today would take more than 50 days to complete the same trip!

Granted, we paddle for pure pleasure today. Voyageurs were driven by time, and pleasure was a bonus earned at the end of the trek. If there were no rapids to run, canoemen would be on the water by three a.m. or earlier, stopping at eight a.m. for a simple breakfast, often fish or venison procured along the way. Lunch was a wad of pemmican, probably traded from the Red River Métis. There was a pipe stop every hour or so until camp was made by ten p.m. Voyageurs averaged 55 strokes per minute — the same grueling pace that Andrea and I set when we race.

Most canoemen did not marry, chiefly because they were not reliable. Many took "wives" at transfer points and rendezvous posts, spontaneous arrangements made according to local customs, unbinding and opportunistic. Portage work became the testing ground of young men, forced to haul a minimum of two 90-pound packs on each carry, often pushing the limit to four or five packs. Hernias were common and often caused an excruciating death; add

to this broken limbs, compressed spines and severe rheumatism. No wonder many an early canoeman would sleep sitting up for fear that his heart would stop.

Most canoemen could not swim. It was far easier to run the rapids than to unload, portage through bug-infested scrub and then repack again at the end of the trail. Canoes often upset and men drowned. David Thompson writes in his journal about an attempt to run the Dalles des Morts — "Death Rapids" — a violent stretch of rapids on the Columbia River upstream from Revelstoke, British Columbia (now submerged beneath the waters of Lake Revelstoke Reservoir). The canoemen

> *preferred running the Dalles; they had not gone far then to avoid the ridge of waves which they ought to have kept. They took the apparent smooth water, were drawn into a whirlpool, which wheeled them round in its vortex, the canoe with the men clinging to it went down end foremost, and [they] were all drowned. At the foot of the Dalles, search was made for the bodies, but only one man was found, his body much mangled by the rocks.*

Allowed and encouraged by Company officials, the bawdy revelry that defined the gatherings at the rendezvous posts included gambling, feasting, heavy drinking, fights and impulsive marriages to local Native women. There were few rules or decrees or commandments that held the men responsible for their actions; it was characteristic and expected pleasure that in some way made up for the hardships of the work.

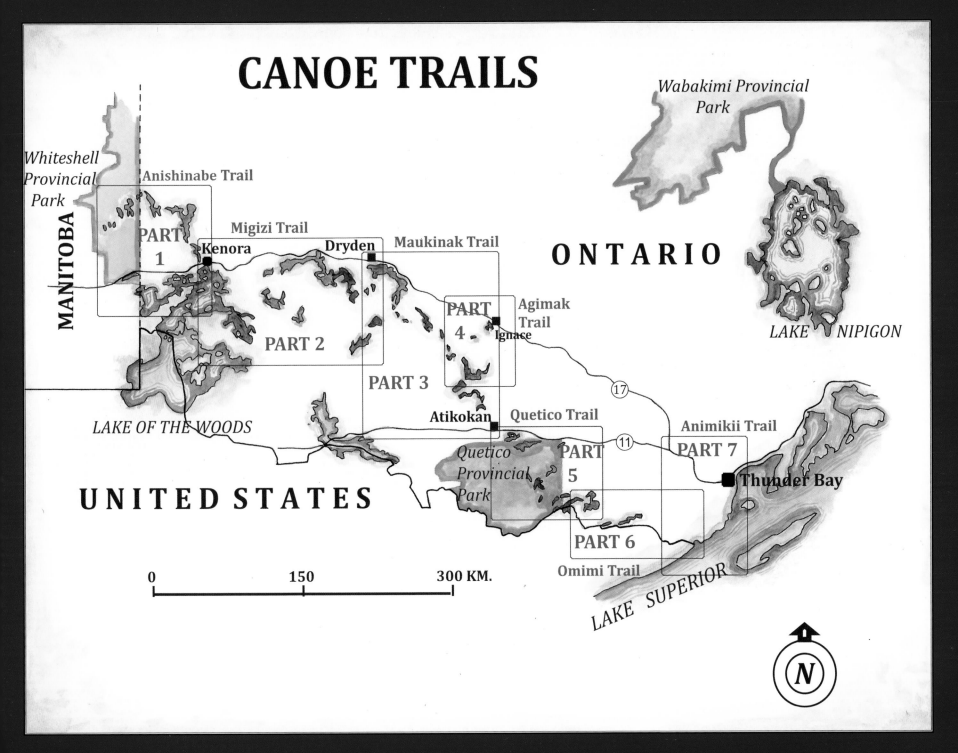

CANOE TRAILS

Wabakimi Provincial Park

Whiteshell Provincial Park

Anishinabe Trail

MANITOBA

PART 1

Migizi Trail

Kenora

Dryden

Maukinak Trail

ONTARIO

PART 2

PART 4

Agimak Trail

Ignace

LAKE NIPIGON

PART 3

LAKE OF THE WOODS

17

Atikokan

Quetico Trail

Animikii Trail

UNITED STATES

Quetico Provincial Park

PART 5

11

PART 7

Thunder Bay

PART 6

Omimi Trail

LAKE SUPERIOR

0   150   300 KM.

N

May your travels be crooked, winding, lonesome, dangerous, leading to the most amazing view.
May your mountains rise into and above the lands.
— Edward Abbey

Chapter 2

How To Use This Book

This book is primarily a guide to the Trans Canada Trail's Path of the Paddle canoe route as it was first designed. In no way does it represent the full inventory of what is available to the paddler or nature enthusiast. Time and space considered, it features the most practical and interesting linear canoe trail; it also includes the author's choice of challenging routes. The maps have been hand-drawn as accurately as possible. The detailed inset maps have been drawn from actual field assessments, while the portages have all been measured, often cleared, and accurately depicted on the maps.

Diagrams of specific rapids are not intended to make the running of whitewater easier for the inexperienced paddler. It is also important to remember that navigable channels may vary with water levels. Some rivers and lakes are under the influence of control dams, so their water levels can change at any time in the paddling season, depending on the amount of rainfall. It is suggested that the paddler use a secondary map and possibly a GPS to complement this guidebook.

A General Note about Adventure Canoeing

Paddlers often need a break, and that's the great thing about portaging — it offers the traveler a chance to rest, snack and stretch cramped legs. This book indicates some choice places to hike and explore the country away from the canoe corridor. Off-route hikes often take in high vistas, waterfalls and other features you wouldn't normally see if you simply stuck to the prescribed main trail.

As with any outdoor activity, there exist inherent risks (without some uncertainty and danger, life on the trail would be quite prosaic). Hiking and nature observation on their own pose little threat to life and limb, barring a sudden urge to free-climb a precipitous rock face in bare feet. Water sports, on the other hand, require at least a basic understanding of the skills required for personal safety and well-being.

Whitewater paddling and open-water kayaking can be dangerous fun. For each route in this guide, the applicable skill requirements or level of expertise is indicated. Please carefully read over the following section; it will help you decide which route matches your level of skill.

Water Levels and Hydrology Patterns

It is next to impossible to make a perfectly accurate average assessment of any river. The best I can do is to make the variables known to the paddler — forewarned is forearmed! The paddler's ability to adjust to environmental changes, including fluctuating water levels, is part of the overall skill required to make responsible and safe judgment calls. The information gathered in these pages regarding water levels has been based on average conditions that prevail from June through to early September, when channels are clearly defined. This period is considered the "normal" canoeing season.

High-Water Conditions
(typical during spring thaw, late April through May)

Extreme high-water conditions are very dangerous, and they render some of the detailed rapid charts in this book valueless. An exception is where they note spring-level portage landings above dangerous water, which are quite often different from normal summer takeout points. Most rapids will become unrecognizable — voluminous, often with flooded portage landings and very strong currents throughout. Because of the low temperatures of both water and air, classification of the route goes up a notch.

Creeks and small rivers without rapids are better to navigate in the early season, while larger rivers will present more difficult situations and greater risks. The advantages of high-water levels include smoother ledges, submerged rock gardens, exciting deepwater wave action, and straight-running channels. Concentration must focus less on spontaneous technical moves and more on keeping water out of the canoe. Obvious problems or risks involve longer rescue times because of the strong current, hypothermia, swamping by big waves, and the added danger of hitting snags (fallen timber, also called "sweepers" or "strainers"). It is best to check with local sources or the Ontario Ministry of Natural Resources (OMNR) office for current conditions.

Low-Water Conditions
(typically late July through September)

Water levels that are lower than those described in this book may necessitate more lining, wading or portaging. Rock gardens — characteristic of most lower Canadian Shield rivers — may become rockier, actually constricting main channels, while ledges become more pronounced, forming actual drop-offs. Obstacles or obstructions generally become more visible and main channels are better defined. The potential for getting hung up or broaching on "pillow rocks" (rocks just below the surface that push up the water slightly — easily missed if you aren't following the water patterns) means that good technique is necessary.

Because the water volume is lower, you have more adjustment time while maneuvering. Ferries and eddy turns have to be executed with diligence. Low-water conditions sometimes allow more playtime along rapids that are normally too difficult to run during high-flow periods. Those who possess good whitewater skills and creative technique also have an opportunity to shorten or eliminate some portages. Some creeks and small rivers lose their appeal quickly as water levels drop; rivers such as the Falcon should be run in the early season.

Skill Classifications

The following skill-level categories are predicated on the paddler's ability to safely handle a standard open recreational canoe, sea kayak or standup paddleboard. Each classification indicates the necessary skills required, suitable route characteristics and the types of difficulty or hazard that should be manageable.

Novice or Beginner
Skills Required

- Primary flat-water skills but little or no experience or knowledge of moving-water techniques.
- Capable but not proficient at navigating swifts or easy Class I rapids only.
- Technical rapids are avoided (or portaged around), but a higher grade may be attempted if accompanied by a more skilled paddler.
- Kayakers avoid large open-water crossings or dangerous coastlines.

Landscape Profile

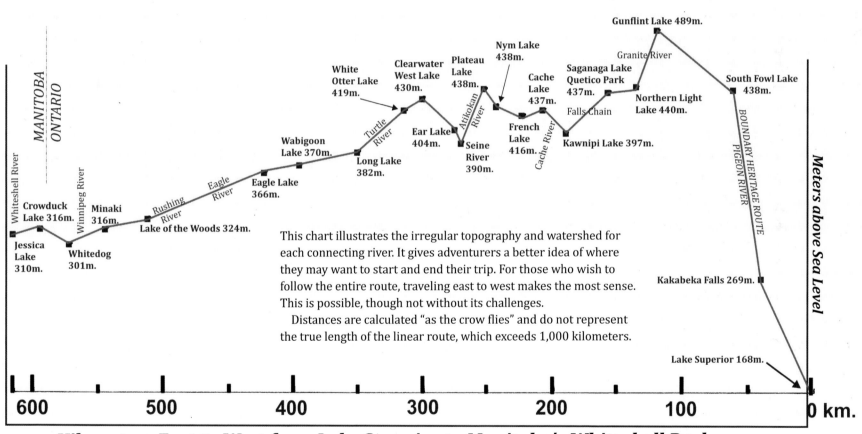

This chart illustrates the irregular topography and watershed for each connecting river. It gives adventurers a better idea of where they may want to start and end their trip. For those who wish to follow the entire route, traveling east to west makes the most sense. This is possible, though not without its challenges.

Distances are calculated "as the crow flies" and do not represent the true length of the linear route, which exceeds 1,000 kilometers.

Kilometers East to West from Lake Superior to Manitoba's Whiteshell Park

Running rapids on the Pigeon River.

Route Characteristics

- Predominantly flat water, with some river or creek links that may have swifts or very minor rapids with the option to portage.
- Portages not excessively long or difficult.
- Water temperature exceeds 16°C (60°F) from June through August.
- For sea kayakers, smaller lakes with numerous islands.
- Trips are shorter and close to access points.

Hazards or Concerns

- High winds on larger lakes.
- During buffer season, cold weather and water or a sudden rise in water levels on rivers.

Experienced Novice

Skills Required

- Basic whitewater skills.
- Proficiency with safely navigating Class I and Class I technical rapids; may attempt higher-class rapids if accompanied by more skilled paddler.
- Class II rapids and higher are portaged.
- Some basic lining skills (roping the canoe up or down rapids).
- Kayakers can safely navigate larger waves or swells that are less than 0.75 m. (2 ft), and make crossings of up to 2 km (1.2 mi).

Route Characteristics

- River or creek gradient usually consistent and gradual, with sporadic drops (beaver dams, heavy swifts, easy rapids).
- Portages generally easy, but with a few classic steep pitches, wetland

bogs or longer hauls (more than 1 km).

- Water temperatures above 16°C (60°F) during normal paddling season.
- For kayakers, larger lakes and easy portage routes.
- Trips generally 1 week to 10 days.

Hazards or Concerns

- High winds on larger lakes.
- During buffer season, cold weather and water or a sudden rise in water levels on rivers.
- Potential for capsizing in easy-grade rapids above or close to dangerous chutes, falls or continuous rapids.

Intermediate

Skills Required

- Proficiency in paddling skills.
- Ability to safely navigate up to Class II technical rapids without difficulty.
- Class III rapids run only with safety and rescue precautions in place and/or accompanied by an advanced paddler.
- Full understanding and application of technical maneuvers.
- Canoe extrication and rescue techniques mandatory.
- Kayakers can safely navigate smaller breaking waves or swells of 1 to 1.5 m and make open-water crossings of 2 to 5 km.
- Self-rescue techniques mandatory.

Route Characteristics

- Longer trips that may include spring high-water conditions, where water temperatures are lower than 16°C (60°F).
- Portages may be precipitous, longer than 2 km and partially obstructed or overgrown.

- Environmental conditions generally moderate.
- Kayakers may paddle Lake Superior under moderate conditions.

Hazards or Concerns

- Cold weather and cold water risks with longer paddling season.
- Greater risk of capsizing in larger rapids.
- Temptation to run more difficult rapids.
- Kayakers may get caught by sudden wind changes farther from the mainland.

Advanced or Expert

Skills Required

- Extensive whitewater experience.
- High-level skills, including all technical rescue and extrication procedures.
- Stamina and endurance under duress, with a high level of self-control.
- Kayakers are adept at self-rescue or roll recovery and can safely navigate extreme wave conditions.

Route Characteristics

- Longer, more remote and physically challenging.
- Water and air temperatures may be extreme but within parameters of paddling season.
- Portages extremely difficult, long or non-existent.
- Kayakers have no difficulty paddling Lake Superior or visiting offshore islands.

Hazards or Concerns

- Cold weather and cold water risks much higher.
- Equipment must suit extreme conditions: wet or dry suits, added flotation for canoes, option for spray-covers for bigger rapids or environmental conditions.

How to Organize Your Trip

Trip planning is an essential element in making sure that your canoe venture unfolds smoothly. You would do the same if you were planning a visit to a luxury resort, and you don't want any surprises along the way. There are several ways to approach each trail in this guidebook, depending on your skill level and how much time you have.

Once you've selected a route, the next thing to determine is how to get to and from there by way of access points. I used my mountain bike on the shorter trips, but because this is a linear route of significant length, you will need to plan your shuttles in advance — not a problem if you have two vehicles and allow for extra driving time. Shuttles can be arranged by contacting local outfitting businesses, lodges or taxi services; for example, in Atikokan the local taxi driver shuttled our vehicle for a decent price. Make sure you park in a designated parking area and refrain from leaving valuables in your vehicle. Pack a set of booster cables in case your battery goes dead.

Let someone know where you are going. SPOT messages (see page 42) can be a fun way for your friends or family to track your progress. Go over your gear carefully, making sure everything is waterproofed and tightly organized. Use a checklist when putting your kit together.

Pack extra food in case you get delayed by weather, and build extra time into your trip. An average day on any of these routes would cover 12 to 15 kilometers — a slow to moderate pace that includes portaging. Average canoe speed is 3.5 to 5 kph, depending on wind speed and direction.

Quetico and La Verendrye Provincial Parks do not have campsites marked on their maps; campsites are indicated on the routes in this guidebook so that paddlers can plan their trips better. More detailed topographic (1:50,000) or provincial (1:100,000) maps can be ordered ahead of time. You can also print out maps from Google Earth, along with any GPS coordinates that you feel are necessary. If you just use the maps in this book (which is possible), you may want to bring along a GPS unit as well. Cellphones and smartphones are handy devices that work on some of these routes, and weather apps can be useful for satellite imaging that warns of approaching storms.

Although all these routes can be paddled in either direction, the optimum course, based on prevailing winds and downstream currents, is indicated in the text. Take this into consideration when you plan your trip.

About the Maps

All the route maps in this book have been hand-drawn to the 1:100,000 scale used in provincial maps. They are accurately drawn from field assessments and can be used with a GPS (Global Positioning System) topographic map program. For reasons explained in "Technology and Navigation Aids" (see page 42), GPS coordinates are not marked on the maps; coordinates for specific locations can be mapped using Google Earth. The Canadian 1:50,000 topographic charts have been a canoe-tripping standard for decades, but some of their information may be out-of-date. It is recommended that you research paddling routes to acquire information that may be available from other sources. Based on material the author has reviewed, the information in this book is the most accurate.

About the Map Legend
Portages
Portage trails are marked with a red line and a square P symbol. The portage length is indicated in meters, which compares to the number of paces using a long walking stride.

River and Creek Obstructions
Falls are indicated by a blue symbol, unrunnable rapids by a red bar, and runnable rapids by a black bar. Obstructions that require a portage are marked accordingly, usually with a red line.

Paddling Route
Winds often affect the safe progress of an adventure trip, so the maps indicate the optimum paddling route with a solid red line. This takes advantage of lee-shore protection and adds scenic appeal and a greater chance of discovery through exploration. Route distances are shown in 5-kilometer increments for easy planning.

General Map Legend

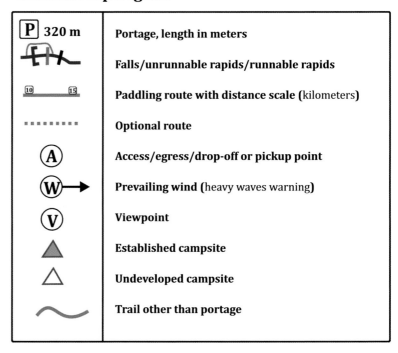

P 320 m	Portage, length in meters
	Falls/unrunnable rapids/runnable rapids
10 15	Paddling route with distance scale (kilometers)
	Optional route
A	Access/egress/drop-off or pickup point
W →	Prevailing wind (heavy waves warning)
V	Viewpoint
▲	Established campsite
△	Undeveloped campsite
~	Trail other than portage

Optional Route
Optional routes are indicated with a broken red line. Some optional routes have not been field-assessed by the author.

Access Points
An A symbol is used to indicated access, egress and drop-off or pickup points. Parking is usually restricted to access points at either end of the trail section, or as otherwise indicated. Remote parking is optional. Shuttle drop-offs and pickups are recommended.

Prevailing Wind

A wind-direction symbol is used for lakes with more than one kilometer of open water and where paddlers have to engage in a potentially dangerous crossing. In most cases it represents the prevailing seasonal wind, typical during the paddling months.

Viewpoint

There are numerous hiking trails along the Path of the Paddle routes, many of which offer access to incredible vistas. Particularly spectacular views are indicated by the V symbol.

Established Campsite

A solid green triangle usually indicates a campsite that has a firepit and maybe a box privy. These sites can typically accommodate three or more tents.

Undeveloped Campsite

A white triangle with green borders indicates a site suitable for camping that may not have a firepit or box privy and may accommodate only one or two tents. These sites are usually used when established sites aren't available or are too far away.

Trail Other Than Portage

A green line indicates an established hiking trail.

Sample Map

I THINK ASSUMPTIONS WERE MADE WHEN THE SALESPERSON SAID "ALL YOU NEED IS HAP'S GUIDE BOOK".

Chapter 3

Helpful Information

If a man walks in the woods for love of them half each day, he is in danger of being regarded as a loafer. But if he spends his days as a speculator, shearing off those woods and making the earth bald before his time, he is deemed an industrious and enterprising citizen.
— Henry David Thoreau

Climate and Ecological Zones

Looking at the natural boundaries or ecological zones, the Path of the Paddle heartland is contained wholly within the Great Lakes–St. Lawrence Forest Region. The climate is cool temperate, with well-defined seasons. The forest is mixed deciduous and coniferous — red and white pine, jack pine, balsam fir, yellow birch, ash and maple. Ice-out is generally from very late April to about May 10 (sometimes earlier or later) and snow showers are not unusual anytime during the month of May. Summers are comfortably warm, as are the water temperatures (except for Lake Superior). By late September the night temperatures may dip below freezing, and October can bring snow showers and cool days.

The Anishinabe Trail, along the Winnipeg River into Whiteshell Provincial Park, marks the transition to warm boreal forest. Gone are the great white pines, replaced by jack pine, black and white spruce and aspen. Both ecozones lie within the southwestern edge of the Precambrian or Canadian Shield, which is typified by ancient rock outcrops, escarpments, "pool and drop" rivers, and a congenial mix of lake, upland and wetland features. Just west of Shoal Lake and Lake of the Woods is parkland — a lowland mix of aspen and birch and open grassland prairie. Prickly pear cactus makes its way into the Manitoba-Ontario border regions.

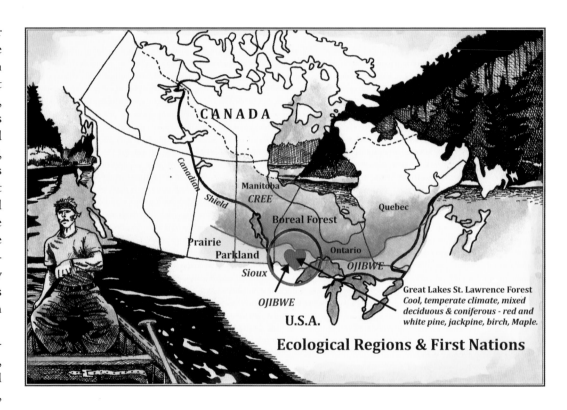

Ecological Regions & First Nations

Great Lakes St. Lawrence Forest
Cool, temperate climate, mixed deciduous & coniferous - red and white pine, jackpine, birch, Maple.

There is a marked correlation between ecological zones and aboriginal territories. Cree First Nations occupy the boreal forest lands, the Ojibwe predominate in the Great Lakes–St. Lawrence region, and the Siouan Assiniboine people reside on the prairie veldt. In the past, skirmishes along the border regions, particularly between the Ojibwe and their neighbors, were frequent and violent.

Spiritual Places

It is a privilege and a source of great pride to travel these waters. We also have to remember that we are travelling on traditional routes that are still used, in many instances, by people of the First Nations. As such we need to be respectful of their habits, the cultural propriety required and the importance of aboriginal spiritual sites. The Canadian Shield region of Canada contains hundreds of First Nations spiritual representations. To the untrained eye they can easily be missed as you paddle by. There are numerous pictograph (rock painting) sites, chiefly teaching sites that were used by local healer shamans to depict anything from hunting forays to powerful medicine symbols. Don't even think about adding your own contribution.

Petroforms (rocks arranged in patterns), petroglyphs (stone carvings) and large dolmen stones can also be found throughout the region. Leave them alone. Do not rearrange stones, and refrain from building inuksuks — they are part of neither Algonkian culture nor your own.

Blindfold Bay pictographs.

Native Spiritual Beliefs

The differences between the ideologies of First Nations and white imperialists became apparent upon first contact. How one group usurped the other's land for their own needs and greed was governed by the control and distribution of trade within the new-found territories. In the process, the Native peoples relinquished many of their traditional practices, becoming almost wholly dependent on acquiring what they needed from "the post." And while white explorers and traders relied on the Natives for furs, meat and guiding services, neither group trusted the other.

The white man thought the aboriginals lazy, vague and phlegmatic, a presumption based on the fact that they were not driven by profit. The term savage encompassed both their non-Christian beliefs and their impassioned barbarity in battle. The Anishinabeg, on the other hand, believed the white man to be stupid, untrustworthy and spiritually deficient — and for good reason. The Europeans could not survive alone in the wilds, engineered their own failures with peculiar regularity, and displayed total impiety toward the land.

For us to be able even to attempt to understand Canada's first peoples, we need to understand their connection to the environment. Native spiritual faith and shamanic or "healing" practices may have evolved more than 20,000 years ago, originating in central Siberia when Asia and North America were joined under a thick sheath of ice. More recently, associated religious rites seemed to have spread north from the Ohio Valley in 700–500 BCE. Burial mounds, rock paintings, petroforms and excavations such as the "Pukaskwa Pits" near Lake Superior are visual evidence of Native theology. Much of their religion survived through these iconic representations and in oral traditions.

To the Anishinabeg, all animate and inanimate objects possessed a spiritual pith or energy. Their lives involved continual mollification of the spirits, both benevolent and evil, that had absolute control over fertility, availability of food and social position. Specific geographic locations, such as the Teggau Lake and Blindfold Bay pictograph sites, were revered as places of "harmonic convergence" — sacred spaces where the physical world of upright consciousness could meld with the incorporeal spirit world.

Illness was brought on not by some physical breakdown but by the invasion of an enemy or evil spirit that subdued the body of the possessed and occupied their soul. The shaman — more correctly, healer — would be summoned to enter the spirit world to retrieve the soul and suck out the invading evil entity, a practice very similar to exorcisms performed in Christian Roman Catholicism.

The Algonkian peoples, a linguistic group of the woodland Canadian Shield, used "shaking tent" or sweat lodge ceremonies to induce a spiritual trance. (The latter was more widely used, since the shaking tent was unavailable to anyone but the tribal healer.) The sweat lodge — the "womb of Mother Earth" — acted as a dream enhancer, purifying the soul by summoning of the four powers of creation: air, fire, earth and water. Native "law" supports the idea that certain powers do not mix, and that Nature will punish those who do not respect that law.

The law includes respecting spiritual sites found along the Path of the Paddle corridor. To appease the spirits dwelling in such places, Natives were required to leave gifts or offerings such as medicine bundles or prayer sticks, tobacco or wampum (strings of shell beads, later replaced by cheap glass ones supplied by European traders in the 1800s). Failing to honor this practice could prove fatal — even for white men, as in the case of Alexander Henry, the explorer and free-trader, who set up shop in 1767 at Michipicoten, at the east end of Lake Superior. He writes in his journal about a fishing expedition along the Superior coast:

The mischievous *payhunsuk*.

On the first night, we encamped on the island of Naniboujou, and set our net. We certainly neglected the customary offerings, and an Indian would not fail to attribute it to this cause, that in the night there arose a violent storm, which continued for three days, in which it was impossible for us to visit our net . . . the storm abated, and we hastened to examine the net. It was gone.

The number four is very powerful. There are the four winds of the universe, the four directions, four basic elements, four races of humankind and four stages of life. A good medicine healer will have at least four important visions. As well, the interplay between art and religion is extremely important to First Nations — something that Carl Jung also felt was necessary, uplifting and empowering to the human spirit. The Path of the Paddle, being so rich in First Nations spiritual symbology, allows us to get a firsthand look into the elements of a culture that we may fail to understand otherwise.

When it comes to First Nations land claims and environmental issues, it is easy to understand why a rift often develops within Native bands. Protecting traditional lands is important to some, while developing resources for profit may appeal to others. Regardless, First Nations have the right to protect their traditional territory and to share in the profits from resources harvested on their territorial lands . . . so long as that harvest is carried out in a sustainable fashion. Colonial ideals, consumerism, greed and avarice were something new to First Nations, and after four centuries bureaucrats and politicians are still trying to figure out why "Indians" just don't follow the rules thrown at them. But after four centuries of trying to convert the "pagans" to European standards, our politicians now say it's okay to be aboriginal (a little late in the day!).

For those who may think that Canada lacks otherworldly creatures

Evil *wendigo*, the flesh-eating monster.

Nebaunaubaequae — an Ojibwe symbol of the incorporeal nature of water.

Who says Canada doesn't have any boogeymen?"

(aside from sasquatch and the occasional haunted farmhouse), here's something that may surprise you. The more time one spends in wild places, the more opportunities there are to experience the supernatural. A plethora of spirits, sprites, tricksters and wraiths live within the confines of the natural world. To the Anishinabeg, the existence of both benevolent and malevolent spirits is very real. The *maymaygwense*, or "stone people," reside within the rock walls of pictograph sites. Then there are the infamous Great Hare Nanaboozhoo, the buffoon and manipulator; Mishepeshu, the underwater cat; Paguk (or Bakaak), the flying skeleton (you don't want to hear the rattling of his bones as he flies overhead on a dark night); and the crafty Payhunsuk, who sits beside your tent at night and climbs into your dreams. And there's Nebaunaubaeque — watch out for this one — a symbol of the incorporeal nature of water that appears to men as a woman and to women as a man, seducing or enticing the victim and then drowning them. The most feared, of course, is the evil *wendigo*, the flesh-eating giant that seeks out those who flounder in the wilderness, sneaking up on the victim in the mist; its terrible voice can be heard from miles away.

I have witnessed some very strange things over the years, unexplainable events and happenings, so I've gained just a little bit of knowledge that helps me stay on the path. My very best advice is to leave tobacco at any spiritual site, and be respectful. Look after the Earth Mother and she will provide for you.

Choosing a Canoe

It was Bill Mason who vaulted the classic "prospector" canoe to widespread popularity. Canoe manufacturers jumped in and began producing copies of the iconic boat for hungry markets. That was back in the 1970s and early '80s, when canoes were heavy and made of fiberglass resin, aluminum and later ABS (Royalex). Bill's cedar and canvas canoe likely weighed in at around 80 pounds. Today we have a lot of options, each involving a tradeoff in weight, durability and function. But Bill's love of the prospector still makes great sense: it's an all-round good design, and best suited for the trips in this guidebook.

Materials have evolved, along with a general distaste for long portages. Canoes are lighter, although the price tag goes up as the weight goes down. A lighter canoe, made of Kevlar, carbon fiber or the new Innegra (which replaced ABS), weighs as little as 32 pounds for a 17-foot craft — a dream to carry on the portage. The tradeoffs can be in carrying capacity, wind resistance and temperament. Light canoes, if not secured at the campsite, can easily blow away, and if you're camping alone, this could present an embarrassing problem. But heavy canoes — like that old several-layer fiberglass canoe borrowed from your uncle's cottage — could easily result in broken friendships or divorce.

I am a solid advocate of quality. If you want to invest your time and money wisely, choose the right canoe for the job. In this guidebook, the routes require a devotion to shrewd planning. Most trips fail because of improper planning and poor-quality gear. I've put together a few helpful tips:

There are several narrow, meandering creeks on these routes. A 16-foot canoe handles these better than a longer canoe — the more rocker, the better the maneuverability.

Canoes should be a minimum of 16 or 17 feet long, upgraded to

Still morning along the Quetico Trail.

"expedition" class — an extra layer of resin at key points along the hull — and with skid plates on each stem, which work like bumpers. The added weight (5–10 pounds) is well worth it, and the canoe will still weigh less than 50 pounds.

Tighten all the nuts and bolts before you head out, and make sure you take along a repair kit and a multi-tool.

For tips on canoeing and portaging techniques, see facing page.

Canoeing & Portaging Tips

- Make sure the canoe(s) is pulled well up from shore and tied off. Summer storms can whip up in the middle of the night.
- Practice hoisting a canoe properly — one person should be able to handle this.
- Follow the suggested route: in the lee of the winds and close to the shore, not down the middle of the lake.
- Start paddling early to beat the morning wind. Camp early and enjoy the afternoon.
- It's not necessary to tie off your packs in the canoe. All gear should be packed in waterproof barrels or canoe dry bags that float; only thwart bags (day packs) should be fixed to the canoe. This is important in case of an upset, to easily facilitate a canoe-over-canoe rescue.
- Keep the load below or at the gunwale line and properly balanced. This is crucial for stability and handling.
- Avoid a lot of loose stuff. It's a pain in the ass at the portage, adds time and work to your day, and results in a lot of lost items.
- It's courteous to keep portage landings clear.
- Organize your day according to wind and weather conditions. It's always better to wait out a storm or sit tight during high afternoon winds, then paddle in the evening or early morning to keep to your schedule. Allow extra time in your trip for this.
- Tie canoes together catamaran-style if you have to make a dangerous crossing or simply want to sail down a lake. Leave a minimum 18-inch space between the canoes.
- Take one extra paddle per canoe.
- Keep your canoe party together and within sight of each other.
- Have an extra set of maps stored away just in case.

The dreaded portage — an important cultural component of the Great Canadian Trail.

Standup Paddleboarding

The notion of standing up on a board and using a paddle to propel yourself actually originated in Africa, where it was common practice to stand up in canoes, especially when trying to sneak up on an enemy. There is also a connection with 16th-century Hawaiian surf paddlers. In the United States, Waikiki surf instructors started using paddles to greet incoming swells as early as the 1940s.

In the past few years, standup paddleboarding, or SUPing, has dominated the paddlesport industry with new designs and technique. The US Outdoor Foundation's 2015 report on paddlesports listed SUPs as the most popular among first-time participants, with a median age of 28. Almost three million people engaged in the sport in 2014, 76 percent being males 25 to 44 years old. At first the popularity of SUPing rarely cruised beyond flat-water paddling and short, cottage-type tours around the lake, but Swift Canoe and Kayak, for example, has been designing boards and rigging for a growing market of expedition paddlers. It's easy to understand why SUPs are attractive to first-time paddlers — they are easy to control in the wind (as opposed to solo canoeing), they are half the price of a decent Kevlar canoe, and the view is better from a standing position.

Since this is not a how-to book, it is assumed that expedition paddlers will already have researched the equipment and are adept at some form of outdoor travel by canoe or kayak.

Equipment Needs

+ **Board:** determined by the paddler's weight, skill and intended use. Larger, longer boards — 12.6 to 14 feet in length, with three fins instead of one — will track better for lake paddling. You also need a board that will carry your weight plus the weight of your gear. Inflatable boards have become popular for expedition paddling,

Photo credit: Scott Parent

especially if you intend to run shallow, rocky rivers and creeks.
+ **Paddle:** should be quality carbon fiber and 6 to 10 inches longer than your height. You will also need a spare "breakdown" paddle securely fastened to the board or load.
+ **Leash:** the type can vary for flat water and rivers. A coil-type leash will stay out of the water.
+ **Traction pad:** should be beefy.
+ **Deck tie-downs:** essential for your gear, either bungee or net type.
+ **auto pressure valve (APV):** for releasing internal board pressure.
+ **Fins:** should be detachable. This make the board more maneuverable for meandering creek travel.
+ **Clothing:** suitable for cold or hot conditions. Have a wet or dry suit for cold conditions, and stuff you don't mind getting wet for warm conditions.
+ **Personal flotation device (PFD):** should be good quality and comfortable to move in.

* **Dry bags:** pretested for leaks, plus a pack to carry them in for portaging.

Play It Safe
* Test-load your board before you get out there, so there will be no surprises.
* Load weight for expedition SUPing should be evenly distributed front and back. For whitewater or brisk headwinds, shift the weight forward and kneel on one knee for stability.
* Stay close to shore if water or air temperatures drops below 15°C (60°F).
* Minimize gear, but take two sets of maps, a repair kit and a spare fin.

Best Places to Paddleboard
* **Anishinabe Trail:** both routes in their entirety (portaging required)
* **Lake of the Woods:** one of the finest destinations in North America (no portages)
* **Migizi Trail:** Eagle Lake (no portages)
* **Maukinak Trail:** White Otter and Clearwater West Lakes (one short portage)
* **Agimak Trail:** White Otter and Clearwater West Lakes (one short portage)
* **Quetico Trail:** Northern Light and Saganaga Lakes (one short portage)
* **Omimi Trail:** Gunflint Lake to Arrow Lake Provincial Park (portaging required)
* **Animikii Trail:** Superior route (portage at takeout)

Water Quality

Outside of the interior lakes and rivers, which are typically lower than the surrounding land, it is best to filter or treat your drinking water. Use of a water purifier is recommended for these areas:

* all of the Animikii Trail
* all of the Anishinabe Trail
* Lake of the Woods
* Eagle and Wabigoon Lakes (Migizi Trail)
* Agimak Lake (Agimak Trail)

In the interior, "dipping" right from the canoe is still practiced by canoe camps and individuals. This is fine, so long as it is done well out from shore on the larger lakes and not along creek systems, where there is a lot of animal activity.

Expedition Kayaking

Inuit hunters developed the kayak to hunt seals and even small whales (the ancient Aleuts of Alaska called these speedy boats iqyaks), and archeological remains of kayaks date back at least 4,000 years. The evolution of materials from wood and skin to fiberglass, rotomolded plastic and on to Kevlar and carbon fiber has improved the maneuverability of kayaks, increasing their cruising speed, cargo capacity, tracking and long-distance comfort. The longer the kayak, the straighter it tracks, but most solo touring kayaks range from 10 to 18 feet, and up to 26 feet for tandem boats.

Expedition paddling certainly has its drawbacks when it comes to portaging over longer, more arduous trails. The over-the-shoulder carry is tiresome, but luckily some manufacturers build in cockpit pads so the kayak can be carried directly over your head, like a canoe. The advantage that kayaks have over canoes is that they are less likely to be affected by wind conditions on bigger lakes. Kayaks are also easier to handle solo if you are just at the beginner stage of the sport. Gear has to be compact and stored in waterproof dry bags that fit neatly into bulkheads or flotation chamber hatches. If you plan on portaging, make sure you also use a "canoe pack" to carry the dry bags in.

Equipment Needs
- **Kayak:** If maneuverability is important (for example, on meandering creeks), a shorter touring craft is preferable. For general lake touring with no rivers or creeks or portaging planned, a longer kayak with a detachable skeg or rudder for tracking is ideal. Check your bulkhead and hatches for leaks before you head out.
- **Safety gear:** paddle leash, repair kit, paddle float for self-rescue, bilge pump and sponge, spare "breakdown" paddle, towline (painter), navigation light, flares and a whistle or air horn.
- **Personal Flotation Device (PFD):** should be fitted for weight, approved and comfortable.
- **Packing:** Weight should be evenly distributed. Limit deck gear to a waterproof deck bag (I like to bungee my sleeping bag/dry pack behind the cockpit for back support). Either wear the skirt or keep it handy, along with rain gear, water bottle and navigation aids.

Play It Safe
- For cold water or air temperatures, wear a wet or dry suit, waterproof gloves and storm-proof outerwear — 8°C (46°F) is the critical water temperature.

- If you don't know how to roll and right a touring kayak or perform a self-rescue using paddle floats, think carefully about off-season paddling or attempting a trip on Lake Superior.
- It is always best to travel with someone else or in a group.

Best Places to Kayak

Anishinabe Trail: Falcon River to Kenora (early season only); Kenora to Whiteshell, MB (full season, either direction, portaging required)

Lake of the Woods: a "bucket list" destination for sure

Migizi Trail: Stewart Lake to Ingall Falls/Eagle Lake tour (a couple of easy portages)

Maukinak Trail: Wabigoon Lake/Long Lake Tour; White Otter Lake

Agimak Trail: if you don't mind the portaging, entire route is excellent; or cut the trip in half by parking at the Moosehide/Devil's Gap Lake access point

Quetico Trail: French and Pickerel Lakes; Northern Light and Saganaga Lakes tour

Omimi Trail: Northern Light and Saganaga Lakes tour; Arrow Lake to Gunflint Lake

Akimikii Trail/Lake Superior: Chippewa Park to Pigeon River

Technology and Navigation Aids

There was a time, not so long ago, when navigational prowess depended on your ability to decipher three-dimensional reality from two-dimensional maps. The 1:50,000 topographical map series were the standard navigation maps and the compass was about as high-tech as you could get. And even the topo maps were suspect, as they weren't initially designed for canoe travel. Today we are fortunate that the commercial outdoor trade has favored backcountry travel with state-of-the-art navigational technology. It's now impossible to get lost (well, it still is possible, but you really have to work at it).

Maps

I love maps. I still carry the 1:50,000 topo map, just because I don't trust technology (and I'm a bit nostalgic). I like to have the big picture in front of me; perhaps it's also because my eyesight isn't quite up to par these days and I hate squinting at my GPS screen. The reality is that you don't need to purchase paper maps anymore. You can even download Google maps of your route in great detail. The maps in this book have been drawn to 1:100,000 scale and can be used for reference along with a GPS unit. And if your GPS acts up, a paper map in a waterproof pouch can be a trip saver. Refer to each trail information page for map references.

Global Positioning System (GPS)

GPS units are invaluable for backcountry travel. Most now come with a good topographic map feature and you can make quick calculations of distance and time. They are also handy for pinpointing a location during emergencies (in conjunction with a satellite phone). The disadvantage of the GPS is the size of the screen; it is sometimes difficult to convert a 2-D image to a ground reference. And paying too much attention to your GPS can get you in trouble when navigating whitewater rivers.

GPS co-ordinates have been left off the maps in this book for three reasons: (1) too much information crowds the map; (2) they detract from the true experience of wilderness travel and using real visual references; and (3) locking on to key wayfinding co-ordinates tends to make the paddler adhere to straight-line projections, which can draw him or her offshore in order to cross from point to point. The GPS co-ordinates for any reference point in this book can be determined by using Google maps.

GPS units should be tethered and stored in a waterproof case, along with two sets of spare batteries.

Spot Satellite Messenger

SPOT satellite messenger beacons are GPS tracking devices that use the Globalstar satellite network. They cannot receive data but allow you to send short text messages to specific phone numbers or Internet addresses. They can transmit a "breadcrumb trail" of GPS points to a web page and can connect to emergency services. They are surprisingly inexpensive.

Satellite Phone

The sat-phone has become a standard piece of equipment for most expedition paddlers. You can call directly for emergency services or arrange to have a member of your party who everyone hates airlifted out (don't forget to ask the floatplane pilot to bring in pizza and beer). Everybody likes to be connected these days, for whatever reason, and it makes good sense to cover all the bases, especially if

Tablets and Cellphones

Surprisingly, cellphones do work on much of the Path of the Paddle route system, as indicated on the map to the left. Coverage is restricted to the Highway 11 and 17 corridors for up to 15 air kilometers on either side (that's an estimate only). Cellphones are also handy for taking photographs and videos. If you're going to drop something in the water or onto a rock, it's probably going to be your cellphone. Make sure it at least has a shatterproof case and a waterproof home when not in use.

Drones

Believe it or not, some paddlers have taken to the skies to see what's ahead. Drones are being used more and more by whitewater paddlers for scouting canyons. I suggest leaving them at home.

Chargers

There are various solar and fuel-burning chargers on the market, but they aren't cheap. Unless you plan on setting up a base camp and have time for the charger to actually do its job, for the average trip you won't need to bring one. It's cheaper just to purchase a spare battery.

you have a paddler with a medical condition. Pack the phone in a waterproof case and make sure the battery is fully charged before you leave, or take a spare.

Permits

Crown Land Camping

Canadian citizens are allowed to camp without charge for up to 21 days on Crown land; foreign visitors may also camp, provided they pay a fee of $10 per night. Crown land camping permits, along with fishing permits, are readily available at most outfitting depots, outdoor stores and tourist lodges. The non-resident Crown land camping program was developed in 1984 to address concerns about competition between residents and non-residents, to generate non-tax revenue for the province, to stimulate commercial tourism by encouraging non-residents to use local commercial tourist establishments, and to limit fishing pressure.

I was working as a park ranger in Temagami in the 1980s. The use of newly built forestry roads was uncontrolled, allowing mechanized sportsmen (both local and non-resident) access to once remote lakes. The province did not have the manpower to monitor the proliferation of roads, and the result was depletion of fish and game resources in short order. Instead of closing off logging roads into wilderness areas, the Ontario Federation of Anglers and Hunters, along with local sporting resorts, pressured the Ontario government to adopt an "open gate" policy and the Crown land permit system.

Regulated Green Zones

In 1989 Northwest Ontario implemented Regulated Green Zone (RGZ) restrictions. This is unique to the region; RGZs could never have been implemented in Northeast Ontario, which has a long-established non-mechanized recreation industry, and the environmental movement (specifically in Temagami) has forced the government to be more transparent. RGZs are supposed to allow day use by non-residents but no camping; overnight accommodations have to be at a registered tourist accommodation facility. The District of Atikokan was made an exception to the rule because of the number of canoe parties passing through the area. Canoe parties are allowed to camp at a site for only one night, then must move on. This applies to Dashwa, Crowrock and Clearwater West Lakes and the Maukinak Trail.

I brought up this discrepancy with Ontario's Environment Commissioner, Gord Miller, and he knew nothing of the Green Zone restrictions, which leads me to believe that they were a closed-door agreement between local tourist operations and local Ministry of Natural Resources offices. Paddlers put little pressure on fishing resources, whereas motor campers would park for long periods of time in remote areas to access fishing lakes. Instead of regulating road access, the government implemented an unfair program that seriously undermines the growing paddlesport industry.

When the Ontario Ministry of Natural Resources was approached by Trans Canada Trail during initial Path of the Paddle discussions, it was noted that canoe outfitters with foreign clients would be restricted from camping along some of the routes. The suggestion was made of amending the Public Lands Act so that foreign canoe tourists would be able to camp but along a linear route only. To my knowledge, nothing has been done to date. The RGZ name implies that some sort of "green space" is being protected, but all it does is placate the local hunting and fishing resorts.

It is up to individual non-residents whether or not they canoe through a Green Zone with just a Crown land permit. The OMNR office in Dryden can be contacted for information about Green Zones in that district. A non-resident who camps on Crown land outside the regulated Green Zones and who has rented a "camping unit" (tent) from a registered Ontario tourist outfitter is not required to purchase a Crown land camping permit.

Fishing and interior camping permits are required for non-residents.

Crossing the border? You will need pre-clearance.

Entering Canada from the United States

Anyone wanting to paddle into Canada without going through customs at Pigeon River needs to get a Remote Area Border Crossing (RABC) permit. Canada Customs allows a bearer of this permit to cross into Canada without reporting to a port of entry. The permit is valid from Pigeon River Park to (and including) Lake of the Woods, the Canadian shore of Lake Superior and Cockburn Island. Applications can be mailed to

Citizenship and Immigration Canada
Suite 108, 221 Archibald Street North
Thunder Bay, ON P7C 3Y3
Phone: (807) 624-2158.

The cost is $30 Canadian per family. Expect 4–6 weeks for delivery or go to www.cic.gc.ca/english/visit/rabc.html.

Quetico Provincial Park Permit Reservations

From Canada/USA: 1-888-668-7275
From outside Canada/USA: (416) 800-0676

Boundary Water Canoeing Area

There is a quota system in place for the BWCA. Permits are required at all entry points.
Website: www.bwca.org
Phone: 1-877-550-6777

Fishing Licenses

Fishing licenses are required for both residents and non-residents. They are readily available at outfitting stores. Check regulations and restrictions on the Ontario Parks website: www.ontarioparks.com.

No-trace Camping

Government bodies have little money to invest in cleaning up our messes, which is why we need to be vigilant about our housekeeping habits when out on the wilderness trail. It's our responsibility to practice no-trace camping etiquette. Generally speaking, paddlers are pretty careful about this, but after working as a park ranger in Temagami, I know that there will always be a small percentage of "dirty campers."

Fires should be restricted to safe bedrock firepits only. The alternative is to use a camp stove when this is not an option. Firepits should be left clear of garbage and food residue and firewood should be left for the next party. Do not clean fish at the campsite. Pack out any garbage that you create or find, at the campsite and along the portage trail. Do not cut or deface live trees or build permanent structures.

When it comes to taking a dump in the woods, people still don't get it right. By the end of the summer some popular tenting sites have become poop minefields, with garlands of toilet paper strung from the trees. Canoe-camp leaders need to educate new campers about proper disposal of fecal matter, and others need to learn that messy toilet habits can ruin the experience of those who use the campsite next. One of the chief contributing factors to crappy campsites is the nighttime dump, when the perpetrator fears straying too far from the sanctity of the tent. Or it might be bug season and there isn't enough time to bury the business properly. Both are bad excuses for appalling habits.

Everywhere I go these days I run into newly built "inuksuks," traditionally waymarks or anthropomorphic rock monuments built by Inuit hunters. This really has to stop. They have no place in the lower Shield regions, nor do we have the right to appropriate First Nations cultural practices. Members of a well-established canoe organization took it upon themselves to construct inuksuks all the way down the

More than ever, it is the responsibility of each camper to practice good campsite etiquette.

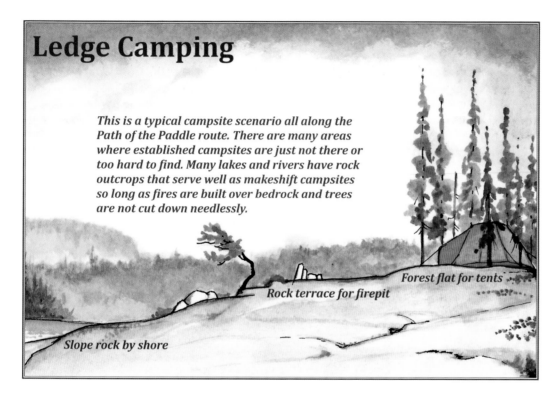

Ledge Camping

This is a typical campsite scenario all along the Path of the Paddle route. There are many areas where established campsites are just not there or too hard to find. Many lakes and rivers have rock outcrops that serve well as makeshift campsites so long as fires are built over bedrock and trees are not cut down needlessly.

Forest flat for tents

Rock terrace for firepit

Slope rock by shore

Some routes have few established campsites but many accessible bedrock ledges.

Seal River in northern Manitoba. Of course the local Sayesi Dene people were outraged — the Inuit had been their traditional enemies, and inuksuks are not part of Dene culture. They are not a component of Algonkian First Nations culture either.

Don't know what to do about garbage? First of all, take items that aren't in tin cans, bottles or excess packaging. Food scraps can be burned, along with tin cans (if you have any), but only while the fire is burning well enough to incinerate what you don't want to pack out in your garbage bag. You don't want smelly garbage either; I use a small barrel lined with an industrial garbage bag for this. Repair kits, the first-aid kit and other items go into the same barrel. After a two-week eight-person expedition I will have less than 5 pounds of garbage, about one-third of a small barrel. And most of the garbage we bring out is not ours.

> **Recommended**: *The Hennessy Ultralite Backpacker hammock (https://hennessyhammock.com) can solve the problem of tenting on rough ground. Used by US Special Forces, it sells for around US$160.*

Wildlife Photography

The Path of the Paddle, Canada's heartland canoeing region, is a photographer's dream. Not only does it have the highest concentration of Native pictographs anywhere in the Canadian Shield, but the Shield itself defines the rugged landscape of this country in spectacular fashion. It's not unusual that more paddlers are taking pictures than packing a fishing rod these days. And good-quality digital cameras have come a long way in size and professional capability — easy to pack, simple to edit and cheap to operate. What hasn't changed is the natural behavior of wildlife, environmental conditions that present photo opportunities, and the way in which the camera should be stored.

Contrary to what some paddlers believe, the wildlife residing in wild places won't be lined up along the shore waiting for their pictures to be taken. Often experiences with wildlife are accidental, sudden and sometimes confrontational. It's hard to decide whether to leave the camera out while paddling, instead of safely tucked in a Pelican case or dry bag. I've seen cameras go overboard at portage landings because the owner forgot to close the case lid or zip the bag properly.

A lot of animals, such as moose, are early risers, so it's best to break camp at a decent hour if your route includes a creek or wetland environment — both prime habitats for moose. Wind conditions and noise play a huge factor in photographic success with wildlife. Banging paddles against the gunnels or social exchanges while paddling do not bode well for viewing opportunities. Here are a few extra tips:

- Use a waterproof case for storage.
- Take an extra camera battery and memory card.
- Avoid damp conditions, or use a waterproof camera.
- Don't disturb nesting birds. Loons and swans, for example, are shore nesters.

Moose calves and bear cubs... best to keep your distance and leave them alone.

- Bears and moose swimming in the water will capsize a canoe if you get too close.
- Be cautious about photographing moose or bears with young.
- Do not disturb archeological or spiritual sites. This includes moving rocks and splashing water on pictographs.

Bears, Bugs and Other Critters

Bears

* Avoid heavily used campsites in the summer.
* Keep a clean campsite, firepit and gear.
* It's handy to carry "bear bangers" or pepper spray, just in case.
* Guns are not necessary, and there's too much paperwork involved if you shoot a bear.
* Don't get between a mother bear and her cubs. Back away slowly.
* Don't keep food in your tent.
* Clean fish away from the campsite.
* Dogs can bring a bear into camp or really piss one off.
* Pack food in barrels. Hanging a food pack is like leaving a piñata for bears.

Other Critters

* Rabbits will eat leather straps, especially in the spring.
* Mice can build a nest and bear young overnight — in your canoe pack.
* Squirrels will eat holes through canvas and nylon to get at the gorp bag or other nut snacks.
* Porcupines and beavers will eat the wood gunnels of canoes.
* A cow moose with calf can be unpredictable and dangerous.
* Trying to portage with a bull moose blocking the path always works in his favor.

Bugs

* Loose, light-colored protective clothing is best.
* Bug jackets are a must in spring, and a screened tent is handy for groups (there'll be fewer mutinies).
* Avoid foods containing potassium.
* Avoid high concentrations of DEET — it melts plastic and messes up your wood paddle grip.

A clean campsite is your best protection against unwanted bear visits.

Ticks are local and seasonal and shouldn't deter from trip enjoyment.

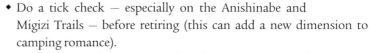

* Bugs are attracted by carbon dioxide, so stay calm.
* Forget about garlic or vitamin B1 pills.
* Avoid fragrances, devices that emit sound waves, wristbands with repellant claims, and anything with metoflu-thrin in it (it may pose a risk to your nervous system).
* Do a tick check — especially on the Anishinabe and Migizi Trails — before retiring (this can add a new dimension to camping romance).
* Don't let any of the aforementioned deter you from paddling. It all comes down to experience and common sense. Bugs are an important part of the ecosystem — just be smart about it. Blackflies and ticks are seasonal; mosquitoes, deerflies and horseflies can be tolerated; and stable flies and no-see-ums just add a little pizzazz to the whole mix. It's all part of the adventure!

Outdoor Living

I always have trouble with the word *survival* when it comes to outdoor adventures. There are reasons why some paddling trips embrace the ridiculous, tempt fate or push all the facets of wilderness living to become tests of survival. But if you take care of the fundamental requirements for human survival and well-being — a good tent properly pitched, suitable weather-worthy clothing, the ability to light a warming or cooking fire, adequate food — then a paddling adventure rises to a higher level. This is what I call "outdoor living."

Food is an important part of the paddling experience. Nutrition and sustenance aside, food is a great morale booster. If properly thought out and prepared, a tripping menu can whet appetites, not incite riots. I've had a paddler's cookbook on the backburner for years. Although this guidebook is not intended as a "how-to" publication, there are three recipes I would like to share with readers. Whether you're a grease-burner or an alfresco chef de cuisine, master these recipes and you will satisfy the culinary desires of the fussiest camper.

Bannock

Bannock, an unleavened flat bread (sometimes called scones in Scotland), originated either with the Scots (the word is Celtic) or with North American first peoples. The first Scottish use was recorded in 1000 CE; it was later defined as a staple food in 1562. Scottish bannock was traditionally made with barley and oatmeal; the dough was formed into a circle and baked on a flat stone that had been heated in a fire. Pre-contact "Indian bread" — what Path of the Paddle Anishinabeg call *pakwejigan* — was made from pounded maize (corn) or *wabanomin* (rice), various types of roots, tree sap and berries. But bannock became a staple along the frontier canoe routes of Canada.

If anything can get screwed up over a campfire, it will be the bannock.

The ingredient mix is incidental; it's the right cooking method — one that doesn't burn the outside while leaving the innards raw — that's the secret. There are two ways to cook bannock: in a good frying pan with a lid or in a reflector oven. The heat source is all-important; you want the temperature to be moderate, not too hot.

For campfire cooking in a frying pan, I scrape hot coals over to the cooking side and keep the flames under tight control. Turn the pan often and keep the lid on; this speeds up the cooking and keeps blackflies from coating the topside of your bannock. Once one side is browned, re-grease your pan and flip it over. (Baking your bannock in a reflector oven may be considered cheating by some, but there's an art to it — prop it either against a hot fire or over a primus-type stove.) The important thing to remember is to turn your pan often.

If you're frying over a gas stove, the heat is not well distributed, so it will quickly burn in the middle. It's more work, but in this case you have to hold the pan over the stove and keep moving it around so the edges of the bannock cook at the same time as the middle.

Basic Bannock (feeds 4 for lunch)
Ingredients

1 cup	unbleached white flour
1 cup	whole wheat flour
1/2 cup	cornmeal or steel-cut oats, optional (for crunchiness)
1/2 tsp	salt
1 tbsp	baking powder (aluminum-free)
1/2 tsp	powdered egg, optional (helps make it lighter if using heavy flours)
	Optional seasonings: Italian spice, fennel, basil, oregano, or cinnamon and brown sugar (for sweet bannock)

2 tbsp	oil or butter, divided
1/2 cup	water
	Honey or other sweetener, to taste

Preparation

1. Mix dry ingredients and place in resealable plastic bag, then in a nylon ditty bag.
2. When ready to cook, place 1 tbsp oil or butter in frying pan to heat up.
3. Meanwhile, mix sweetener into water. Add just enough water to dry ingredients to make a "dry" dough. (If it's too sticky, add flour as needed.)
4. Spread dough in pan and cover with lid. Turning pan frequently, cook until bannock is browned on one side.
5. Add remaining oil or butter to pan and flip bannock over. Cook until other side is brown and crisp.
6. Cut into wedges, pour yourself a cup of wine and enjoy.

Variations

Selkirk Bannock: There are several variations for making a wicked bannock. A baker named Robbie Douglas of Selkirk, Scotland, opened his shop in 1859, and his Selkirk bannocks became an instant sensation. More like a fruitcake, the dough is infused with raisins, brown sugar and butter.

Atikwa Bannock: Add fried-up chunks of ham or bacon and chunks of cheese to the dry ingredients, and go a little heavier with the cornmeal. Flavor with a mixture of rosemary, basil and oregano. A sure hit on cold mornings, serve it with campfire coffee and slices of orange.

Going Green

On longer canoe trips, the food item we miss most is a green salad. After half a century of expedition planning and leading, I have managed to create the perfect mix of fresh salad ingredients that can last several weeks. If you opt for a lighter load and stick with dehydrated or freeze-dried meals, you will sacrifice a lot of goodness for the sake of weight. Personally, I like to chop and dice — it keeps clients happy, nutritionally balanced and less flatulent.

Saganaga Salad
Dressing

1/4 cup	olive oil
1/2 cup	balsamic vinegar
Pinch	each salt and pepper
1 tsp	Dijon mustard
1 tbsp	maple syrup
Dash	each thyme and oregano

Mix and store in a small watertight Nalgene bottle.

Salad

For short trips:
- Romaine lettuce (fresh romaine will last well up to a week if you keep your food pack out of the sun and keep the lettuce in its plastic bag)
- Cherry tomatoes (pack in a Nalgene container)
- Cucumbers, preferably English (keep in a dry place out of the sun)
- Other short-lived ingredients

For long trips:
- Cabbage, chopped fine or chunked
- Diced carrots (pack in a paper bag and spread out to dry every evening)

- Minced fresh garlic and/or onion
- Chopped tamari almonds, dried cranberries or unsalted sunflower seeds
- Fennel, sesame seeds and other preferred seasonings
- Minced or candied ginger
- Peel from your organic oranges (to add zest to your salad)

Coffee

Legend dates coffee-drinking to a thousand years ago, but its use wasn't authenticated until the 15th century, in the Sufi monasteries of Yemen. Coffee consumption spread through the Middle East, India, Africa and Europe before it ever came to North America. The word *coffee* comes from the Dutch *koffie*, borrowed from the Turkish *kahve*, borrowed from the Arabic *qahwah* or *quwwa* (meaning "power" or "energy"). In the world today, more than 2.25 billion cups of coffee are consumed daily.

Coffee farming was originally carried out in the shade of trees that provided habitat for many insects, animals and birds — a model of sustainable biodiversity and ecological logic. Coffee was produced without using chemicals and fertilizers, while the fruit trees used for shade provided income for the local people. In the 1970s and '80s, the US Agency for International Development, along with sponsor corporations, injected $80 million dollars into Latin American coffee production to shift it to high-yield technology. Shade trees were replaced by sun-cultivation techniques in order to increase yield over a shorter period. Deforestation, chemical fertilizers and pesticides eventually led to a loss of biodiversity; from 1990 to 1995, 37 of the 50 countries with the highest deforestation rates were coffee producers.

Fortunately there has been a revival of shade-grown coffee farming that uses more environmentally sustainable techniques. Please look for shade-grown free-trade or organic coffee brands.

To the Path of the Paddle Ojibwe, coffee is *makate-mashkikiwabo* — "dark-colored medicine water." Certainly the stimulating effect of the caffeine (a psychoactive drug) in coffee has long graced campsites as a morning motivator and a day-end indulgence. In 2012 the National Institutes of Health found that higher coffee consumption was associated with a lower risk of death. So, paddlers out there, drink heartily, no matter how you brew your java.

For budding neophytes, I'm sure instant will suffice, but if you cherish a good cup of coffee in the morning, you can leave behind the gadgets (Bodums, vacuums, percolators, drips). I've probably brewed more wilderness coffee than most baristas have served lattes, and my clients complain only when the coffee ration (always generous) is gone and the grounds have been scattered as compost. After a hard day on the trail, when the clients start getting a little paddle-weary, camp is made and the coffee pot goes on the fire irons. That's when shots of Irish whiskey get passed around — a fine additive for coffee, but only after the canoes have been hauled up on shore for the night.

Bush Coffee
Equipment
- 12-cup steel coffee pot with a strong handle
- grill or fire irons
- a good fire

Ingredients
12 cups	lake, river or creek water
3/4 cup	regular-grind shade-grown coffee (1 tbsp per cup, or 3 handfuls)

Preparation
1. Fill coffee pot with water up to 1 inch (2.5 cm) from spout. Bring to a boil over fire.
2. Add coffee and stir. Take pot off fire and prop it up where it will stay hot but not boil. Stir again after 5 minutes.
3. Pick up pot and swing in a full circle about 10 times; this centrifuges the grounds to the bottom of the pot, so don't bother adding eggshells or cold water to do the same thing. Before swinging, make sure area is clear of low-hanging branches or guy ropes. (The first morning out, clients always think their guide has gone mad and is about to toss the coffee pot into the lake. Pour. It takes practice, but you'll be thanked for the results . . . and the entertainment.)

Variation
Migizi Mocha: If you have leftover coffee in the evening, mix it with hot chocolate and Canadian (rye) whisky. Stir with a cinnamon stick.

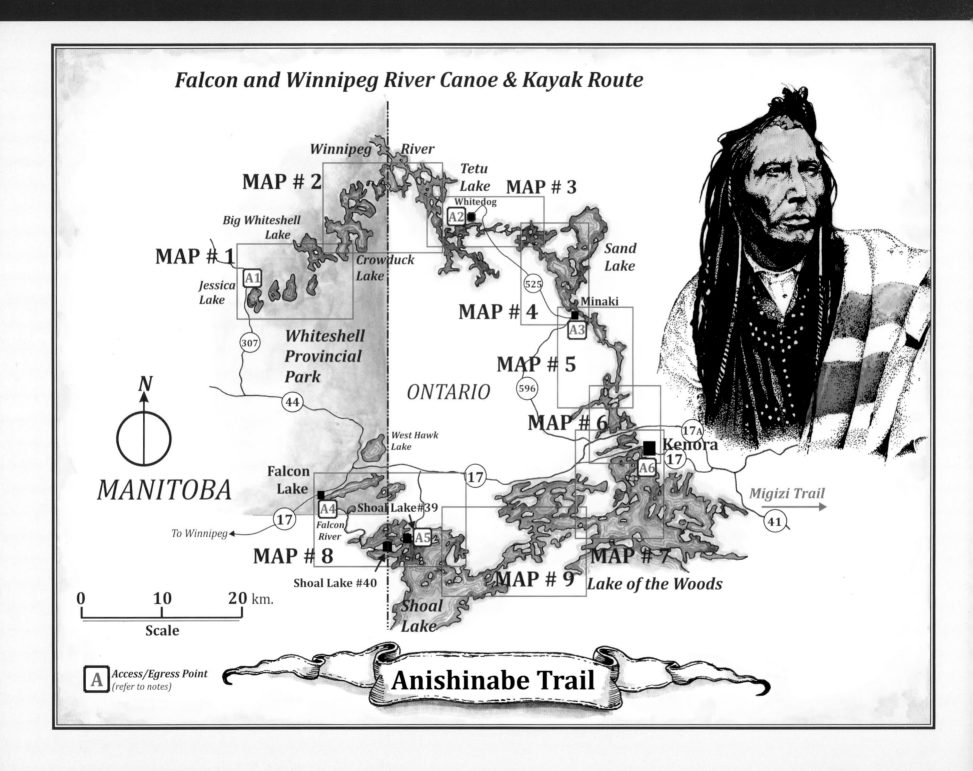

Falcon and Winnipeg River Canoe & Kayak Route

MAP # 2

MAP # 1

Winnipeg River

Big Whiteshell Lake

Tetu Lake

Whitedog

A2

MAP # 3

Sand Lake

A1

Jessica Lake

Crowduck Lake

Whiteshell Provincial Park

307

525

Minaki

MAP # 4

A3

MAP # 5

596

ONTARIO

44

MAP # 6

17A

N

West Hawk Lake

Kenora

A6

17

MANITOBA

Falcon Lake

17

Migizi Trail

A4

Shoal Lake #39

41

Falcon River

A5

To Winnipeg

17

MAP # 8

MAP # 7

Lake of the Woods

Shoal Lake #40

MAP # 9

Shoal Lake

0   10   20 km.

Scale

A Access/Egress Point
(refer to notes)

Anishinabe Trail

Chapter 4

Part 1
Anishinabe Trail

Anishinabe Trail name has been changed to "Linoo Oowan" (translation unknown).

Topographic Map Locations
1:50,000 scale
Falcon River–Shoal Lake route: 52-E/14 – 52-E/11 – 52-E/10 – 52-E/9
Winnipeg River route: 52-L/3 – 52-L/2 – 52-E/15 – 52-E/16

*A*nishinabe (also Anicinape or Anicinabe, often shortened to Nishinabe), is the name for a culturally related group of First Nations peoples of Canada and the United States. It includes the Odawa, Potawatomi, Mississauga, Oji-Cree, Algonquin and Ojibwe (also Ojibwa or Ojibway) peoples. The Anishinabeg speak Anishinaabewowin, which belongs to the Algonquian language group. Their traditional territories are the woodlands and warm boreal regions surrounding Lake Superior and west to the prairies. The word *Anishinabe* is sometimes mistaken as a synonym of *Ojibwe*, but it refers to a much larger group of tribes. There are several meanings to the word, including "people from whence lowered" or "the good humans," meaning those who are on the right path, given to them by the creator, Gitchi Manitou, or Great Spirit. The Ojibwe historian, linguist and author Basil Johnston maintained that its literal translation is "beings made out of nothing," or "spontaneous beings," since the Anishinabe people were created by divine breath.

The Anishinabe Trail(s) passes through the heart of traditional Ojibwe territories. It seems fitting that Canada's Canoe Route begins here, in appreciation of the cultural significance of a great people, of the canoe as an iconic craft that defined a huge part of our history, and of Canada's first trails. (The trail was recently retitled Linoo Oowan, a name of unknown origin.)

The adventurer has a choice of two routes: the Falcon River and the Winnipeg River. The Manitoba portion of the Trans Canada Trail (TCT) had been built as far as Falcon Lake. It seemed a natural choice to connect the land-based trail with the Path of the Paddle water route by way of the Falcon River, even though it was a seasonal connection; the attributes of the Falcon outweighed the reality of a shortened paddling season. Manitoba Trails opted for the High Lake route because they had pushed the TCT to the Falcon Resort. Shoal Lake 39 First Nation later complained that they were not consulted; in the end, the Winnipeg River was selected as the counter to a surfeit of challenges.

Route 1: Falcon River Route
Maps 1, 1A, 2, 3

Classification experienced novice

Distance 107 km (66 mi), with 30 km (19 mi) on river

Duration 3 to 4 days

Portages one 10 m (33 ft) lift-over (2 optional through Fox Lake)

Season mid-May to July (river only)

Preferred craft canoe (kayak or SUP in early season only)

Campsites semi-remote/undeveloped; on river only

Access Falcon Lake Beach (river) or Kejick (lake section only)

Egress Kenora (refer to Map 3)

Water Characteristics and General Hazards

- Gentle spring current on Falcon River during spring high water.
- Wind conditions on Shoal Lake may present problems (keep to the lee of islands).
- Wood ticks present during early season, along with blackflies and mosquitoes; proper dress is essential.
- Stay away from main boat channels, as boaters may not see you.

Features

- The marsh environment of Falcon River hosts innumerable wildlife species and rates extremely high for photography opportunities, nature study and birding.
- Late May through early June is prime time for canoe, kayak or SUP.
- Only one short lift-over to contend with.
- Fox Lake is an optional side route; it gets you off the main boat channel as you approach Lake of the Woods.
- Paddlers should contact the band office of Shoal Lake 40 First Nation to ask permission to pass through reserve lands
- The lake portion of this route from Kejick to Kenora offers a laidback weekend jaunt through a labyrinth of channels and islands at the junction of two impressive lakes.

Points of Interest

- A stopover at the Olympia Mine site is well worth the extra effort. Mining and lumbering date back to the 1870s.
- Steamboats moved great numbers of settlers from Kenora to Fort Frances. The last steamer to operate on the lake was the *Mather*, which was pulled from service in 1960. Many of the steamers taken out of service were dismantled and sunk.
- Lake of the Woods lies at the heart of the highest concentration of aboriginal pictographs (paintings) and petroglyphs (rock carvings) in North America.
- Lake of the Woods is in the transition zone between the northern boreal forests to the north, the Great Lakes forest regions to the south and the prairie grasslands to the east. There is no better place to see this than along the Vernon interpretive nature trails, a 5 km (3 mi) hike through old-growth red pine, bur oak and ironwood, grassland marsh and Canadian Shield rock, all representing the varied vegetative and geological uniqueness within shouting distance of Kenora.

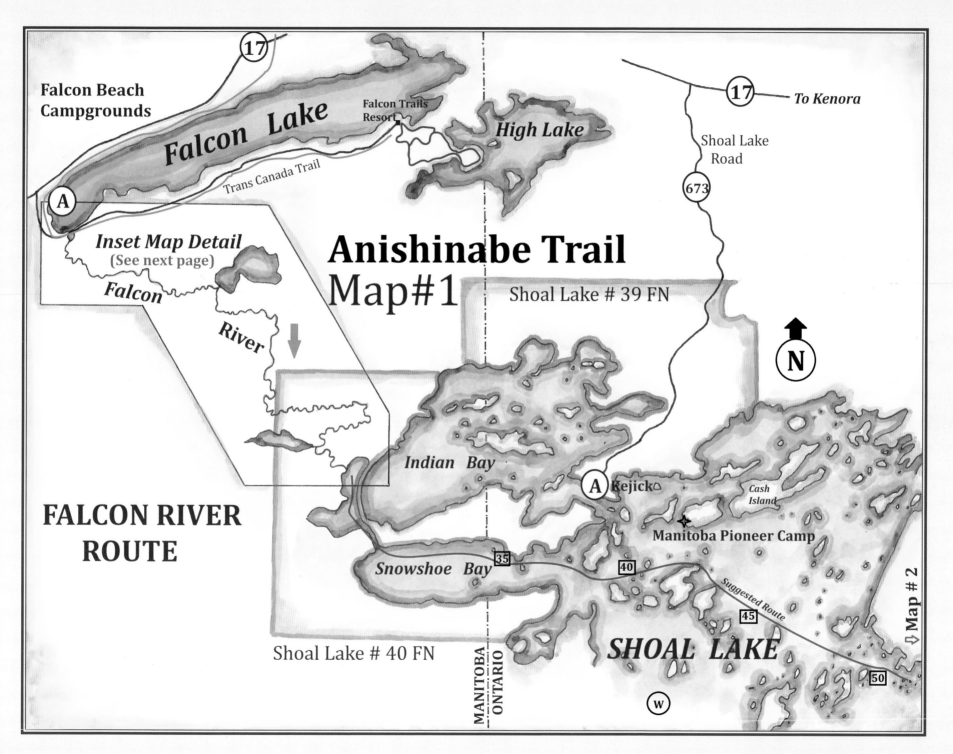

Falcon Beach Campgrounds

Falcon Lake

Falcon Trails Resort

High Lake

Trans Canada Trail

17

17 — *To Kenora*

Shoal Lake Road

673

Anishinabe Trail
Map#1

Shoal Lake # 39 FN

Inset Map Detail
(See next page)

Falcon

River

N

A

Kejick

Cash Island

Manitoba Pioneer Camp

Indian Bay

FALCON RIVER ROUTE

35

40

Suggested Route

45

Snowshoe Bay

Shoal Lake # 40 FN

MANITOBA
ONTARIO

SHOAL LAKE

50

W

⇩ Map # 2

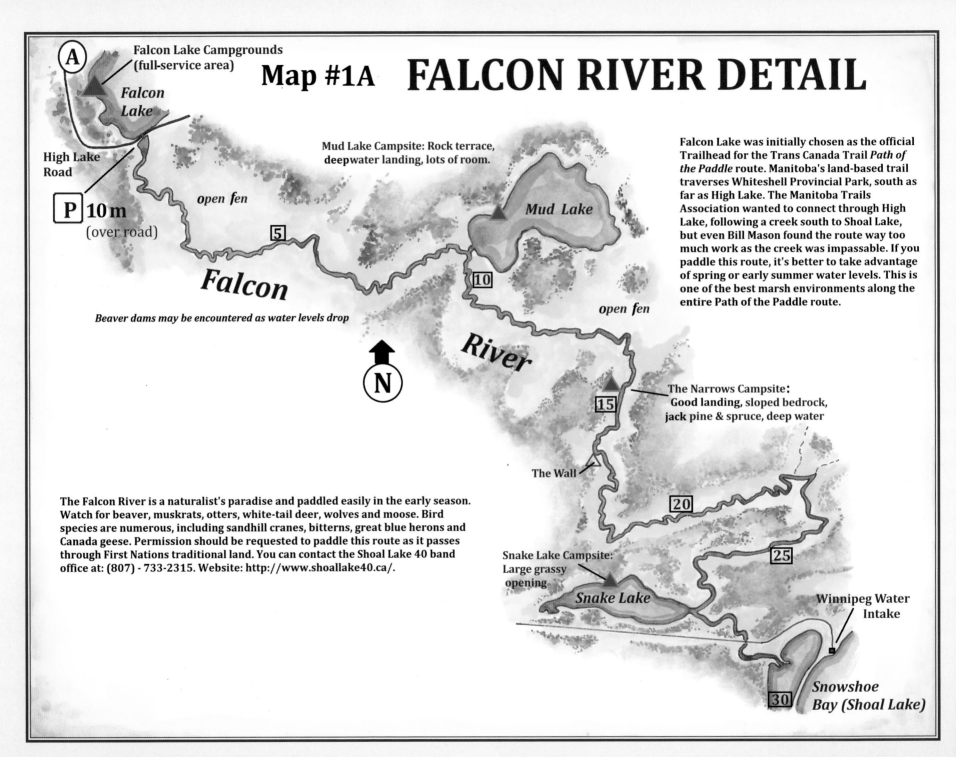

Map #1A FALCON RIVER DETAIL

A

Falcon Lake Campgrounds (full-service area)

Falcon Lake

High Lake Road

P 10 m (over road)

open fen

5

Falcon

Beaver dams may be encountered as water levels drop

N

Mud Lake Campsite: Rock terrace, deepwater landing, lots of room.

Mud Lake

10

open fen

River

15

The Narrows Campsite: Good landing, sloped bedrock, jack pine & spruce, deep water

The Wall

20

25

Snake Lake Campsite: Large grassy opening

Snake Lake

Winnipeg Water Intake

30

Snowshoe Bay (Shoal Lake)

Falcon Lake was initially chosen as the official Trailhead for the Trans Canada Trail *Path of the Paddle* route. Manitoba's land-based trail traverses Whiteshell Provincial Park, south as far as High Lake. The Manitoba Trails Association wanted to connect through High Lake, following a creek south to Shoal Lake, but even Bill Mason found the route way too much work as the creek was impassable. If you paddle this route, it's better to take advantage of spring or early summer water levels. This is one of the best marsh environments along the entire Path of the Paddle route.

The Falcon River is a naturalist's paradise and paddled easily in the early season. Watch for beaver, muskrats, otters, white-tail deer, wolves and moose. Bird species are numerous, including sandhill cranes, bitterns, great blue herons and Canada geese. Permission should be requested to paddle this route as it passes through First Nations traditional land. You can contact the Shoal Lake 40 band office at: (807) - 733-2315. Website: http://www.shoallake40.ca/.

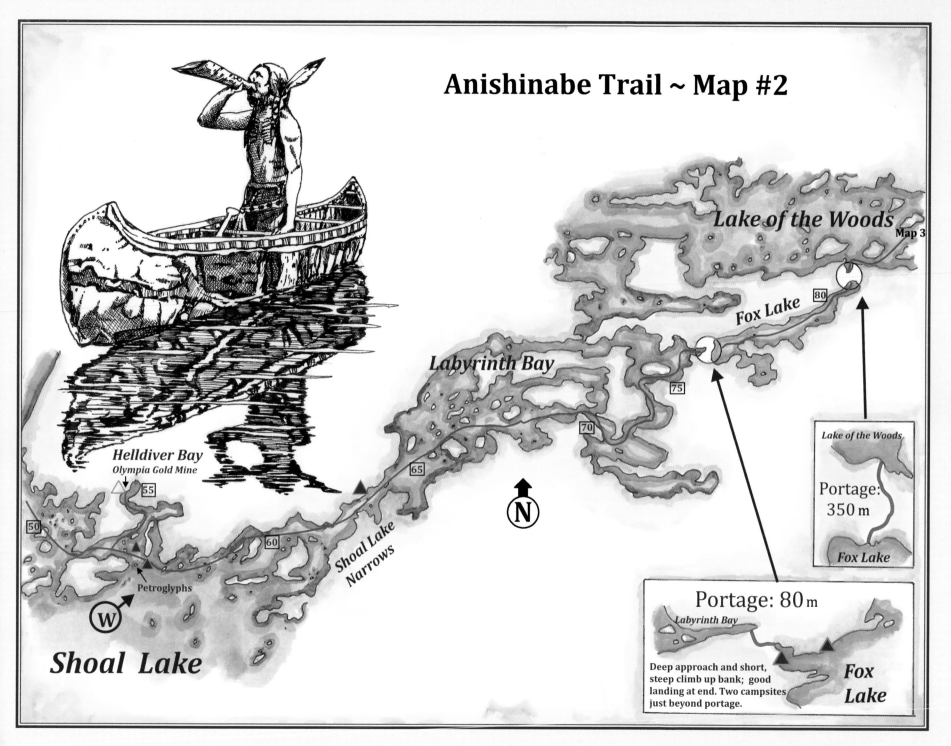

Anishinabe Trail ~ Map #2

Lake of the Woods

Map 3

Fox Lake

80

Labyrinth Bay

75

70

65

N

Helldiver Bay
Olympia Gold Mine

55

50

60

Shoal Lake
Narrows

Petroglyphs

W

Shoal Lake

Lake of the Woods

Portage:
350 m

Fox Lake

Portage: 80 m

Labyrinth Bay

Deep approach and short,
steep climb up bank; good
landing at end. Two campsites
just beyond portage.

Fox
Lake

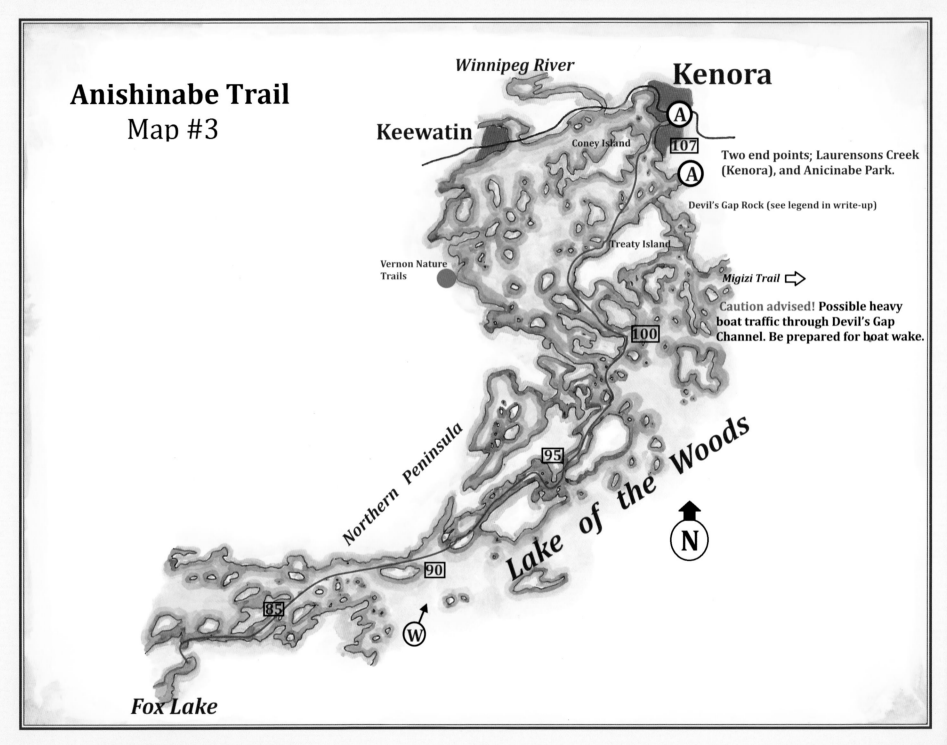

Anishinabe Trail
Map #3

Winnipeg River

Kenora

Keewatin

Ⓐ

Coney Island

107

Two end points; Laurensons Creek
(Kenora), and Anicinabe Park.

Ⓐ

Devil's Gap Rock (see legend in write-up)

Treaty Island

Vernon Nature
Trails

Migizi Trail ⇨

Caution advised! Possible heavy
boat traffic through Devil's Gap
Channel. Be prepared for boat wake.

100

Northern Peninsula

Lake of the Woods

95

N

90

W

85

Fox Lake

Falcon River Diary, late May

I stand at the road edge for some time, looking across the great field of winter-tired grasses, the Falcon meandering slowly southward, red-winged blackbirds flitting about the reeds. I take a deep breath as if getting ready to lift up a great weight, thinking how far it is to Lake Superior from here, not as the crow flies but as the fish swims. No straight lines in the wilderness. Day one of a long journey.

I scoop up a vial of river water and tuck it into my day pack. I'll give it to an elder at Shoal Lake and ask his permission to paddle through band territory, maybe get a blessing of the river water. I push my canoe off the shore and paddle quietly for 15 minutes. Rounding a sharp bend, I see a rather large timber wolf standing on top of a beaver lodge. Our eyes meet briefly. He bounds off through the sedge to a copse of spruce and disappears. I'm not alone. There is so much activity on the river, over the marsh, in the air, the water, everywhere.

Later A shallow lake off the river, over a flooded beaver dam. Mud Lake is aptly named. I scout for a possible campsite and see a rock outcropping on the north shore. It looks habitable and friendly, even good swimming, deeper than the rest of the lake off the shore. An old firepit and a ring of rocks encrusted with lichen. Perhaps ghosts still reside here. Too early to camp.

Unwanted guests Before the river ends I follow a channel into Snake Lake. There is a grassy open area perfect for tenting. A one-pot meal cooked on a stove and not an open fire. Not my preference, but there is no firepit. Exhausted. First days are like that. I'm sitting on my camera case and after a few minutes I notice the ground around me moving — insects of some kind, making headway up my boots and onto my legs. I pick one up; it flattens itself between my thumb and forefinger, as if it's doing pushups. I squeeze it, expecting it to pop, but it's hard. I curse

and stand up, brushing them off my pants; shake out my shirt; rake my fingers through my hair. *Ticks!* I retreat to my tent and strip down, finding several in the folds of my clothes.

No trespassing! The City of Winnipeg water intake, no trespassing signs everywhere. There is bad energy here. I paddle hard until I reach the open water of Snowshoe Bay and find clarity.

Ogitchida I meet Daryl Redsky at the reserve's beach. Tall and muscular, he arrives with his daughter riding on his back. His handshake could crush walnuts. He is in his early fifties and wears his hair in a tight faux-hawk. He has a broad smile and a soft voice, but he belongs to a network of aboriginal advocates known as warriors. He prefers the Anishinabe word *ogitchida*, meaning "big heart, a person who has love of the people and the land." Daryl is a veteran of the Canadian army and has led protests and blockades across Canada, including at Grassy Narrows. He trains people from his community in the art of peaceful protest.

He takes me to see an elder and I give him the vial of water. The elder is puzzled. "He's okay," Redsky explains. "He even has a Nishinabe name — *Mahingan Webidaw*. The water, it's from the river. It needs a blessing."

History Notes

In the early 1900s, engineers recommended Shoal Lake as a supply of water for the burgeoning city of Winnipeg. It was perfect. The water was crystal clear and the elevation was ideal for constructing a 137 km (85 mi) aqueduct. A delegation in 1906 reported: "There is practically no habitation, with the exception of a few Indians and an odd mining camp and no possibility of contamination from the source." To facilitate construction, the Native community of Shoal Lake 40 was shunted to a peninsula, which became an island when engineers cut a channel to divert the tannin-stained water of Falcon River away from the aqueduct intake.

—*Josiah Neufeld, "Sucked Dry: A First Nations Suffers So Winnipeg Can Have Water," The Walrus, February 23, 2015, https:// thewalrus.ca/sucked-dry/.*

Falcon River Diary, late October

My friend Jeremy Brown, a Métis from Kenora, drops me at Kejick. I pack my camping gear into the kayak hatches and set off into big water. I have been married for three weeks — a sweetheart from my past — and we've had Celtic rings custom made. I've only kayaked about 2 kilometers when I notice my ring has fallen off into the deep, cold waters of Shoal Lake, a lake so immense that I can see nothing of the far shore. Islands break the anger of the waves. Droplets of water freeze as they speed across the kayak deck. Next morning I find my ring, dancing

around in one of the storage hatches. This will be a good day, once the ice thaws in the coffee pot.

Labyrinth There are no boats here in the marshlands, just the last straggling clusters of loons, socializing until the shore freezes. Strange to see cactus plants (*Opuntia fragilis*) so far north, on the shores of Lake of the Woods. Inconspicuous spiny desert plants, as odd as the white pelican, which one associates with ocean coastlines. Some local anglers believe the pelicans are guilty of eating game fish like walleye and bass, and they are killed indiscriminately. Pelicans are surface feeders though, and they feast on shiners, cisco and sunfish. They like the peace and safety of the small rocky islands. So do I.

A diversion through Fox Lake — easy portages, even with the kayak. I feel so far removed from the immensity of Lake of the Woods. Once out on the big lake, I get only glimpses of the vastness, between the islands that shield me from south winds. The sun warms my hands through mitts that are covered with a crust of ice. I lean back and soak in the warmth. I think Bill Mason has best described the mystic beauty of Shoal and Lake of the Woods:

> *The morning mists that envelop the islands of Lake of the Woods hold special meaning to me. As a camper at Manitoba Pioneer Camp, I enjoyed our morning dip off what was called Senior Point. The air was cold but the water felt warm, clean and inviting. After my swim I would wrap up in a towel and watch the swirling mists between the distant islands . . . on clear days there was only a watery horizon between the islands, because the lake beyond was so large. It was called Shoal Lake.*
>
> —*Bill Mason,* **Canoescapes**
> *(Erin, ON: Boston Mills Press, 1995)*

Daryl Redsky and daughter at Shoal Lake.

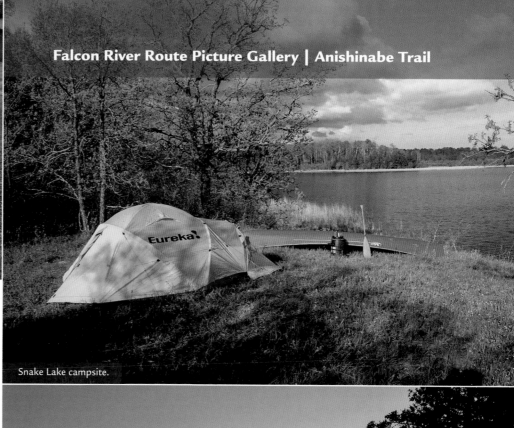
Falcon River Route Picture Gallery | Anishinabe Trail

Snake Lake campsite.

PRIVATE PROPERTY
NO TRESPASSING
BEWARE OF DOG

To add insult to injustice, "No Trespassing" signs were erected on Shoal Lake 40 FN traditional lands.

Lake of the Woods in the morning.

Route 2: Whiteshell & Winnipeg River Route   *Anishinabe Trail*

Maps 4, 5, 6, 7, 8, 9

Classification experienced novice

Distance 160 km (99 mi)

Duration 7 to 8 days

Portages 2, totaling 845 m (0.5 mi)

Season mid-May to mid-October

Preferred craft canoe, kayak or SUP

Campsites mix of established and undeveloped sites on rock outcrops and beaches

Access Reed Falls (Hwy 307 to Jessica Lake)

Egress Keewatin or Kenora

Water Characteristics and General Hazards

♦ Passive current on the Whiteshell River. The Winnipeg is a powerful river with a strong current wherever shorelines come together. This will not pose a problem for paddling downstream, but those taking advantage of prevailing lake winds will be paddling from west to east and will have to contend with the current at various places along the route. If you play the eddies near the shore, progress upstream through the narrows is not difficult.

♦ Several large lakes along this route. The route maps indicate preferred pathways depending on the direction of the wind; it generally hails from the southwest to west during prime paddling season (with variations).

♦ Caution advised when water temperatures are low. Add more time to your trip in case of wind, and avoid large sections of open water.

Features

♦ The Winnipeg River (it means "murky water" in Cree) was used by First Nations for thousands of years, then later as a major fur trade route to the interior. Where the Whiteshell River meets the Winnipeg River system through Whiteshell Provincial Park, there are many petroforms (stone placements), indicating ancient use of the region for ceremonies, travel, hunting and fishing and community gatherings.

♦ The Winnipeg flows 235 km (146 mi) from Lake of the Woods at Kenora to Lake Winnipeg. The watershed is 106, 500 sq km (41,100 sq mi), one-quarter of which is in northern Minnesota.

♦ The river was the main route from the Great Lakes to western and northern Canada before the coming of the railroads. This route was notorious for its many rapids and portages and exacted many casualties.

♦ The Winnipeg has several large dams, mostly below this portion.

♦ The wild rice beds of the Whiteshell lakes and the spruce and jack pine forests of the warm boreal region meet the majesty of rock and pine along the Winnipeg — a blending of two very different waterways that will not disappoint the adventurer.

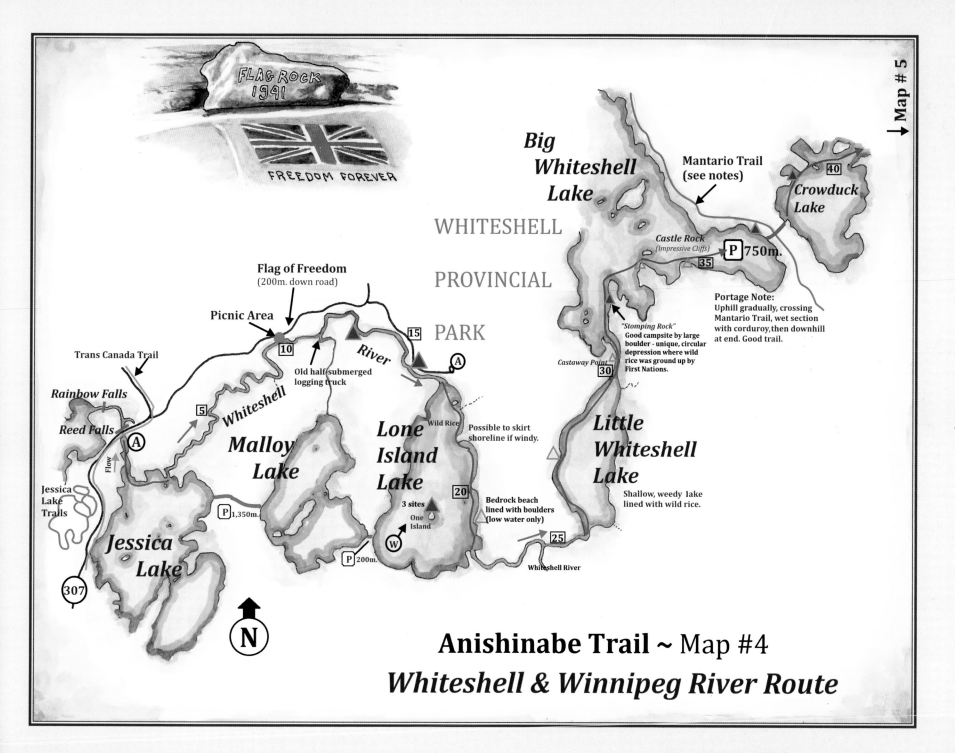

FLAG ROCK 1941

FREEDOM FOREVER

Big Whiteshell Lake

WHITESHELL

PROVINCIAL

PARK

Mantario Trail (see notes)

40

Crowduck Lake

Castle Rock *(Impressive Cliffs)*

P 750m.

35

Portage Note: Uphill gradually, crossing Mantario Trail, wet section with corduroy, then downhill at end. Good trail.

Flag of Freedom (200m. down road)

Picnic Area

10

15

River

A

"Stomping Rock" Good campsite by large boulder - unique, circular depression where wild rice was ground up by First Nations.

Old half-submerged logging truck

Trans Canada Trail

Rainbow Falls

Reed Falls

A

Whiteshell

5

Malloy Lake

Flow

Jessica Lake Trails

P 1,350m.

Jessica Lake

307

N

Lone Island Lake

Wild Rice

Possible to skirt shoreline if windy.

20

3 sites

One Island

W

P 200m.

Bedrock beach lined with boulders (low water only)

Whiteshell River

25

Castaway Point

30

Little Whiteshell Lake

Shallow, weedy lake lined with wild rice.

Anishinabe Trail ~ Map #4
Whiteshell & Winnipeg River Route

Map #5

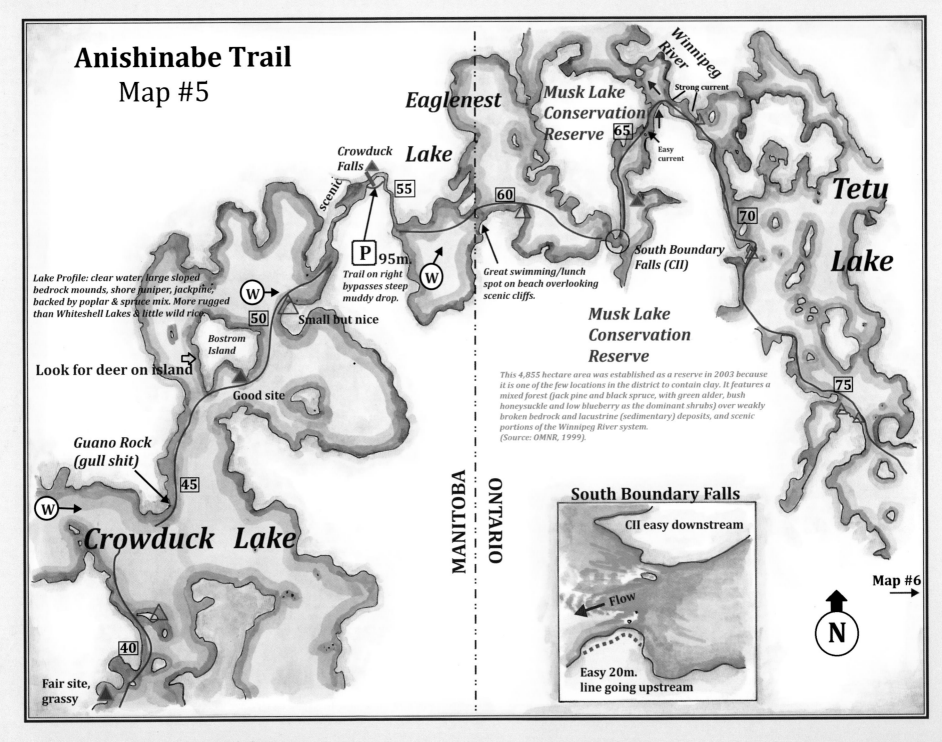

Anishinabe Trail
Map #5

Eaglenest

Lake

Winnipeg River

Musk Lake Conservation Reserve [65]

Strong current

Easy current

Tetu Lake

Crowduck Falls

[55]

[60]

[70]

[P] 95m.
Trail on right bypasses steep muddy drop.

(W)

Lake Profile: clear water, large sloped bedrock mounds, shore juniper, jackpine, backed by poplar & spruce mix. More rugged than Whiteshell Lakes & little wild rice.

(W)

[50]

Small but nice

Great swimming/lunch spot on beach overlooking scenic cliffs.

South Boundary Falls (CII)

Bostrom Island

Look for deer on island

Good site

Musk Lake Conservation Reserve

This 4,855 hectare area was established as a reserve in 2003 because it is one of the few locations in the district to contain clay. It features a mixed forest (jack pine and black spruce, with green alder, bush honeysuckle and low blueberry as the dominant shrubs) over weakly broken bedrock and lacustrine (sedimentary) deposits, and scenic portions of the Winnipeg River system. (Source: OMNR, 1999).

[75]

Guano Rock (gull shit)

(W)

[45]

MANITOBA | **ONTARIO**

South Boundary Falls

CII easy downstream

Crowduck   Lake

Flow

Map #6 →

[40]

(N)

Fair site, grassy

Easy 20m. line going upstream

Anishinabe Trail
Map #6

Previously known as the Islington Band of Saulteaux or Whitedog First Nation, Wabaseemoong Independent Nations is made up of the communities of Whitedog, One Man Lake and Swan Lake. The lifestyle is similar to that of Grassy Narrows. Ontario Hydro flooded the lands in the 1950's, seriously disrupting wild rice harvesting, trapping and traditional economic activities. In 1969, to make matters worse, mercury-poisoning of the English-Wabigoon River system directly affected the people living along these waterways. Before the mercury contamination, Whitedog depended on commercial fishing and tourism. This disruption has led to a high level of unemployment in the community.

Tetu Lake

Wabaseemoong 29 FN

Note: Access by permission only.
Band Office: 807-927-2068

Whitedog
(A)

Pelican Rock

80

85

90

Strong Current

River

95

100

Winnipeg

Whitedog Falls

W

105

Map 7

525

Rough Rock Lake

Whitedog Falls Portage

P 1,100m.

(A) 525
Boat Launch

Dangerous Current

525
Whitedog Generating Station

N

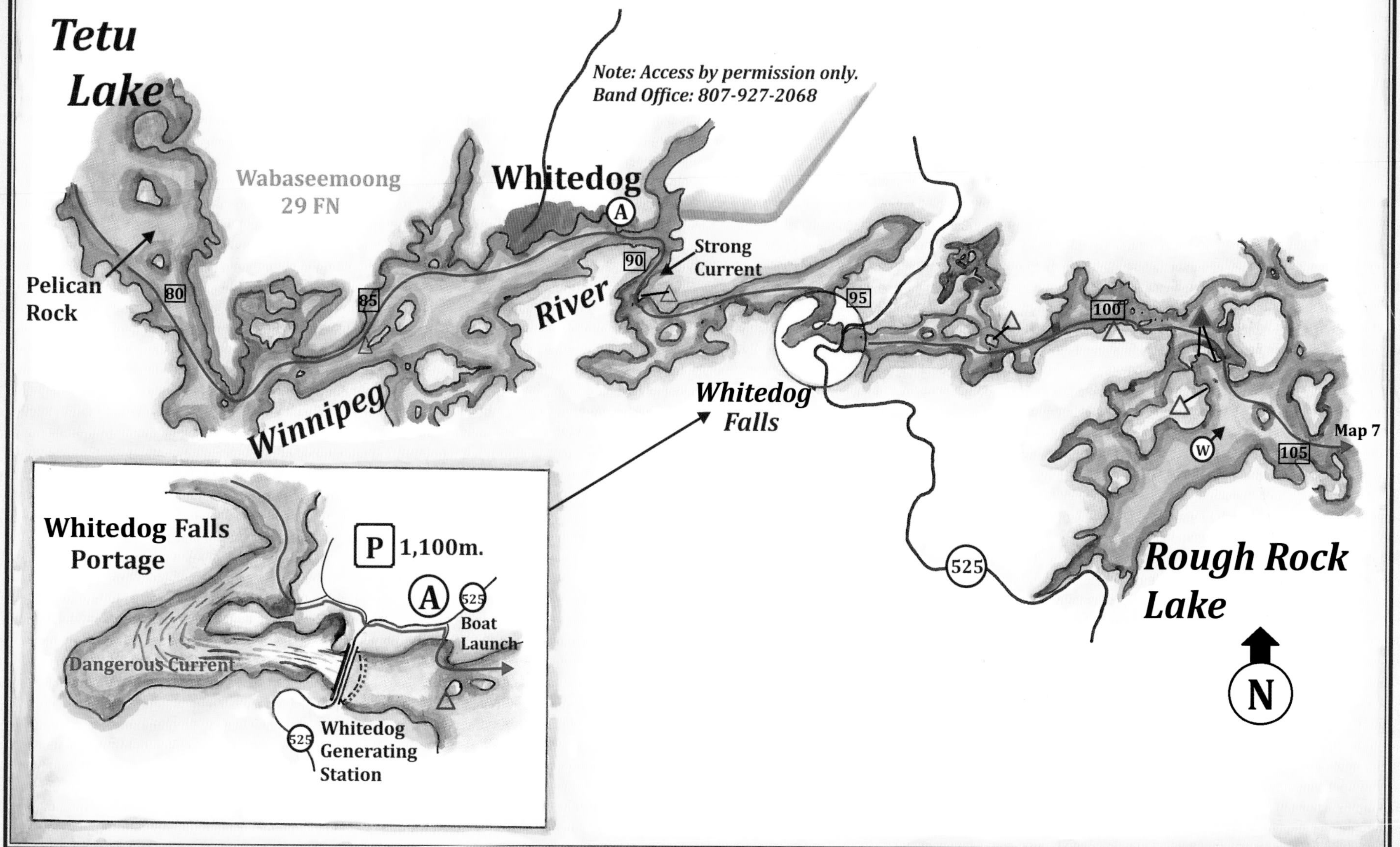

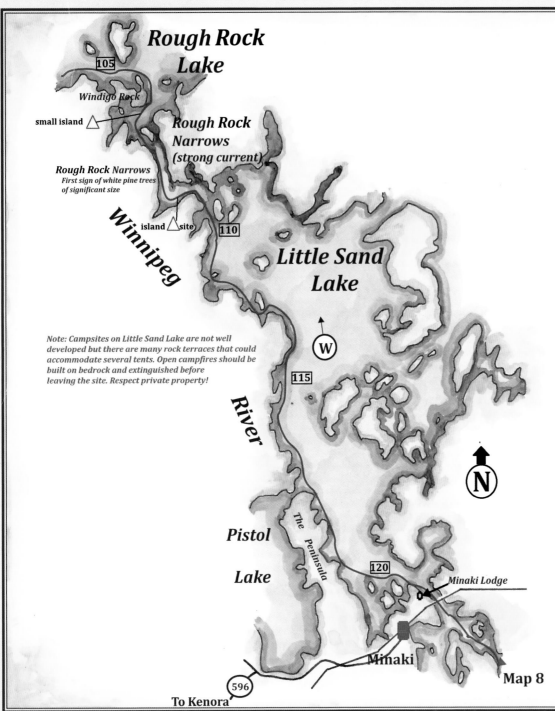

Anishinabe Trail
Map #7

Rough Rock Lake

105

Windigo Rock

small island △

Rough Rock Narrows (strong current)

Rough Rock Narrows
First sign of white pine trees of significant size

island △ site

110

Little Sand Lake

Winnipeg

Note: Campsites on Little Sand Lake are not well developed but there are many rock terraces that could accommodate several tents. Open campfires should be built on bedrock and extinguished before leaving the site. Respect private property!

W

River

115

N

Pistol Lake

The Peninsula

120

Minaki Lodge

596

Minaki

Map 8

To Kenora

MINAKI LODGE (*min-a-ki* is Ojibwe for "beautiful water") was formerly part of the CN hotel chain, originally built in 1914 by the Grand Trunk Pacific Railway - it burned down in 1925. It was rebuilt more lavishly, using Scottish stone masons, Swedish woodworkers and English gardeners. Thirty trainloads of soil were brought in from a farm in Manitoba to build a golf course on the rock of the Canadian Shield. It was owned for a short period by the Ontario government which spent $50 million on upgrades and then sold it at a loss. This "white elephant" has since been owned by a local First Nations band, a Calgary real estate developer and a Texas land speculator. The main lodge burned down in a spectacular fire in 2003 and the resort has remained closed ever since.

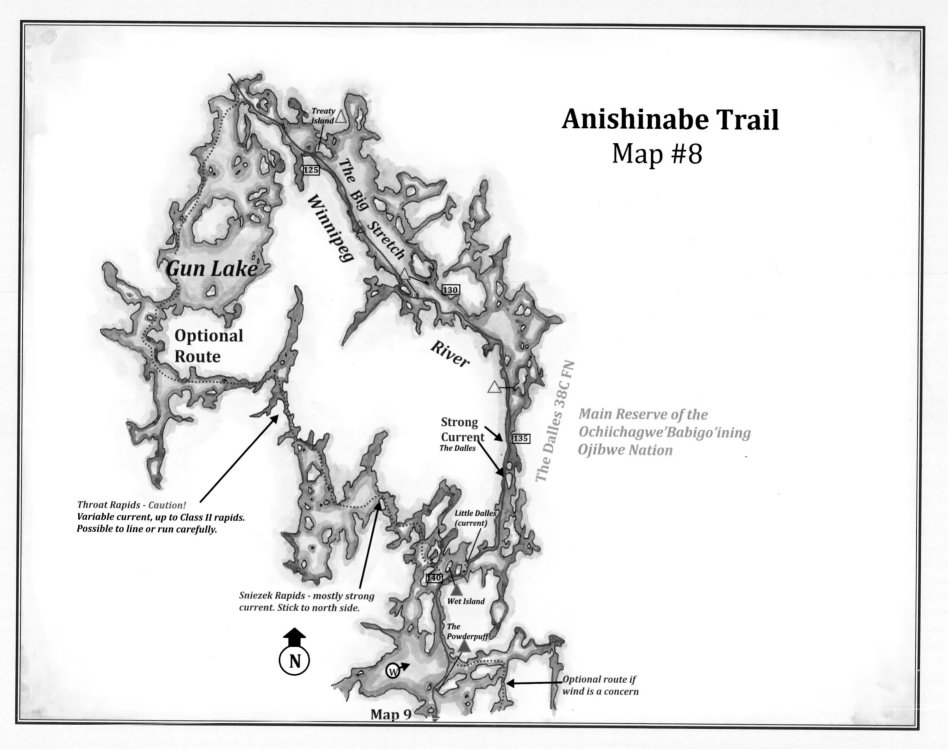

Anishinabe Trail
Map #8

Treaty Island △

125

Winnipeg

The Big Stretch

130

Gun Lake

Optional Route

River

The Dalles 38C FN

△

Strong Current
The Dalles

135

Main Reserve of the Ochiichagwe'Babigo'ining Ojibwe Nation

Throat Rapids - Caution!
Variable current, up to Class II rapids.
Possible to line or run carefully.

Little Dalles (current)

Sniezek Rapids - mostly strong current. Stick to north side.

140

Wet Island

The Powderpuff

N

W

Optional route if wind is a concern

Map 9

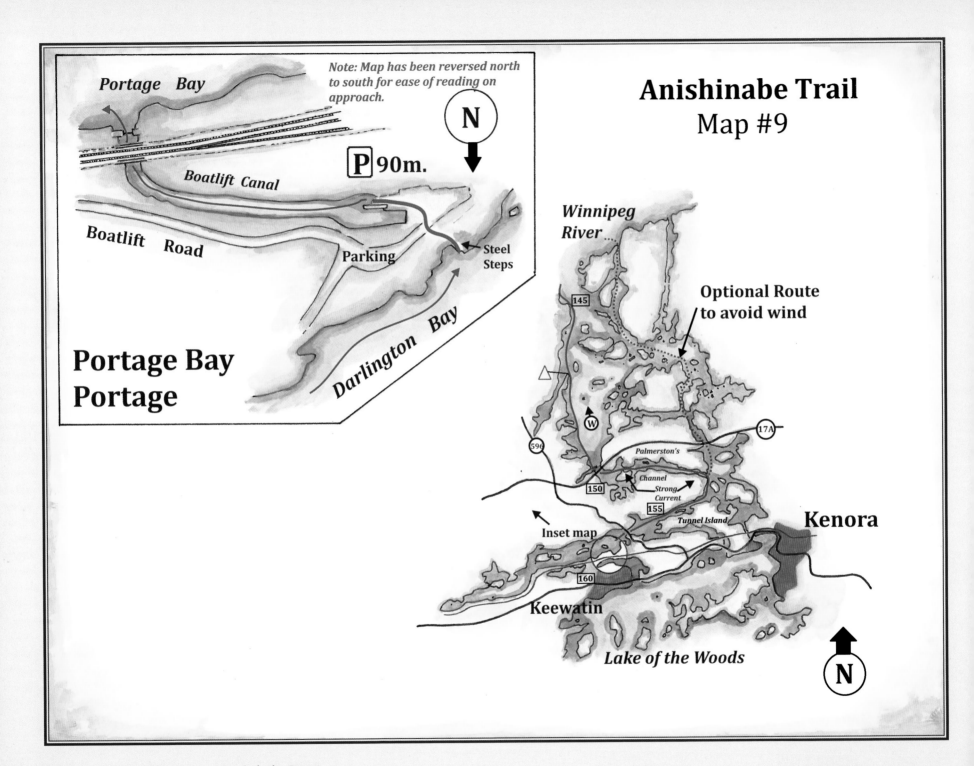

Portage Bay

Note: Map has been reversed north to south for ease of reading on approach.

N

P 90m.

Boatlift Canal

Boatlift Road

Parking

Steel Steps

Darlington Bay

Portage Bay Portage

Anishinabe Trail
Map #9

Winnipeg River ...

145

Optional Route to avoid wind

W

596

17A

Palmerston's

150

Channel Strong Current

155

Tunnel Island

Inset map

Kenora

160

Keewatin

Lake of the Woods

N

Whiteshell and Winnipeg River Diary, August

First days are always crazy, with few exceptions. Re-outfitting after a two-week expedition down the Bloodvein with clients. A lot of driving, too much bad road coffee and restaurant food. So nice to be mapping out this section of water trail with Andrea, my wife, as solo tripping does have its drawbacks. We pack quickly, stop at the LCBO for Irish whiskey and two large cans of Sapporo beer (they don't crush in your pack like other beers) and pick up our shuttle driver Bill, a retired teacher from Kenora who will take our vehicle back to town, then head east and north into Whiteshell Provincial Park. Steely Dan on the radio. Two hours later we arrive at the picnic area that straddles Reed Falls on Jessica Lake. We notice a Trans Canada Trail signpost beside the garbage can — our starting point.

Flag of Freedom We stop for lunch at a grassy opening squeezed between the river and the road. The owner of Jessica Lake Lodge has told us about the Flag of Freedom, a short hike along the road, so we take a look. Impressive bit of local history. Back at our canoe there are two Native men looking out at the river. They say they are checking out the wild rice, and they can tell what kind of season it will be just by looking from the shore. Their faces are weathered but they are not old. One tells us of a depression in the rock just past the narrows into Big Whiteshell Lake, where the Anishinabe would grind rice. "It's pretty interesting," he tells us. "You should see it if you can find it." He laughs. We did find it and it was very interesting.

Mantario Trail The block of land east and south of Big Whiteshell and Crowduck Lakes is the Mantario Wilderness Zone. No motorized access, hunting, resource extraction or development is allowed. It runs as far as the Ontario border. It is not surprising that, across

History Notes

The Whiteshell River, also known as la rivière Pichikoka, was used by the explorer La Verendrye in 1733 as an alternative to the Winnipeg River. The name Whiteshell is related to the small white sacred seashell known as megis, which some aboriginal people believe the Creator used to breathe life into the first human. Megis shells are symbolic of both the Creation and the "upright path" of life as established for the Anishinabe people. These shells are still used by healers of the Midewiwin society for healing and initiation.

the border in Ontario, the adjoining land is only partly contained by the Musk Lake Conservation Reserve, which has little protection status.

The Manitoba Naturalists Society created the trail in cooperation with the Manitoba Parks Branch in the early 1970s. It is the longest trail in the western Canadian Shield. Outcrops of ancient rock, pristine lakes and streams, peat bogs and sensational viewpoints typify the trail. It often follows granite ridges and makes use of existing beaver dams and primitive bridges to cross streams. A typical backpacking trip would take three to four days to complete, but a marathon race held each October generally completes the track in two days.

Crowduck Falls Andrea and I take our time to explore the falls. It's more of a sloped cascade than a falls, very charming, and it demanded to be explored in bare feet. Eaglenest Lake is actually part

History Notes

In 1962 the Dryden Chemical Company (DCC) began operating a plant that used a chloralkali process with a component of mercury. The plant produced sodium hydroxide and chlorine, which were used in large amounts for bleaching paper being produced by the nearby Dryden Pulp and Paper Company. DCC discharged its effluent directly into the Wabigoon-English River system. In the late 1960s, the people of Grassy Narrows and Whitedog First Nations began noticing symptoms of mercury poisoning (known as Minamata disease after its occurrence in Japan). In 1970 the Ontario government ordered DCC to stop dumping mercury into the river, although it did not place any restrictions on airborne emissions. Mercury dumping continued until 1975, when the company stopped using mercury cells in its process; it closed down a year later. It is estimated that more than 9,000 kg (10 tons) of mercury were dumped into the river between 1962 and 1970.

Fluid energy We get a taste of the power of the big river at South Boundary Falls, and we haven't reached the main channel yet. We push our canoe upstream and make an easy line along flat rocks around the rapids — an easy run if we were going the other way. We pitch camp nearby on a shelf of coarse rock, construct a good firepit out of the square stones scattered about, and cook our dinner. Sapporo in tin cups, a small block of chocolate and a soft mist rising across the bay as the sun touches the serrated tops of the far-shore jack pine.

Native land We work the eddies along the shore against the strong current through the narrows. A good workout. Aside from the occasional surge of current, the wildness of the Winnipeg has been disciplined by the many dams along its course. The landscape is quite stunning, raw and undeveloped, and before long we see the first vestiges of Ontario's provincial tree — the white pine, dominant with its outstretched limbs shaped by strong southwesterly winds, roots grasping shore rocks like clenched fists, soft music emanating from its lofty branches.

Past the derelict vehicles, a picnic bench hanging from a cliff is the village of Whitedog, home of the Wabaseemoong Anishinabeg. I chat with Adrian Bunting, who is sitting on his porch overlooking the river. His daughter sits on his lap; she has the most beautiful brown eyes and a smile that almost touches each ear. He talks of the changes in the village, of the high rate of unemployment; he is prideful, cautious, with an air of sadness in his voice.

Minaki Andrea and I fantasized about staying over at the posh Minaki Resort instead of pitching our tent — dinner in the dining room (the smoky aroma of our clothes would have gone unnoticed); maybe a gin and tonic, iced, with a wedge of lime; a soft bed in a

of the Winnipeg River system; Crowduck Falls tips away from the lake above on its downward plunge to Lake Winnipeg. The landscape is striking, boreal in all respects but more dramatic than further north; abrupt granite cliffs and bold rock outcrops remind me of Temagami or Quetico.

FLAG ROCK
1941

FREEDOM AND TY

History Notes

The Flag of Freedom

When you begin digging into local history, there are always one or two gems of particular interest. This story was related by a longtime resident of Jessica Lake, Bill Scarfe.

During the Second World War, the Manitoba Home for Boys in Portage la Prairie was commandeered by the Canadian Army to house recruits for military training. The boys and staff of the Home were forced to move to "Camp Three" in the Whiteshell Forest Reserve. The camp had been created by the government during the Great Depression of the 1930s to provide work for the unemployed men of Manitoba. They were building a forest-fire access road from Rennie to Green Lake. It was all physical labour, with horses pulling small scrapers and men pushing boulders; they were paid $5 a month and given food and clothing. When Canada joined the war in 1939, they left the camp for better-paying jobs in the military.

Camp Three was nothing more than a collection of shacks: small wood-frame boxes covered with tar paper, with no insulation and heated by converted 45-gallon drums that burned 2-foot split logs. The boys, teachers, caretakers, a cook and a minister — about 30 people — were at the camp over one winter, from October 1940 to June 1941.

In the spring of 1941, with the country at war and patriotism running high, in appreciation of their own freedom it was decided to paint a Union Jack, the flag of the British Commonwealth, for all passersby to see. Bohdan Kuryk, a teacher, with the help of at least one of the boys, chose the location, drew the outline and painted in the colours. Below it was printed "Freedom Forever." For many years the road was known as Flag Road, and the park where Camp Three stood is still referred to as Flag of Freedom Wayside Park.

The painting faded with the years, and by the 1970s only a lack of moss on the rock hinted at where the flag had been. However, more recently Anne Cott, a Big Whiteshell Lake cottager and amateur historian, felt it was important to restore the flag, and she arranged to have it repainted.

large room overlooking the river. Instead the town looks deserted, a bit haggard around the edges, almost too quiet for a once booming tourist destination. We pitch our tent on a rock knoll, quickly eat a one-pot meal and retire to the tent with a dram of Irish whiskey just before it starts to rain.

The big stretch It makes sense that most of the historic campsites are under several meters of water, not to mention any archaeological evidence of First Nations. Beautiful as the Winnipeg River is, finding an established campsite through this stretch can be daunting. However, there are many rock ledges where a camp can be set up, which is convenient if you do all your cooking on a stove rather than an open fire.

Thoughts on the Anishinabe Trail

I saw no other paddler during my solo ventures. It could have been the season and the weather, but neither did my wife and I see anyone during our trips. The Anishinabe Trail is an underutilized paddling resource, far more remote in aspect than I expected and beautiful in fact, with the lingering additive of historical merit. Canadian history was made here.

History Notes

An early description of a trip down the Winnipeg River appears in a book by Alexander Henry, *Travels and Adventures in Canada and the Indian Territories, Between the Years 1760 and 1776*. Henry called the river "Winipegon" and describes his journey:

> *From the Portage du Rat [present-day Kenora] we descended the great river Winipegon, which is there from one mile to two in breadth, and at every league [a British nautical league is 4.8 km/3 mi] grows broader. The channel is deep, but obstructed by many islands, of which some are large. For several miles, the stream is confined between perpendicular rocks. The current is strong, and the navigation singularly difficult. Within the space of fifteen leagues, there are seven falls, of from fifty feet to a hundred [15 to 30 m] in height.*

Whiteshell and Winnipeg River Route
Picture Gallery | Anishinabe Trail

Prehistoric wild rice stomping rock 'pot-hole' depression on Big Whiteshell Lake.

Winnipeg River

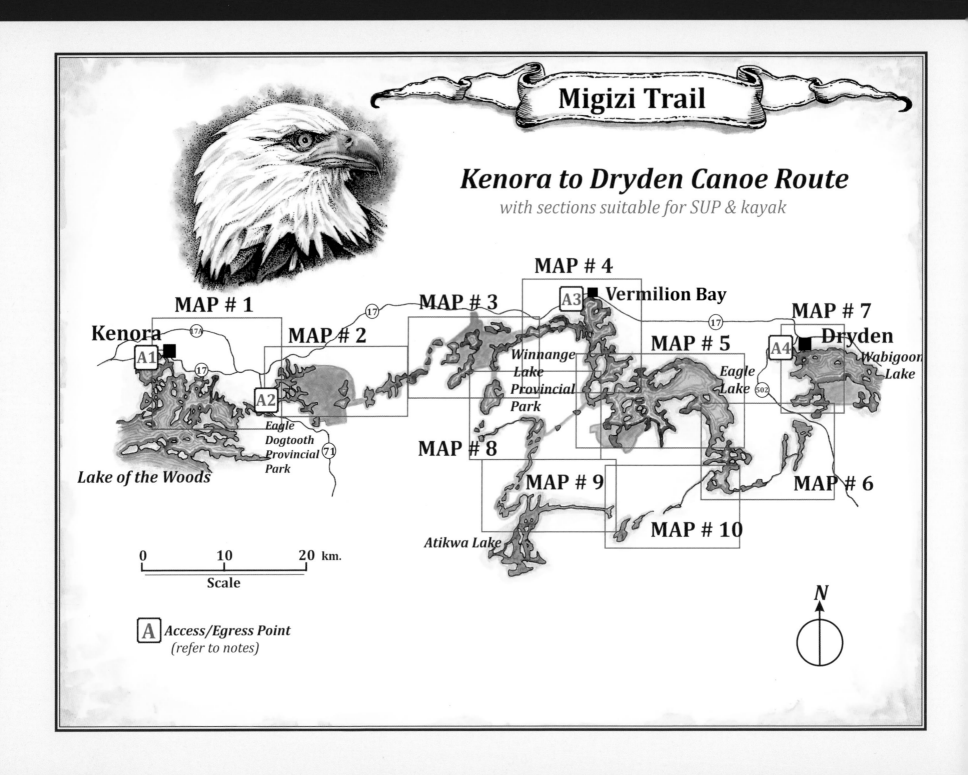

Migizi Trail

Kenora to Dryden Canoe Route
with sections suitable for SUP & kayak

MAP # 1

MAP # 2

MAP # 3

MAP # 4

MAP # 5

MAP # 6

MAP # 7

MAP # 8

MAP # 9

MAP # 10

Kenora

A1

A2

A3 — Vermilion Bay

A4 — Dryden

Lake of the Woods

Eagle Dogtooth Provincial Park

Winnange Lake Provincial Park

Eagle Lake

Wabigoon Lake

Atikwa Lake

0   10   20 km.
Scale

A Access/Egress Point
(refer to notes)

N

Chapter 5

Part 2
Migizi Trail

Topographic Map Locations
1:100,000 scale (provincial series)
Rat Portage Bay 52-E/NE – Blue Lake 52-F/NW –
Wabigoon Lake 52-F/NE – Rowan Lake 52-F/SW
1:50,000 scale
Dryden 52-F/15 – Kenora 52-E/16 – Longbow Lake 52-E/9 – Feist Lake 52-F/13
– Vermilion Bay 52-F/13 – Dryberry Lake 52-F/12 – Osborne Bay 52-F/14

The Anishinabeg believed that the bald eagle, *migizi*, was a thunderbird in disguise, dedicated to protecting Mother Earth. It is considered the most powerful of all spirits, or manitous, second only to the Great Spirit, Gitchi Manitou — the Creator. The eagle protects, serves and guards the people and flies close to the Creator. That is why the eagle feather is the most sacred of feathers and is most often used by healers to guide prayers back to Gitchi Manitou.

Bald eagles have taken a bad rap. They were once persecuted and blamed for predation of wild salmon and even livestock; some US states offered lucrative bounties for killing eagles, mostly between 1917 and 1970. As with other animals whose parts are considered valuable aphrodisiacs or ceremonial items, the poaching of eagles tipped the balance even further. To exacerbate the eagle's already tenuous hold on survival, the pesticide DDT invaded the food chain, with horrific results for raptors that reside higher on the ecological scale. DDT was banned in the 1970s but by then the eagle was almost exterminated. It has since made a remarkable comeback.

So it is fitting that the next trail on our journey across the heart of the country gives special place to the eagle as a significant and iconic feature. It is seen almost everywhere, particularly near narrow bands of water, creeks and high cliffs. Nests are often built on lofty perches atop pine trees. The eagle's vivid white head stands out against the olive drab of pine and spruce as it perches in the branches watching you paddle by.

Kenora to Dryden Canoe Route

Maps 1, 2, 3, 4, 5, 6, 7 | Challenge Route Maps 8, 9, 10

Migizi Trail

Kenora to Dryden, via Eagle Lake

Classification intermediate

Distance 218 km (135 mi)

Duration 12 to 14 days (15.5 to 18 km per day)

Portages 16, totaling 7,140 m (4.5 mi), 3.5% of distance (below average)

Season mid-May to mid-October

Preferred craft canoe (minimum 16 ft)

Special concerns large lake crossings; wind conditions

Moving water light current; some swifts

Access Kenora (other options on maps)

Egress Dryden (other options on maps)

Kenora to Dryden, via Challenge Route

Classification experienced intermediate

Distance 243 km (151 mi)

Duration 16 to 18 days (13.5 to 15 km per day)

Portages 35, totaling 14,655 m (9 mi), 6% of distance (above average)

Season mid-May to mid-October

Preferred craft canoe (lightweight, 16 ft minimum)

Special concerns some large lake crossings; wind concerns; isolation; difficult portages

Moving water light current; some swifts

Access Kenora (other options on maps)

Egress Dryden (other options on maps)

Features

- The coastal attributes of Lake of the Woods and Eagle Lake make them good kayak and SUP destinations.
- A string of provincial parks and conservation reserves, each with special natural characteristics, protects and highlights some of the finest canoeing waters imaginable.
- Clear-water lakes and dramatic sweeping landscapes take your breath away and provoke the senses.
- Historic and cultural features include rock paintings more than 2,000 years old and *onigum* (portage trails) unchanged through the millennia.
- In the magnificent pine forests it is easy to find solace, adventure and connection.

Route Options

- For those who want to park vehicles in the community of Vermilion Bay for loop trips, there are two options that cut distance and time from the linear configurations. The return route takes either Piskegomang Brook or Barren Brook back to Eagle Lake instead of proceeding east and north to Dryden.
- Kayakers and SUPers are encouraged to use Vermilion Bay as their access point if they want to avoid the portages from Stewart Lake, and to explore the lake islands in a loop configuration.

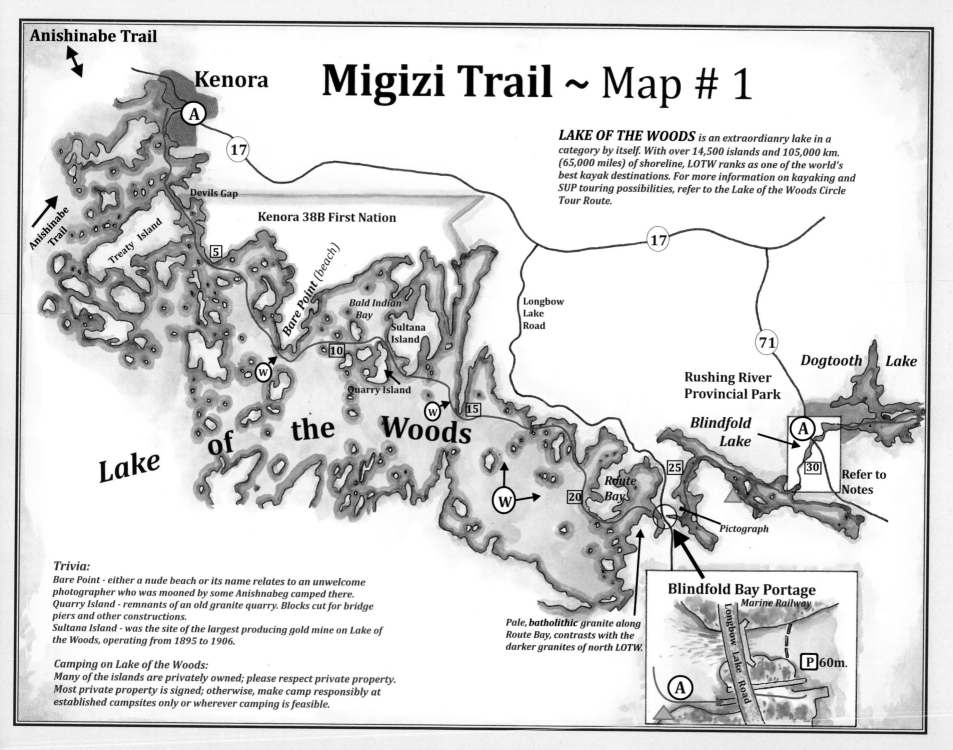

Migizi Trail ~ Map # 1

Anishinabe Trail

Kenora

A

17

Anishinabe Trail

Devils Gap

Kenora 38B First Nation

Treaty Island

5

Bare Point (beach)

Bald Indian Bay

Sultana Island

10

W

Quarry Island

Lake

of

the

Woods

W

15

W

20

Route Bay

25

Pictograph

LAKE OF THE WOODS *is an extraordianry lake in a category by itself. With over 14,500 islands and 105,000 km. (65,000 miles) of shoreline, LOTW ranks as one of the world's best kayak destinations. For more information on kayaking and SUP touring possibilities, refer to the Lake of the Woods Circle Tour Route.*

17

Longbow Lake Road

71

Dogtooth Lake

Rushing River Provincial Park

Blindfold Lake

A

30

Refer to Notes

*Pale, **batholithic** granite along Route Bay, contrasts with the darker granites of north LOTW.*

Trivia:
Bare Point - either a nude beach or its name relates to an unwelcome photographer who was mooned by some Anishnabeg camped there.
Quarry Island - remnants of an old granite quarry. Blocks cut for bridge piers and other constructions.
Sultana Island - was the site of the largest producing gold mine on Lake of the Woods, operating from 1895 to 1906.

Camping on Lake of the Woods:
Many of the islands are privately owned; please respect private property.
Most private property is signed; otherwise, make camp responsibly at established campsites only or wherever camping is feasible.

Blindfold Bay Portage

Marine Railway

Longbow Lake Road

P 60m.

A

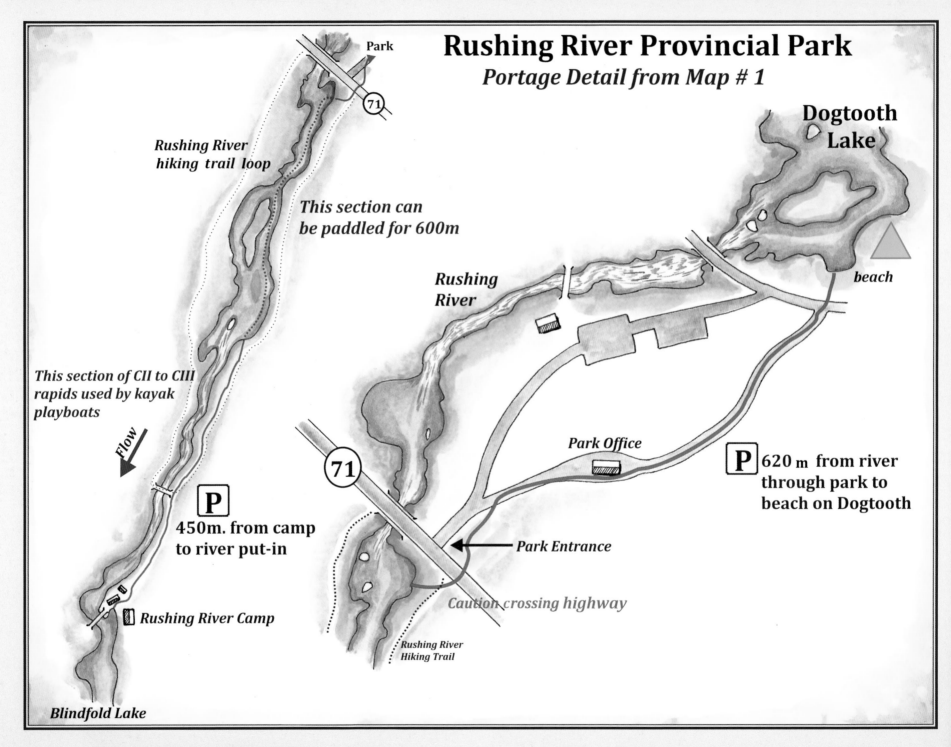

Rushing River Provincial Park
Portage Detail from Map # 1

Park

71

Dogtooth Lake

Rushing River hiking trail loop

This section can be paddled for 600m

Rushing River

beach

This section of CII to CIII rapids used by kayak playboats

Flow

Park Office

P 620 m from river through park to beach on Dogtooth

71

P 450m. from camp to river put-in

Park Entrance

Caution crossing highway

🏕 *Rushing River Camp*

Rushing River Hiking Trail

Blindfold Lake

Migizi Trail ~ Map # 2

Rushing River, Eagle-Dogtooth & Winnange Provincial Parks

Three provincial parks combine to form a link between Lake of the Woods and Eagle Lake. Rushing River is a developed recreational park that features the scenic rapids of the Rushing River. Eagle-Dogtooth is a waterway park that contains regionally significant moraines, wetlands and pine forests. Winnange Lake is a non-operating natural environment–class park established to protect geological features. All three parks support a unique backcountry paddling experience.

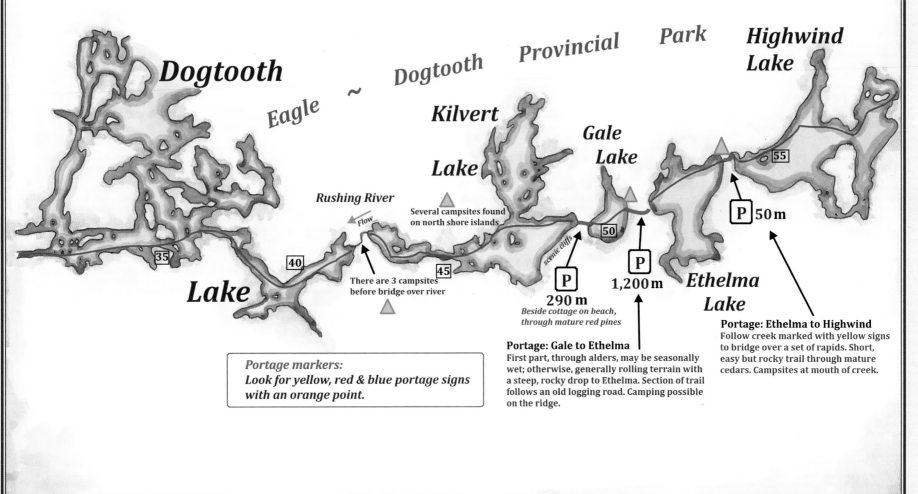

Dogtooth

Eagle ~ Dogtooth Provincial Park

Highwind Lake

Kilvert

Gale Lake

Lake

55

Rushing River

Flow

Several campsites found on north shore islands

scenic cliffs

50

P 50 m

35

40

45

P 290 m

P 1,200 m

Ethelma Lake

Lake

There are 3 campsites before bridge over river

290 m
Beside cottage on beach, through mature red pines

Portage: Gale to Ethelma
First part, through alders, may be seasonally wet; otherwise, generally rolling terrain with a steep, rocky drop to Ethelma. Section of trail follows an old logging road. Camping possible on the ridge.

Portage: Ethelma to Highwind
Follow creek marked with yellow signs to bridge over a set of rapids. Short, easy but rocky trail through mature cedars. Campsites at mouth of creek.

Portage markers:
Look for yellow, red & blue portage signs with an orange point.

Migizi Trail
Map # 3

private cabin — **Cedar Rapids Detail**

swifts through rocks (good channel)

Ⓟ 100 m

Geejay Lake

Flow

17

Pine Road
Experimental Lakes Road
Private past 4.5km

Ⓐ

20m. to creek ▲ **2**

Stewart Lake

Ⓟ **350 m**

Geejay Lake

70

Optional Route

▲ *Cedar Rapids*

Winange Lake

Winnange Lake Provincial Park

Ⓟ **395 m**

Manomin Lake

75 Ⓟ **560 m** *see note*

Eagle Lake

95

Rivet Lake
Lake 109 - one of 58 experimental lakes. See journal notes.

Fish Lake

80

Ⓟ **275 m**

Impressive pine-topped cliffs

90

Porcus Lake

65 Ⓟ **125 m**

Rivet Lake

flow **Eagle River**

Challenge Route Starts Here
Paddlers have the option of taking the Eagle Lake route or the Challenge Route (110 km), which rejoins the Eagle Lake route at mileage 170 (km).

⬇

60

Winange Lake

85

Ⓟ **120 m**
Buzzard Falls: Steep trail at end

Ⓟ **575 m**

Wet sections at start, slow uphill alongside Teggau Creek.

Ⓟ **260 m**

Pictographs

5

Portage: Manomin to Winange
A "pile of rocks," and probably one of the more interesting portages you'll come across. Glacial erratics of enormous proportions are tumbled and stacked, forming grottos and caves - well worth investigating!

Teggau Lake

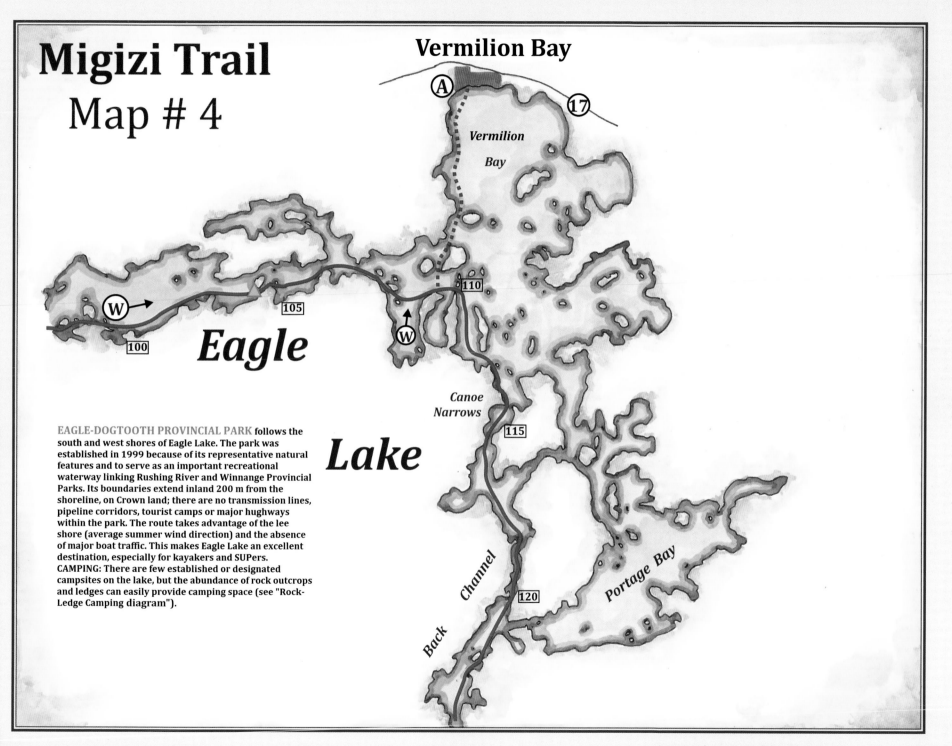

Migizi Trail
Map # 4

Vermilion Bay

Ⓐ

17

Vermilion

Bay

110

Ⓦ

105

Ⓦ

100

Eagle

Lake

Canoe
Narrows

115

EAGLE-DOGTOOTH PROVINCIAL PARK follows the south and west shores of Eagle Lake. The park was established in 1999 because of its representative natural features and to serve as an important recreational waterway linking Rushing River and Winnange Provincial Parks. Its boundaries extend inland 200 m from the shoreline, on Crown land; there are no transmission lines, pipeline corridors, tourist camps or major hughways within the park. The route takes advantage of the lee shore (average summer wind direction) and the absence of major boat traffic. This makes Eagle Lake an excellent destination, especially for kayakers and SUPers.
CAMPING: There are few established or designated campsites on the lake, but the abundance of rock outcrops and ledges can easily provide camping space (see "Rock-Ledge Camping diagram").

Portage Bay

Back Channel

120

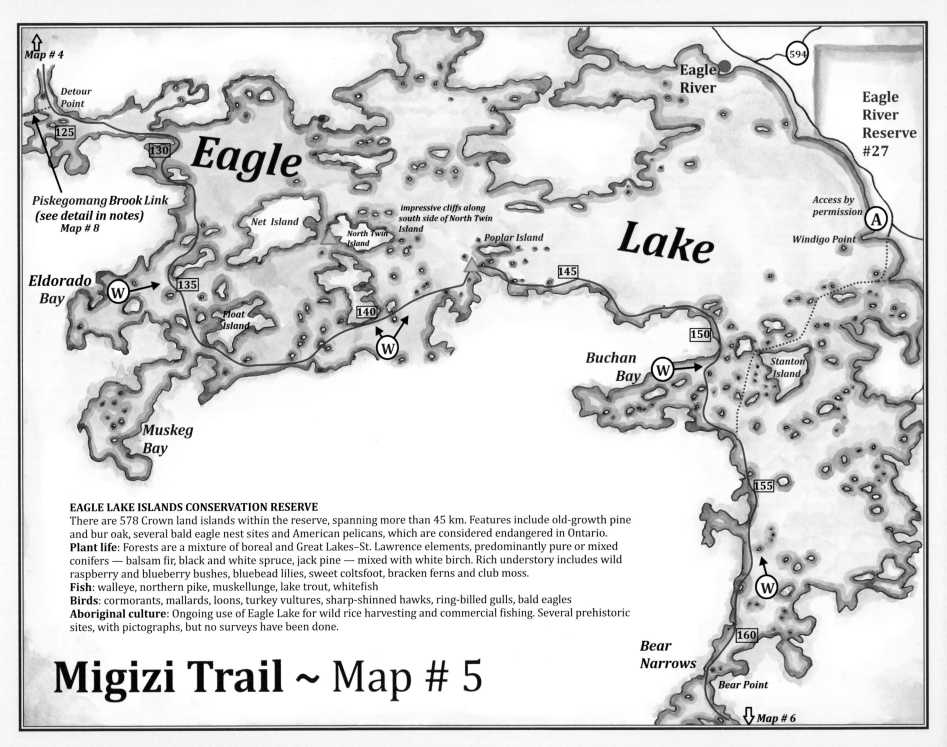

Map # 4

Detour Point

125

130

Eagle

Piskegomang Brook Link
(see detail in notes)
Map # 8

Net Island

*impressive cliffs along
south side of North Twin
Island*

North Twin
Island

Poplar Island

Lake

Eagle
River

(594)

**Eagle
River
Reserve
#27**

*Access by
permission*

(A)

Windigo Point

**Eldorado
Bay**

(W) 135

Float
Island

140

(W)

145

**Muskeg
Bay**

150

**Buchan
Bay**

(W)

*Stanton
Island*

155

(W)

EAGLE LAKE ISLANDS CONSERVATION RESERVE
There are 578 Crown land islands within the reserve, spanning more than 45 km. Features include old-growth pine and bur oak, several bald eagle nest sites and American pelicans, which are considered endangered in Ontario.
Plant life: Forests are a mixture of boreal and Great Lakes–St. Lawrence elements, predominantly pure or mixed conifers — balsam fir, black and white spruce, jack pine — mixed with white birch. Rich understory includes wild raspberry and blueberry bushes, bluebead lilies, sweet coltsfoot, bracken ferns and club moss.
Fish: walleye, northern pike, muskellunge, lake trout, whitefish
Birds: cormorants, mallards, loons, turkey vultures, sharp-shinned hawks, ring-billed gulls, bald eagles
Aboriginal culture: Ongoing use of Eagle Lake for wild rice harvesting and commercial fishing. Several prehistoric sites, with pictographs, but no surveys have been done.

Migizi Trail ~ Map # 5

**Bear
Narrows**

160

Bear Point

Map # 6

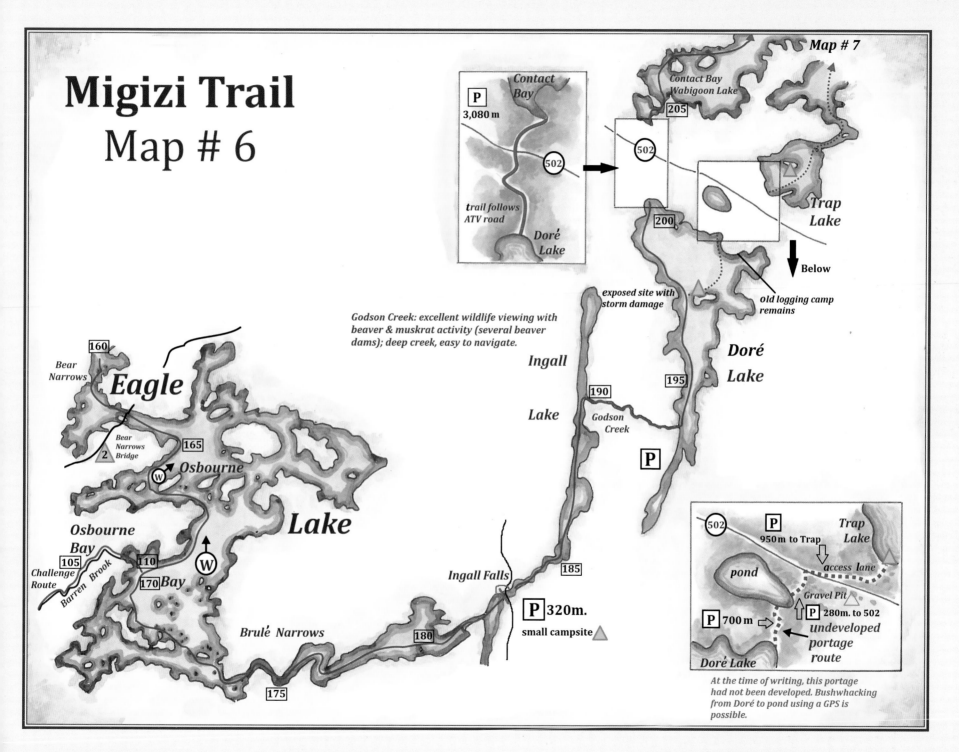

Migizi Trail
Map # 6

Map # 7

Contact Bay

P 3,080 m

502

trail follows ATV road

Doré Lake

Contact Bay Wabigoon Lake

205

502

200

Trap Lake

Below

old logging camp remains

exposed site with storm damage

Godson Creek: excellent wildlife viewing with beaver & muskrat activity (several beaver dams); deep creek, easy to navigate.

Ingall

Lake

190

Godson Creek

195

Doré Lake

P

160

Bear Narrows

Eagle

Bear Narrows Bridge

2

165

W

Osbourne

Lake

Osbourne Bay

105

Challenge Route

Barren Brook

110

170

W

Bay

Ingall Falls

185

P 320m.

small campsite

Brulé Narrows

180

175

502

P

950 m to Trap

Trap Lake

pond

access lane

Gravel Pit

P 700 m

P 280 m. to 502

undeveloped portage route

Doré Lake

At the time of writing, this portage had not been developed. Bushwhacking from Doré to pond using a GPS is possible.

Migizi Trail ~ Map # 7

17

Wabigoon River

Dryden

A

218

Maukinak Trail ⇨

West Arm

Picnic Island

215

Wabigoon Lake

W

Seasonal

Larson Bay

210

Wildcat Bay

205 Contact Bay

From Map # 6

Trap Lake

From Map # 6

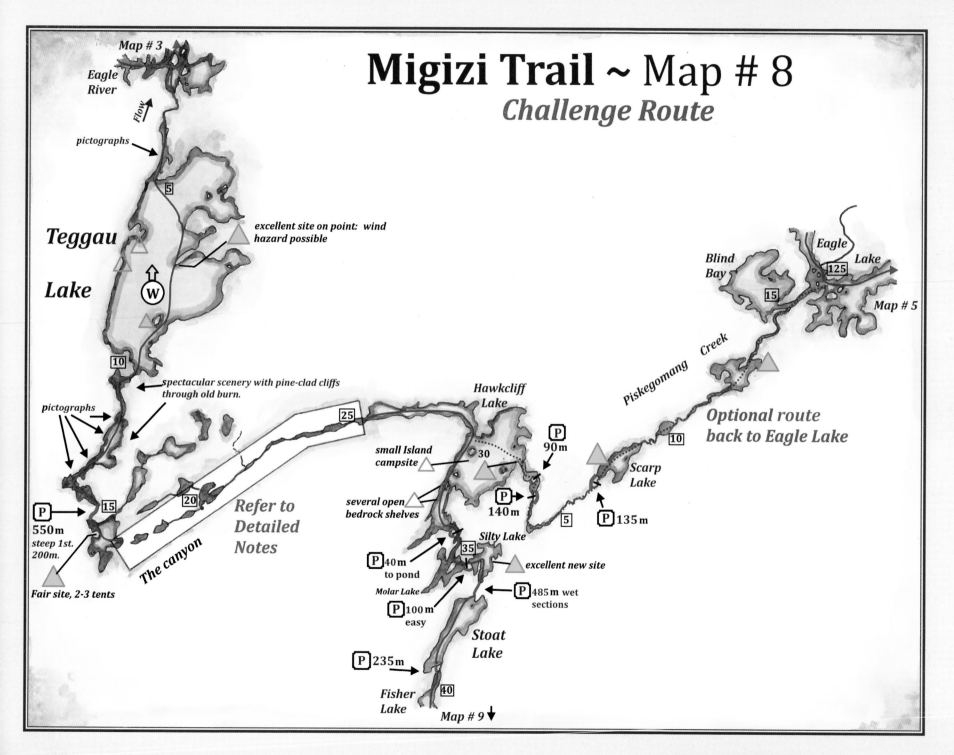

Migizi Trail ~ Map # 8
Challenge Route

Map # 3

Eagle River

Flow

pictographs

5

Teggau

Lake

excellent site on point: wind hazard possible

W

10

spectacular scenery with pine-clad cliffs through old burn.

pictographs

25

The canyon

Refer to Detailed Notes

20

P
550 m
steep 1st. 200 m.

15

Fair site, 2-3 tents

Hawkcliff Lake

small Island campsite

30

P
90 m

P
140 m

several open bedrock shelves

P
40 m
to pond

Silty Lake

35

P
100 m
easy

Molar Lake

excellent new site

P 485 m wet sections

5

P 135 m

Scarp Lake

10

Piskegomang Creek

Blind Bay

Eagle Lake

125

15

Map # 5

Optional route back to Eagle Lake

Stoat Lake

P 235 m

Fisher Lake

40

Map # 9 ↓

Canyon Portages

Portages 1 to 4

1. **200 m.** Skirt left side of grassy marsh to forest edge; cross rocky creek up to pond (wet at end). Marsh may be flooded in spring.
2. **45 m.** Cross creek twice; go through narrow cleft and up beaver dam to a sloped rock outcrop.
3. **600 m.** Steady, gradual uphill, leveling out with a couple of short wet spots. Huge erratic (glacial boulder) at midpoint.
4. **360 m.** Follow narrow creek for about 200 m (lift over where necessary). Portage 160 m across mossy, hummocky mat to open water. Look for bakeapple and pitcher plants.

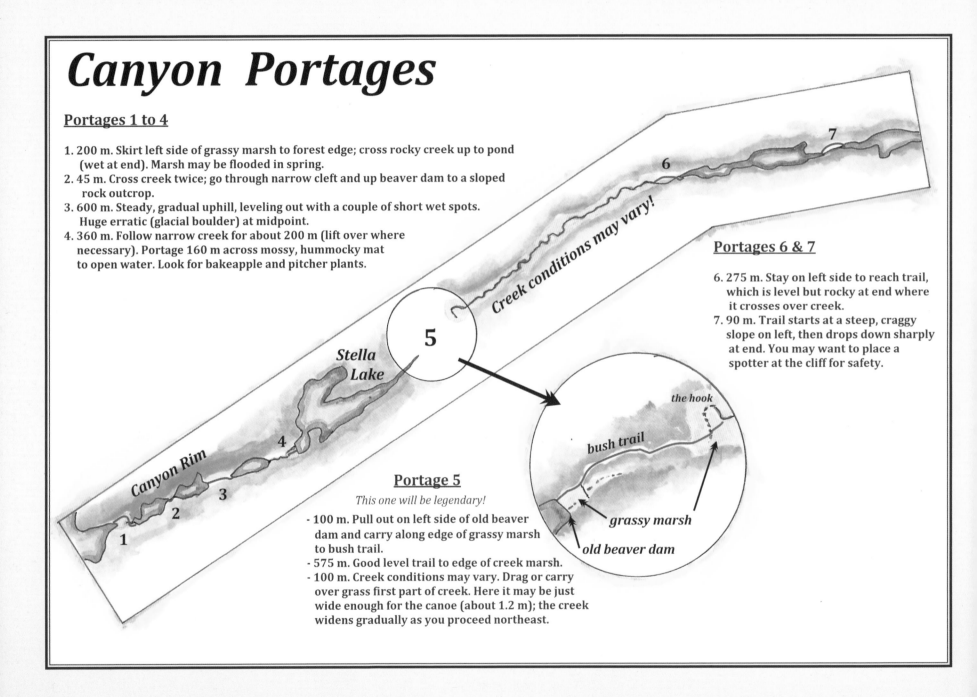

Creek conditions may vary!

Stella Lake

Canyon Rim

Portages 6 & 7

6. **275 m.** Stay on left side to reach trail, which is level but rocky at end where it crosses over creek.
7. **90 m.** Trail starts at a steep, craggy slope on left, then drops down sharply at end. You may want to place a spotter at the cliff for safety.

the hook

bush trail

grassy marsh

old beaver dam

Portage 5

This one will be legendary!

- **100 m.** Pull out on left side of old beaver dam and carry along edge of grassy marsh to bush trail.
- **575 m.** Good level trail to edge of creek marsh.
- **100 m.** Creek conditions may vary. Drag or carry over grass first part of creek. Here it may be just wide enough for the canoe (about 1.2 m); the creek widens gradually as you proceed northeast.

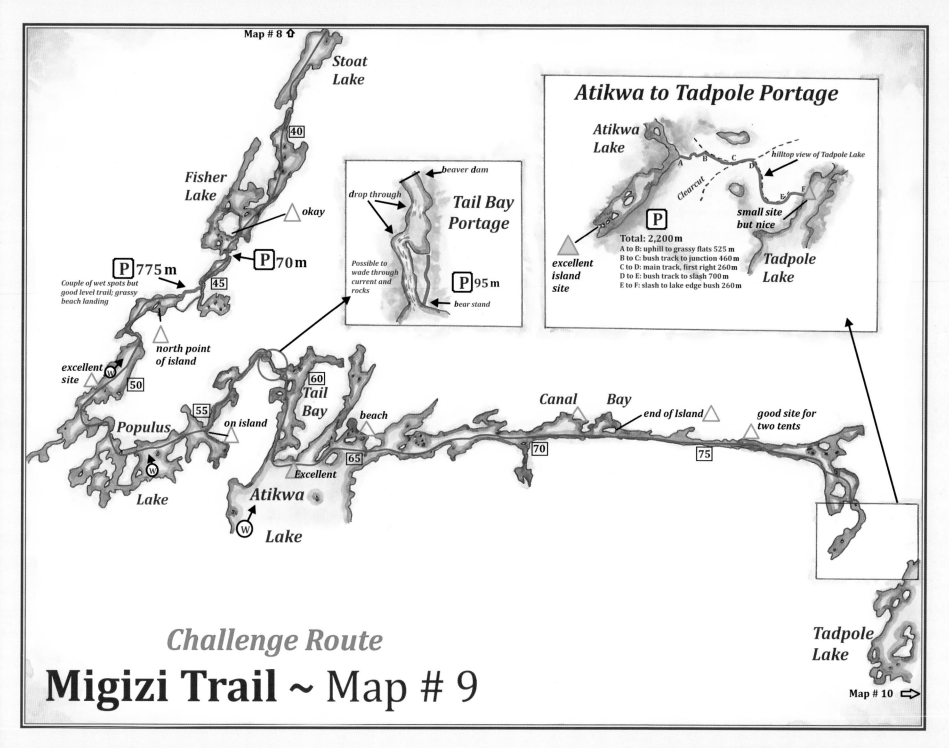

Map # 8 ⇧

Stoat
Lake

40

Fisher
Lake

△ okay

P 70m

P 775m

*Couple of wet spots but
good level trail; grassy
beach landing*

45

△ north point
of island

excellent
site Ⓦ

50

55

Populus

△ on island

Ⓦ

Lake

60

Tail
Bay

△ beach

Excellent

65

Atikwa

Ⓦ

Lake

Tail Bay Portage

beaver dam

drop through

*Possible to
wade through
current and
rocks*

P 95m

bear stand

Atikwa to Tadpole Portage

Atikwa
Lake

A B C

hilltop view of Tadpole Lake

Clearcut

D

E F

△ *small site
but nice*

P

Total: 2,200 m
A to B: uphill to grassy flats 525 m
B to C: bush track to junction 460 m
C to D: main track, first right 260 m
D to E: bush track to slash 700 m
E to F: slash to lake edge bush 260 m

Tadpole
Lake

△ excellent
island
site

Canal   Bay

△

end of Island

△ good site for
two tents

70

75

Tadpole
Lake

Challenge Route
Migizi Trail ~ Map # 9

Map # 10 ⇨

Migizi Trail ~ Map # 10
Challenge Route

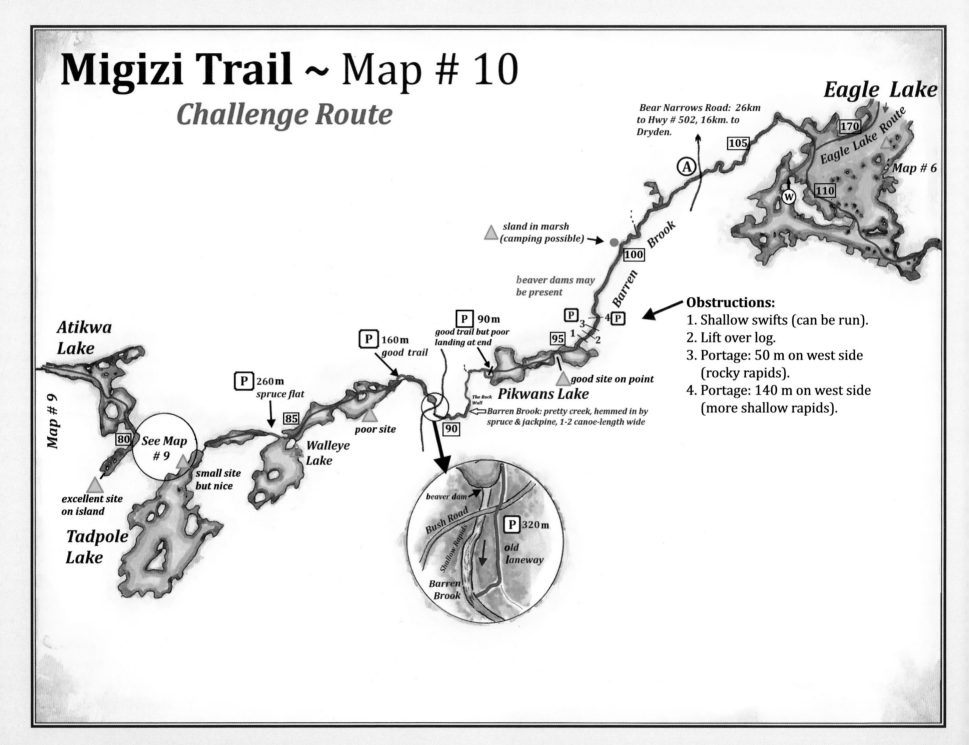

Eagle Lake

Bear Narrows Road: 26km to Hwy # 502, 16km. to Dryden.

Eagle Lake Route

Map # 6

Ⓐ

[105]

[170]

Ⓦ

[110]

△ sland in marsh (camping possible) →

Barren Brook

[100]

beaver dams may be present

[P] 3 4 [P]

Obstructions:
1. Shallow swifts (can be run).
2. Lift over log.
3. Portage: 50 m on west side (rocky rapids).
4. Portage: 140 m on west side (more shallow rapids).

[95] 1 2

Atikwa Lake

Map # 9

[P] 90m *good trail but poor landing at end*

[P] 160m *good trail*

[P] 260m *spruce flat*

△ *good site on point*

Pikwans Lake

The Rock Wall

⇐ *Barren Brook: pretty creek, hemmed in by spruce & jackpine, 1-2 canoe-length wide*

[85]

△ *poor site*

[90]

[80]

See Map # 9

△

small site but nice

Walleye Lake

△ *excellent site on island*

Tadpole Lake

beaver dam →

Bush Road

Shallow Rapids

[P] 320m

old laneway

↓

Barren Brook

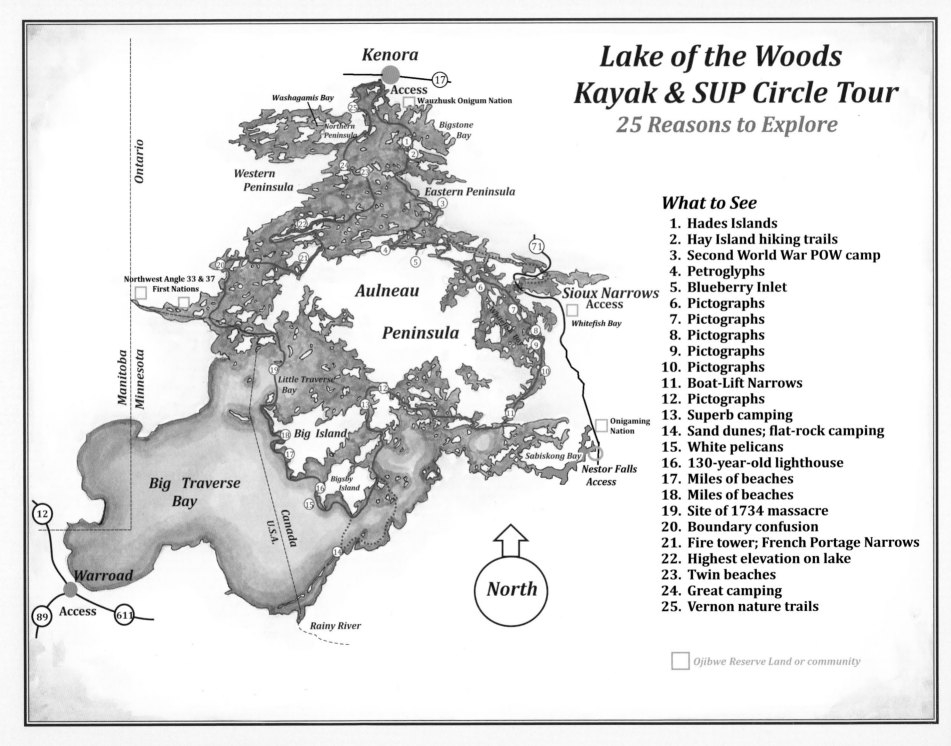

Lake of the Woods Kayak & SUP Circle Tour

25 Reasons to Explore

What to See

1. Hades Islands
2. Hay Island hiking trails
3. Second World War POW camp
4. Petroglyphs
5. Blueberry Inlet
6. Pictographs
7. Pictographs
8. Pictographs
9. Pictographs
10. Pictographs
11. Boat-Lift Narrows
12. Pictographs
13. Superb camping
14. Sand dunes; flat-rock camping
15. White pelicans
16. 130-year-old lighthouse
17. Miles of beaches
18. Miles of beaches
19. Site of 1734 massacre
20. Boundary confusion
21. Fire tower; French Portage Narrows
22. Highest elevation on lake
23. Twin beaches
24. Great camping
25. Vernon nature trails

Ojibwe Reserve Land or community

North

Kenora
Access
Wauzhusk Onigum Nation
Washagamis Bay
Northern Peninsula
Bigstone Bay
Western Peninsula
Eastern Peninsula
Aulneau Peninsula
Northwest Angle 33 & 37 First Nations
Sioux Narrows Access
Whitefish Bay
Whitefish Bay
Little Traverse Bay
Big Island
Big Traverse Bay
Bigsby Island
Sabiskong Bay
Onigaming Nation
Nestor Falls Access
Manitoba
Minnesota
Ontario
Canada
U.S.A.
Warroad
Access
Rainy River

Lake of the Woods Circle Tour

The first European to set eyes on Lake of the Woods was explorer Jacques de Noyon in 1688. He named it Lac aux îles, but the local aboriginal peoples actually considered LOTW to be four different lakes. Geographically, LOTW lies along the longitudinal center of Canada — the heart of the country, so to speak. It became the focal point of early travel between the east and the west. Explorers, traders, voyageurs and surveyors paddled up the long string of lakes and rivers from Lake Superior to Lake of the Woods, then used the only Canadian land route, the Dawson Road, which went as far as Winnipeg. The route continued in use until the 1880s, with the building of the Canadian Pacific Railway.

Since post-glacial times, the Laurel, Blackduck, Cree, Sioux and Ojibwe people have made Lake of the Woods their home territory. Ontario's second largest freshwater lake stretches 88 kilometers (55 miles) from east to west and 104 kilometers (65 miles) from north to south, and it is peppered with more than 14,500 islands. Its shoreline is an impressive 104,000 kilometers (65,000 miles), a distance that would take an average paddler more than 500 years to complete! Without exaggeration, Lake of the Woods, cut from Canadian Shield bedrock and dressed in majestic pines, is one of Canada's most beautiful unspoiled wilderness-class lakes.

Notes from the Map

I have highlighted 25 points of interest on the route map (charted by LOTW kayak explorer and good friend Jeremy Brown of Kenora), but this only touches on the multitude of places to visit. The Lake of the Woods Museum has put together an excellent guide called *The Explorer's Guide to Lake of the Woods*, by Lori Nelson, which complements the marine charts available at several stores in Kenora. Here are some quick descriptions from the circle tour route:

Map on Opposite Page

NUMBER ON MAP	FEATURE	DESCRIPTION
1	Hades Islands	A favorite scenic jaunt through craggy, high-cliffed islands and narrow channels.
2	Hay Island Hiking Trails	Approx. 10 km (6 mi) of excellent hiking. Trail access located on south side of island across from Pipestone Point. Put in at a small beach below an old forest plantation sign, then follow the old trail 200 m to a red pine grove, where the trail intersects with the main 9 km loop.
3	Red Cliff Bay World War II POW Camp #52	There were six known prisoner-of-war camps on LOTW, originally operated as lumber camps. POWs cut wood to supply the Ontario-Minnesota Pulp & Paper Co.
4	small bank/island south of Quartz Island	14 groups of petroglyphs (rock carvings), including circles, symbols, turtles and other animals. To the northwest, on Cliff Island, are pictographs depicting the "bird of omen."
5	Blueberry Inlet	Secluded place to paddle, with many campsites.
6–10	Hayter Peninsula to Picture Rock Island	Many panels of pictographs, depicting turtles, snakes, various manitous and thunderbirds.
11	Boat Lift Narrows	Only portage on the lake (50 m).
12	Painted Rock Island	Pictographs depicting Mishepeshu, the underwater horned cat.
13	Point at the northeast end of Big Island	Camping
14	Sable Island Sand Dunes	Nesting area for endangered piping plover.
15	Three Sisters	Third largest white pelican nesting site in North America, with over 7,000 birds.
16	Ferris Island Lighthouse, off Hooper's Point	Lighthouse (1897) is gone but you can find 100-year-old graffiti.
17–18		Several miles of beautiful beach
19	Massacre Island	In 1736, 22 young voyageurs were massacred, including La Verendrye's eldest son, Jean-Baptiste, and Jesuit priest Jean-Pierre Aulneau, while on their way to Fort William (Thunder Bay) to pick up supplies. The murders were blamed on the Sioux because the voyageurs had been trading with the Ojibwe and Cree, their enemies.
20	Monument Bay	Aside from Alaska, the "northwest angle" is the most northerly point of the US. The boundary protrusion was established after much confusion about boundaries drawn from inaccurate maps.
21	French Portage Narrows	Very narrow cleft of rock and site of an old fire tower, a short distance west of the narrows.
22	Big Narrows Island	One of the highest elevations on the lake, with a commanding view from the top.
23	Shamis Island	*Shamis* is Anishinabe for "bald," referring to the appearance of the island after loggers cut down all the trees. Excellent beaches along the south shore.
24	Crow Rock Island	Another great spot to explore, with interesting rock formations and good campsites.
25	Vernon Nature Trails	5 km of trails through mature pines, marshland and Canadian Shield country.

Migizi Trail Diary

Mapping canoe trails is a multifaceted occupation, sometimes pushing the envelope of time and often enough working outside the normal paddling season, even into the depths of winter. The historical and cultural aspects are an important element of the research, as they lay the foundation for a particular theme. My wife, Andrea, and I traveled to Kenora to explore some of the archeological sites, which are easily visited by ski and snowshoe.

A Métis Connection It's February, and Andrea and I can hardly keep up with Jeremy Brown, our Métis friend from Kenora. His snowshoe gait is suggestive of a much taller person, and he moves easily over the crusted snow. It is easy to imagine that his bloodline exemplifies generations of outdoor living. A line of cliffs rises steeply from the snow-covered rock scree on our left as we edge into Blindfold Lake. Jeremy stops up ahead and points at something at the base of the cliff — rock paintings! The pictographs spread across two rock canvases: a fading moose, a drum, mythical creatures, a pair of inverted canoes, an unrecognizable animal. They draw you in. You want to touch the rock and the paintings, but we simply stand there and take in the moment in silence. We leave tobacco.

Windbound on Atikwa September, eight days out. I'm soloing the 16-foot Swift Dumoine; Andrea and our daughter are in the 17-foot Swift Winisk. Oban, our collie (named after our favorite Scotch), sits in the middle of their canoe, head resting on the gunnel, the craft bobbing in the increasing wave action. I start to slip behind and yell ahead to the others to make a final crossing to a point of land about a kilometer away. Waves start to break and pummel the broadside of the canoe. We pull into a tight channel in the rocks in the lee of the rising winds, unload the canoes and set up camp.

> ### History Notes
>
> Lake of the Woods, including the entire Migizi Trail, lies in the heart of the heaviest concentration of rock paintings in North America. Oxidized iron ore (hematite), probably mixed with sturgeon oil, albumen from gull eggs or bear grease, creates a paint know as red ochre. It is believed that the actual bonding agent — the liquid medium used — was the blood of the *memegwishiwok*, or "stone people," who lived within the stone vault and who proffered their blood to the shaman, a teacher of the upright life or medicine healer.
>
> Specific sites are often chosen by the artist/shaman where the corporeal world offers a portal into the incorporeal world — places of "harmonic conversion" — where magic and ceremony are used to bond the teachings to Mother Earth. Paintings along the Mgizi Trail are more than 2,000 years old.

It's an old campsite, like many others, with a modest firepit, moss and fireweed growing out of half-burnt tin cans. Red pines with long, coarse needles play the wind song, like the sound of a nearby waterfall. Leatherleaf and blueberry shrubs — just enough room for two tents. We sit on the rocks and soak up the sun. No clouds, just wind and wind song. Andrea and I drink the last of the Irish whiskey,

Between Porcus and Geejay Lakes (Map #3) are the "experimental lakes." This sounds a bit sketchy at first and they have been the subject of some controversy, but our route passes through only one of the 58 affected lakes (no. 109). The Experimental Lakes Area (ELA) included small, pristine lakes and their catchment areas, set in a wilderness region unaffected by industrial pollution or human activity. In 1968 the Province of Ontario and the Government of Canada established a research station there, specifically to study long-term ecosystem processes such as the eutrophication of lakes caused by acid deposition, as well as the impacts of mercury on fish populations. Also studied was the effect of flooding wetlands for hydroelectricity on the production of greenhouse gases. Some loading experiments were controversial, such as the dumping of an estrogen used in birth control pills, which led to the extinction of flathead minnows in the test lakes. The Harper government shut down the facility, even though it had won several international awards. Protests from the scientific community and a change in government brought new life to the research station and a new partnership with the International Institute for Sustainable Development. The area is now referred to as the IISD-ELA.

mixed with orange crystals and slices of lime to add zest. Alexa reads her book. Soon enough we all find sleep, slumped on mossy carpets, waking only when the sun tires and the air cools. The day slips into evening and the lake calms. It's quiet enough now to hear the loons.

Exhaustion Slouched among the hummocks and pitcher plants, our water bottles empty, with still a way to go to drag the loaded canoes over the grass to the lake, I pull out three cans of Stella and hand them around. Oban is stretched out on the damp moss, looking more dead than alive. We share a bag of jujubes and wash them down with the cool beer — a strange combination, but it provokes laughter and a charge of rekindled energy. We push on until we see the lake, the three of us pulling on the gunnels, the canoe sliding reluctantly over the uneven mat of spongy moss. With soaked feet we get to the lake, pause for a minute, and then begin our trek back to retrieve the other canoe.

The Longest Day There used to be a route through here, decades ago, but the portage trails have long disappeared. We break camp early. Armed with camp saw, trail axe and a pair of brush loppers, we locate and clear all seven portages — a distance of more than 2 kilometers — while hauling all our gear. We arrive at Hawkcliff Lake near dark and there are no campsites, so we paddle for two more hours, find a terraced rock island and awkwardly set up our tents by flashlight. A one-pot dinner barely finished, each of us too tired even to eat. Sleep is welcome.

Morning Visitor The dog growls, deep and throaty, as if he knows something is out there but isn't sure if it's bigger than him. I'm awake now. Andrea and I hear heavy footsteps in the water along the shore, only meters from the tent. A moose, I figure, by the sound of it. I need a good shot of a bull moose, so I slide out of my sleeping bag and grab my camera. The zipper on the tent door sounds like a chainsaw. I stumble, almost drop the camera. It's a grand bull moose with huge palmated antlers, the morning sun glistening off its chocolate-brown coat, droplets of water shining like diamonds on its back. It's already on the run and into the bush before I can even turn on my camera.

Doré Disappointment October, four years back. Rain — not heavy but persistent, layered and enveloping; cold, on the verge of snow, which would be more welcome. October is like that in the north: one day sunny and deliciously warm, with subtle undertones of change, then, without a hint of warning, tempestuous, savage and unforgiving.

We have been looking for signs of an old portage trail at the north end of Doré Lake, the town of Dryden another day's paddle from here. The thought of a warm motel room, a hot shower and grub not cooked over an open fire has inspired us to keep searching. It was supposed to be here, according to the old MNR charts; but then, most times, their information is not that reliable, and the documentation dates back to the 1960s. We've found endless swamp, a creek choked with deadfall, floating bog and hummocky spruce flats, but no portage, no blazes on trees, no tin cans stuck on lop-sticks, nothing. There was never a portage here.

We bush a campsite in the cold drizzle, kindle a fire and cook supper. Comfort extraordinaire — a kitchen fly stretched overhead, the radiance of a cedar-stoked fire, a pannikin of Scotch and laughter over our struggle to find a portage that didn't exist. As it turns out, we've pitched our tent over an old lumber-camp camboose, rife with collectibles half buried in the forest duff. Next morning we leave the canoe and most of the gear and hike a mile out to the highway, through the worst imaginable — and, I might add, impenetrable — alder snags, muskeg wallows and fallen timber. We're a sorry sight as we stand on Highway 502 in the driving sleet trying to hitch a ride back to Dryden. After an hour, a Native fellow picks us up and drives us to our motel. We apologize for getting his car seats wet, make a token offer to pay him something, but he waves it off and smiles politely. "No trouble," he says. "Yuz guys looked like drowned dogs out there, sorry as hell. Least I could do."

Morning camp on Populus Lake.

Full moon on Atikwa Lake.

Cliffs, clear water and mysterious rock paintings.

Knowing the habitat preferences of wildlife increases opportunity.

Winter trek along the Migizi Trail.

Taking notes on Hawkcliff Lake.

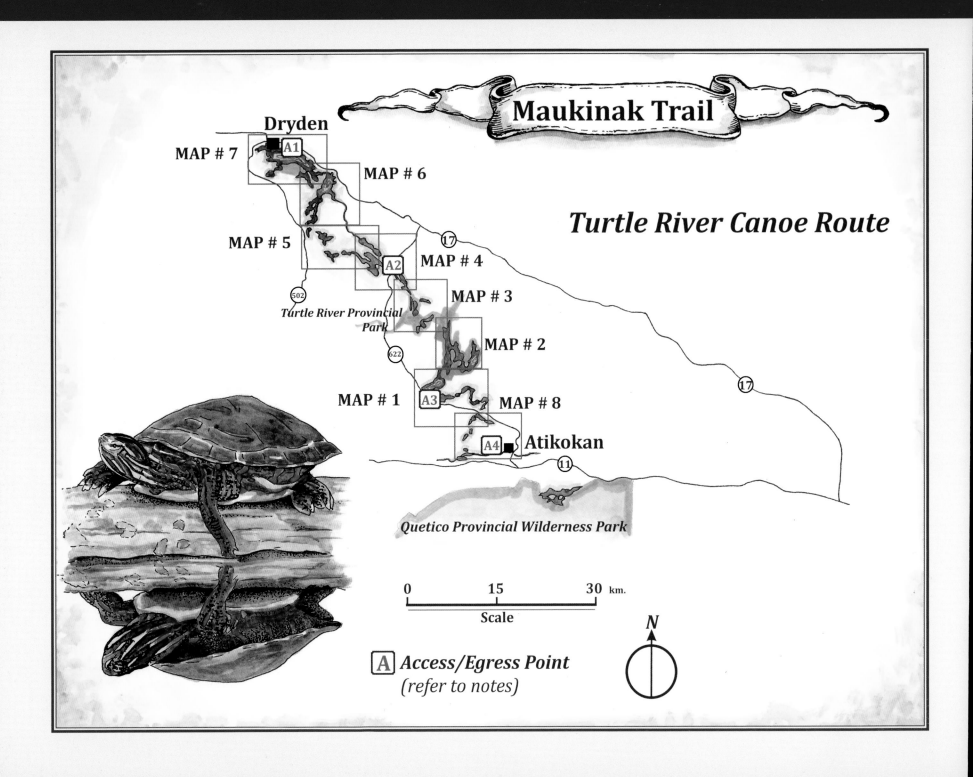

Maukinak Trail

Dryden

MAP # 7

A1

MAP # 6

Turtle River Canoe Route

17

MAP # 5

A2

MAP # 4

502

MAP # 3

Turtle River Provincial Park

MAP # 2

622

MAP # 1

A3

MAP # 8

17

A4 **Atikokan**

11

Quetico Provincial Wilderness Park

0   15   30 km.

Scale

N

A *Access/Egress Point*
(refer to notes)

Chapter 6

Part 3

Maukinak Trail

Topographic Map Locations
1:100,000 scale (provincial series)
Wabigoon Lake 52-F/NE – Gold Rock 52-F/SE – Gulliver River 52-G/SW – Marmion Lake 52-B/NW
1:50,000 scale
Dryden 52-F/15 – Atikokan 52-G/13 – White Otter Lake 52-G/4 – Pekagoning Lake 52-F/1 – Manion
Lake 52-C/16 – Quetico Lake 52-B/2 – Stormy Lake 52-F/8

Mikinaak, mackinak, maukinak . . . no matter how you spell it in Ojibwe, it all means the same thing: the much-honored snapping turtle. The Anishinabeg were known for their fierceness in battle, and that fiery disposition is a dominant characteristic of the snapping turtle when taken out of the water. Anyone who has tried to save a snapping turtle from being run over as it slowly crosses a highway will know that the snapper can arch its head back like a snake — probably why its Latin name is *Chelydra serpentina* — and do a lot of damage with its rapier-like claws. An angry snapping turtle can easily bite off a finger. You can try to pick it up by the shell close to the back legs, but if you have a shovel, even better. Hauling the turtle (which can weigh more than 50 pounds) by the tail will do irreparable damage to its spine.

The Algonkian peoples have various legends about the creation of earth that are certainly no more fantastic than Christian beliefs. Over the centuries of European influence, especially the introduction of Christianity, First Nations creation legends may have become weighted in a certain direction. However, some scholars believe that the biblical writings in Genesis may have borrowed their creation theory from pagan beliefs. Pagan faiths believe in the cyclical nature of Nature and humankind's close association with it; it also predates Christian religions by at least 20,000 years.

In the context of this book, the Anishinabeg story identifies the territory around Lake Superior as the heart of the continent. The Great Flood, or *mush-ko'-be-wun*, wiped out all the people save for Nanaboozhoo (also known as Nanabush) and a few of the animals. Nanaboozhoo floated on a log in search of land, but to no avail. An eternal optimist, he believed that with the help of Gitchi Manitou (the Great Spirit), the four winds and the surviving animals, he could create a new land. He would dive to great depths and bring up some soil with which to make a new earth. But he ran out of breath, and so he returned to his perch on the log beside the few animals and birds. The loon, mink, merganser and turtle all tried but failed. It was the meek little muskrat, *wa-zhushk*, who managed to bring up a pawful of earth (note the emphasis on the capabilities of diminutive creatures). That earth was placed on the back of the turtle. The winds blew from each of the four directions, carrying with them the breath of the Great Spirit. The island grew larger and the winds eventually subsided. A huge island had formed, and that great island became known as North America.

The Path of the Paddle lies within the geographical center or heart of North America, and the Maukinak Trail is the central portion of the Path of the Paddle linear trail. Aside from creation theories and the section's geographical alignment, the turtle is a significant feature along this route. I've often seen enormous snappers floating on the water's surface, basking in the sun, and it's not uncommon to come across a female laying eggs high up on a sandbank. Unlike other turtles, which bury themselves in the bottom mud over winter,

snapping turtles are more cold tolerant; they get enough oxygen by gas exchange through membranes in their mouth and throat. Snappers are also curious at times and may intentionally bump against a swimmer's leg or foot, but if riled or poked, they can easily bite off a finger or toe.

Because the snapper is sensitive to environmental change, Canada has put it on the "special concern" list of species at risk. Painted turtles, on the other hand, can survive nicely in sewage lagoons and polluted wetlands. They are probably the most often seen along the Maukinak Trail, sunning on a log, sometimes several lined up in a row, and slipping noiselessly into the water as you paddle by.

This route combines the best of small rivers and clear-water lakes. There are two distinct routes, each taking advantage of downstream flow — downstream on the Turtle River or downstream on the Eye and Ear Rivers.

Giant snapping turtle — a common denizen along shallow lakes and rivers.

Turtle River Canoe Route
Maps 1, 2, 3, 4, 5, 6, 7 | Challenge Route Maps 5, 6

Maukinak Trail

Classification experienced novice to intermediate

Distance 150 km (93 mi)
challenge route: 175 km (109 mi)

Duration 10 to 12 days
challenge route: 12 to 14 days

Portages 9, totaling 3,730 m (2.3 mi), 2.5% of distance
challenge route: 18, totaling 6,755 m (4.2 mi), 4% of distance

Season mid-May to October

Preferred craft Kevlar canoe; kayak or SUP if touring White Otter Lake

Campsites mostly established sites with firepits

Access Clearwater West Lodge or Anne Bay on White Otter Lake

Egress Dryden

Aside from several easy rapids, the Turtle River is a typical Canadian Shield, "pool & drop" river.

Water Characteristics and General Hazards

- Wind may play a role, primarily as you head northwest along Wabigoon Lake. Otherwise it will likely be in your favor for the first several days.
- Water levels may vary greatly on Turtle River; it is always best to scout rapids before running.
- None of the rapids are technical, just fun and a nice break from lake paddling.

Features

- Clearwater and White Otter Lakes, aside from Teggau on the Migizi Trail, are the clearest lakes along the Path of the Paddle. From here all water flows northwest to Lake Winnipeg.
- There is virtually no development along this route. Paddlers have the option of a challenge route through a chain of outstanding pristine lakes
- White Otter Castle is a must-see, along with the remains of a Second World War POW camp, Native pictographs and scattered erratics — huge boulders dropped from retreating glaciers.

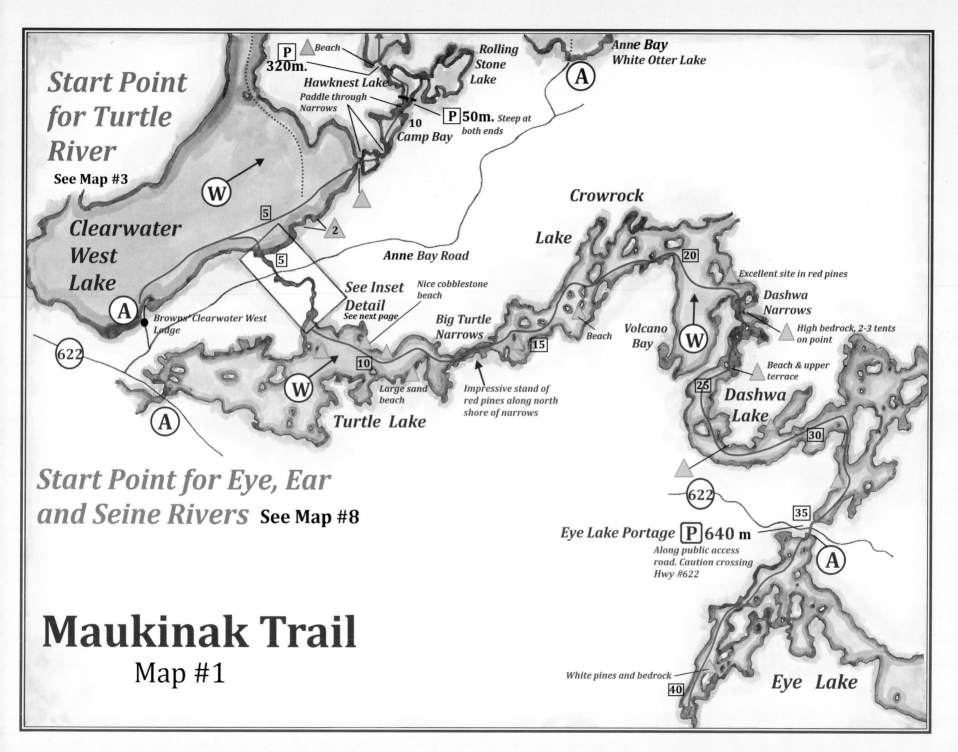

Start Point for Turtle River

See Map #3

Clearwater West Lake

Ⓐ

622

Browns' Clearwater West Lodge

Ⓐ

Start Point for Eye, Ear and Seine Rivers See Map #8

Maukinak Trail
Map #1

Ⓟ 320m.

Beach

Hawknest Lake

Paddle through Narrows

Ⓟ 50m. *Steep at both ends*

10 *Camp Bay*

Rolling Stone Lake

Anne Bay White Otter Lake

Ⓐ

Ⓦ

5

2

Anne Bay Road

See Inset Detail See next page

Nice cobblestone beach

Big Turtle Narrows

5

Ⓦ

10

Large sand beach

Turtle Lake

Impressive stand of red pines along north shore of narrows

15

Beach

Crowrock Lake

20

Excellent site in red pines

Dashwa Narrows

High bedrock, 2-3 tents on point

Beach & upper terrace

Volcano Bay

Ⓦ

25

Dashwa Lake

30

622

Eye Lake Portage Ⓟ 640 m

Along public access road. Caution crossing Hwy #622

35

Ⓐ

White pines and bedrock

40

Eye Lake

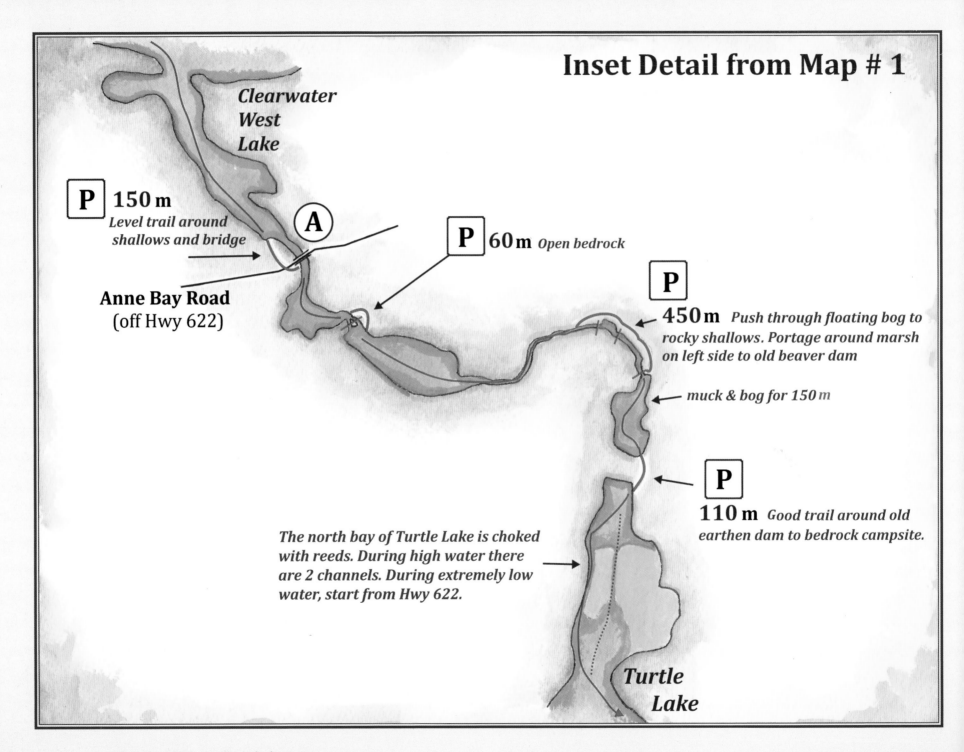

Inset Detail from Map # 1

Clearwater West Lake

P **150 m**
Level trail around shallows and bridge

Anne Bay Road
(off Hwy 622)

Ⓐ

P **60 m** *Open bedrock*

P

450 m *Push through floating bog to rocky shallows. Portage around marsh on left side to old beaver dam*

muck & bog for 150 m

P

110 m *Good trail around old earthen dam to bedrock campsite.*

The north bay of Turtle Lake is choked with reeds. During high water there are 2 channels. During extremely low water, start from Hwy 622.

Turtle Lake

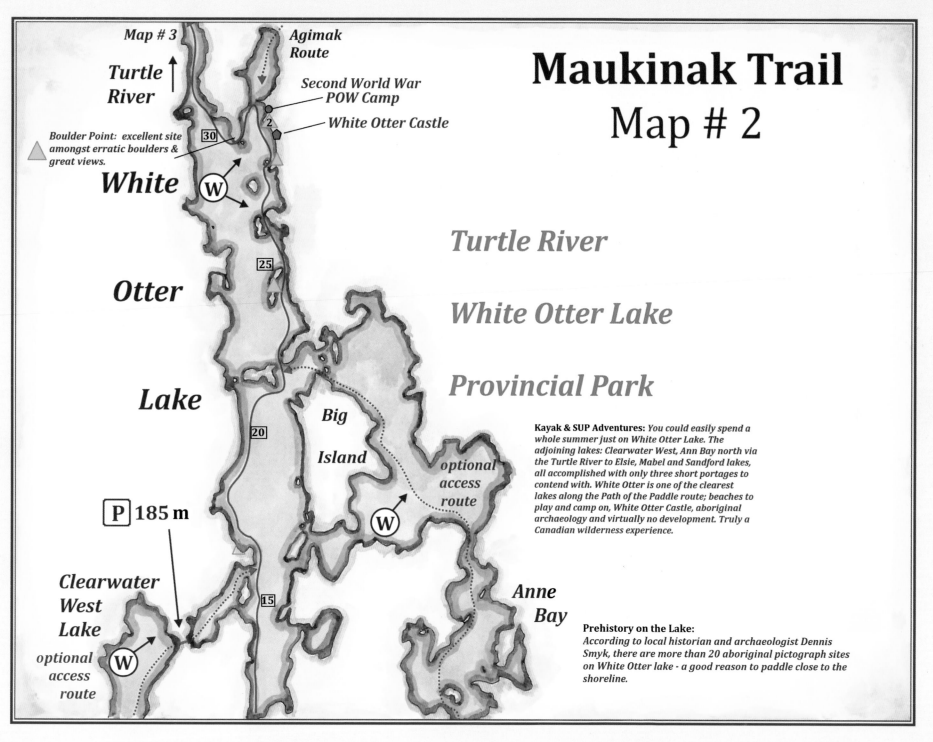

Maukinak Trail
Map # 2

Map # 3

Turtle River ↑

Agimak Route

Second World War POW Camp

White Otter Castle

Boulder Point: excellent site amongst erratic boulders & great views.

White

Otter

Lake

2

30

W

25

20

P 185 m

Big

Island

15

Clearwater West Lake

optional access route

W

optional access route

W

Turtle River

White Otter Lake

Provincial Park

Kayak & SUP Adventures: *You could easily spend a whole summer just on White Otter Lake. The adjoining lakes: Clearwater West, Ann Bay north via the Turtle River to Elsie, Mabel and Sandford lakes, all accomplished with only three short portages to contend with. White Otter is one of the clearest lakes along the Path of the Paddle route; beaches to play and camp on, White Otter Castle, aboriginal archaeology and virtually no development. Truly a Canadian wilderness experience.*

Anne Bay

Prehistory on the Lake:
According to local historian and archaeologist Dennis Smyk, there are more than 20 aboriginal pictograph sites on White Otter lake - a good reason to paddle close to the shoreline.

Maukinak Trail
Map # 3

Bending Lake

Turtle

Inset Box #3
(separate page)

Turtle River

△ Island site, 3 to 4 tents

Inset Box #2
(separate page)

↑ flow

↙ flow

Smirch Lake

△

△ point site in jack pines

River

pictographs

△ rock & jack pines

Dibble Lake Access: Follow Hwy 17 to intersection 22 km west of Ignace. Proceed south for 26 km to Moosehead Road. Follow Moosehead Road for 12 km.

→ **Inset at Right**

Ⓐ

Dibble Lake

△ nice low site over slanted bedrock

△

Ⓟ

Inset Box #1
(separate page)

△

McOuat Bay
White Otter Lake

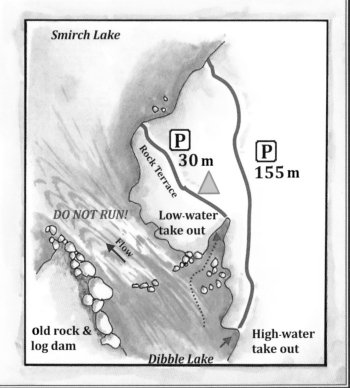

Smirch Lake

Ⓟ **30 m**

Rock Terrace

Ⓟ **155 m**

△

DO NOT RUN!

Low-water take out

Flow →

old rock & log dam

High-water take out

Dibble Lake

Turtle River Rapids

Inset 1 for Map 3

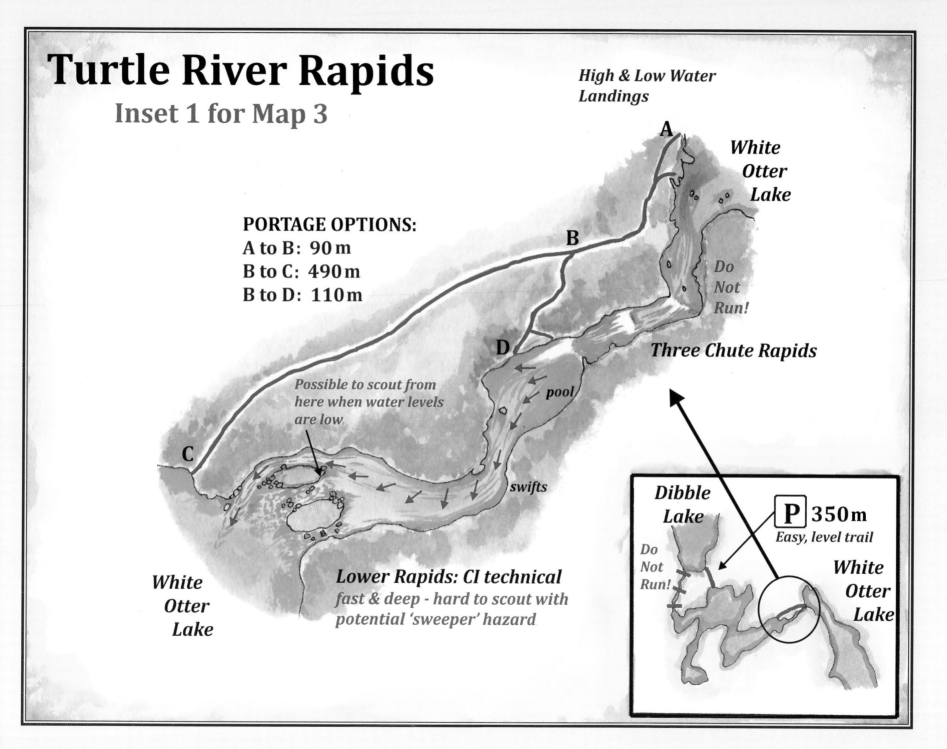

High & Low Water Landings

A

White Otter Lake

B

Do Not Run!

PORTAGE OPTIONS:
A to B: 90 m
B to C: 490 m
B to D: 110 m

D

Three Chute Rapids

Possible to scout from here when water levels are low.

pool

C

swifts

White Otter Lake

Lower Rapids: CI technical
fast & deep - hard to scout with potential 'sweeper' hazard

Dibble Lake

Do Not Run!

P 350 m
Easy, level trail

White Otter Lake

Turtle River Rapids
Inset 2 from Map 3

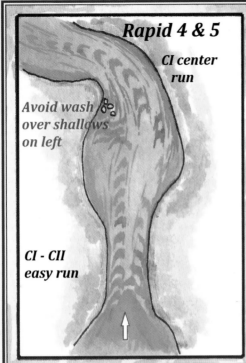

Rapid 4 & 5

CI center run

Avoid wash over shallows on left

CI - CII easy run

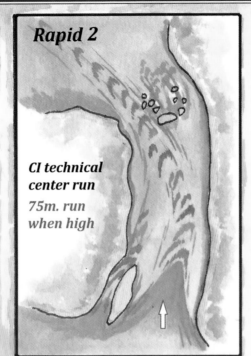

Rapid 2

CI technical center run

75m. run when high

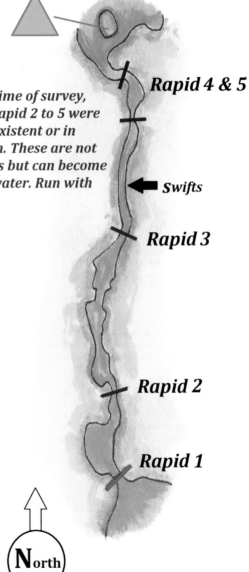

NOTE: At the time of survey, portages for rapid 2 to 5 were virtually nonexistent or in poor condition. These are not difficult rapids but can become rocky in low water. Run with care.

Rapid 4 & 5

Swifts

Rapid 3

Rapid 2

Rapid 1

North

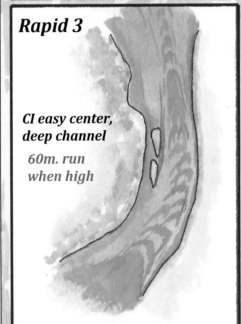

Rapid 3

CI easy center, deep channel

60m. run when high

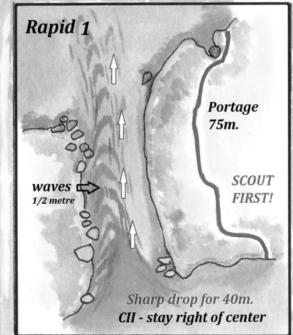

Rapid 1

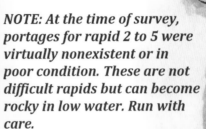

Portage 75m.

SCOUT FIRST!

waves 1/2 metre

Sharp drop for 40m.
CII - stay right of center

Turtle River Rapids
Inset 3 from Map 3

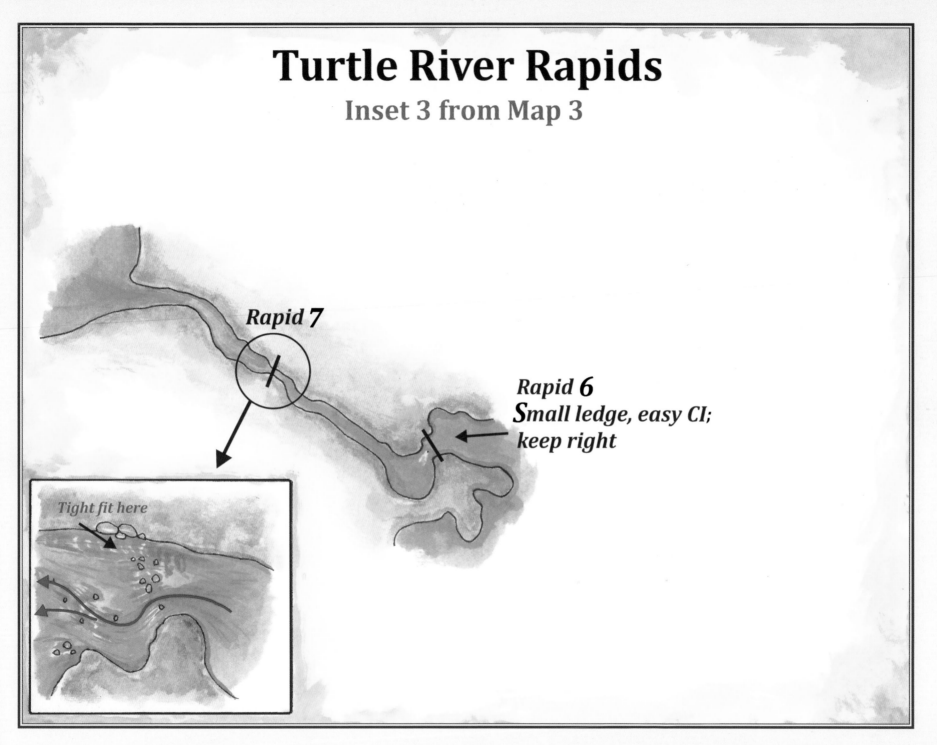

Rapid **7**

Rapid **6**
*Small ledge, easy CI;
keep right*

Tight fit here

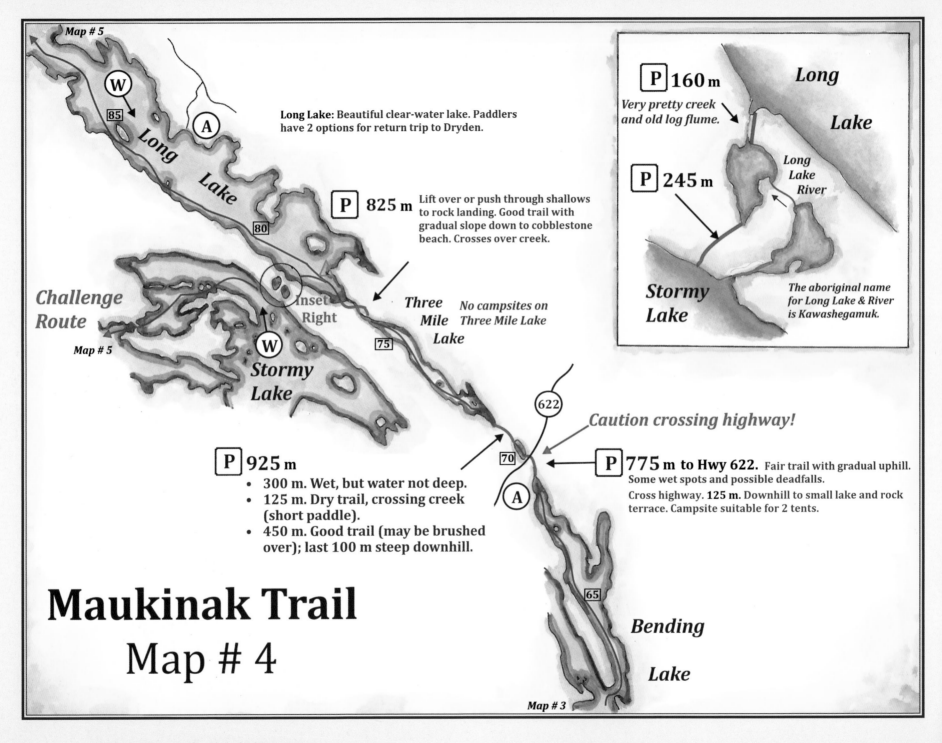

Map # 5

W
85

Long Lake

A

Long Lake: Beautiful clear-water lake. Paddlers have 2 options for return trip to Dryden.

80

P 825 m

Lift over or push through shallows to rock landing. Good trail with gradual slope down to cobblestone beach. Crosses over creek.

Challenge Route

Map # 5

Inset Right

W

Stormy Lake

Three Mile Lake

No campsites on Three Mile Lake

75

P 925 m
- 300 m. Wet, but water not deep.
- 125 m. Dry trail, crossing creek (short paddle).
- 450 m. Good trail (may be brushed over); last 100 m steep downhill.

622

70

A

Caution crossing highway!

P 775 m to Hwy 622. Fair trail with gradual uphill. Some wet spots and possible deadfalls.

Cross highway. **125 m.** Downhill to small lake and rock terrace. Campsite suitable for 2 tents.

Maukinak Trail

Map # 4

65

Bending Lake

Map # 3

P 160 m

Very pretty creek and old log flume.

Long Lake

P 245 m

Long Lake River

Stormy Lake

The aboriginal name for Long Lake & River is Kawashegamuk.

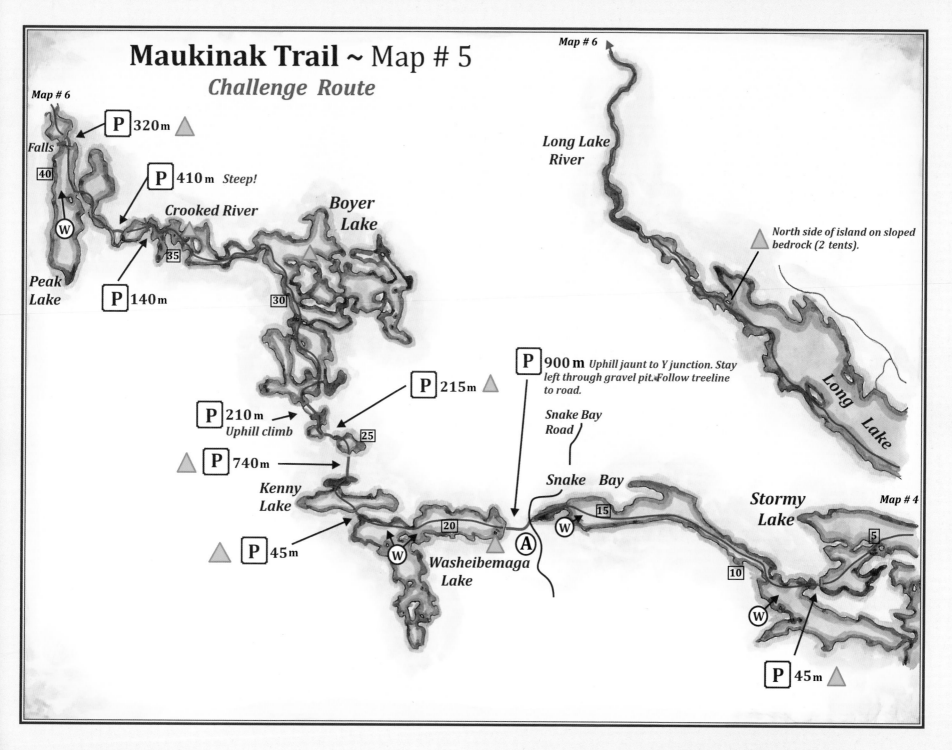

Maukinak Trail ~ Map # 5
Challenge Route

Map # 6

Map # 6

P 320 m

Falls

40

P 410 m *Steep!*

W

Crooked River

Boyer Lake

Long Lake River

P 140 m

35

30

Peak Lake

North side of island on sloped bedrock (2 tents).

P 215 m

P 900 m *Uphill jaunt to Y junction. Stay left through gravel pit. Follow treeline to road.*

P 210 m *Uphill climb*

25

Snake Bay Road

P 740 m

Kenny Lake

Snake Bay

15

Stormy Lake

Map # 4

P 45 m

W

20

A

W

5

Washeibemaga Lake

10

W

P 45 m

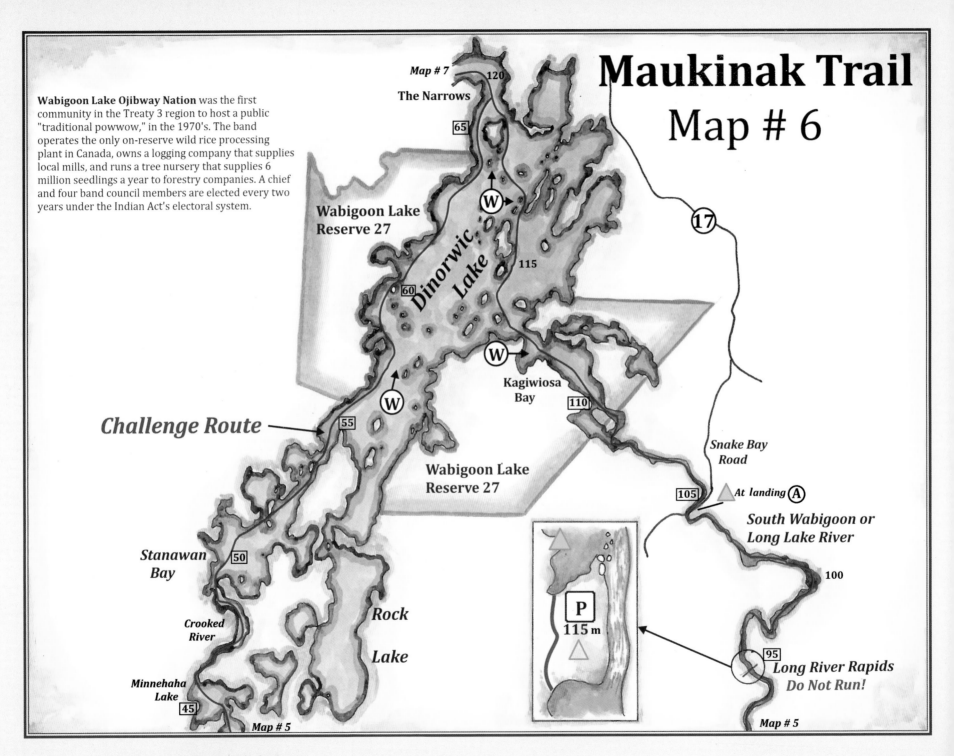

Maukinak Trail
Map # 6

Map # 7

The Narrows

120

65

Wabigoon Lake Ojibway Nation was the first community in the Treaty 3 region to host a public "traditional powwow," in the 1970's. The band operates the only on-reserve wild rice processing plant in Canada, owns a logging company that supplies local mills, and runs a tree nursery that supplies 6 million seedlings a year to forestry companies. A chief and four band council members are elected every two years under the Indian Act's electoral system.

Wabigoon Lake
Reserve 27

Dinorwic Lake

W

115

60

17

W

Kagiwiosa
Bay

110

Challenge Route

W

55

Snake Bay
Road

Wabigoon Lake
Reserve 27

105   At landing Ⓐ

**South Wabigoon or
Long Lake River**

Stanawan
Bay

50

P
115 m

100

Rock

Lake

*Crooked
River*

95

*Minnehaha
Lake*

*Long River Rapids
Do Not Run!*

45

Map # 5

Map # 5

Dryden

(17)

(A)

[150]

Wabigoon

Lake

(17)

Wabigoon

(W)

[145]

[140]

[135]

Bowen Point

The Narrows

[130]

[125]

[120]

(W)

Map # 6

Migizi Route

Kayaking & SUP Adventures

There is virtually no development on the south shore and islands of Wabigoon Lake. Along with the deep bays and islands of Dinorwic Lake, this presents a perfect opportunity to explore. You can easily paddle more than 100 km by simply pond-hopping and circling back to Dryden. Another option is the 85 km trek by way of Long Lake River to Long Lake — a one-way trip that requires a shuttle.

Maukinak Trail
Map # 7

Eye, Ear and Seine River Route
Map 8

Maukinak Trail

Classification experienced novice; easy intermediate if water levels are high

Distance 75 km (47 mi)

Duration 5 to 6 days

Portages 10, totaling 2,990 m (1.9 mi), 4% of distance

Season mid-May to October

Preferred craft Kevlar canoe

Campsites mostly established sites with firepits

Access Clearwater West Lodge or Turtle Lake

Egress Atikokan

Reaching the end of the long portage to Ear River.

Water Characteristics and General Hazards

♦ The Eye and Ear Rivers are not much more than expanded creeks, and water levels drop quickly by midsummer. Most rocky swifts and rapids can be easily lined or waded through.

♦ After midsummer, paddlers should put in at Turtle Lake to avoid the marsh between Turtle and Clearwater West Lakes.

♦ The Seine is dam-controlled and water levels may vary. Swifts can be paddled up or lined, but if the river is swollen (as in the spring) it is suggested that travel be in the opposite direction, downstream on the Seine and upstream on the creeks.

♦ The Atikokan River gets quite shallow by midsummer, which may require some lift-overs to get to the center of town. The takeout below the dam (Sea Plane Base Road) may be a good choice.

Features

♦ An intimate blend of creek, wetland and small lake travel, with excellent opportunities to see wildlife.

♦ Campsites are among the best found along the Path of the Paddle.

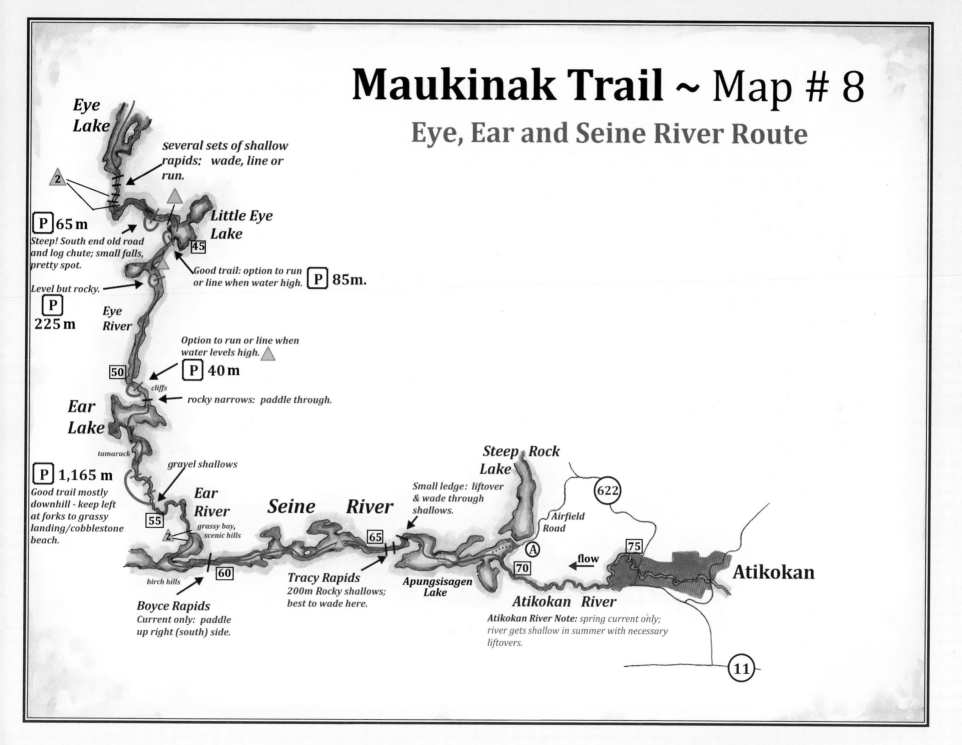

Maukinak Trail ~ Map # 8
Eye, Ear and Seine River Route

Eye Lake

several sets of shallow rapids: wade, line or run.

△ 2

Little Eye Lake

P 65 m
Steep! South end old road and log chute; small falls, pretty spot.

45

Good trail: option to run or line when water high.

P 85m.

Level but rocky.

P 225 m

Eye River

Option to run or line when water levels high. △

P 40 m

50

cliffs

rocky narrows: paddle through.

Ear Lake

Steep Rock Lake

tamarack

P 1,165 m
Good trail mostly downhill - keep left at forks to grassy landing/cobblestone beach.

gravel shallows

Ear River

Seine River

Small ledge: liftover & wade through shallows.

622

Airfield Road

55

△ 2

grassy bay, scenic hills

65

A

75

flow

Atikokan

birch hills

60

70

Apungsisagen Lake

Atikokan River

Boyce Rapids
Current only: paddle up right (south) side.

Tracy Rapids
200m Rocky shallows; best to wade here.

Atikokan River Note: spring current only; river gets shallow in summer with necessary liftovers.

11

Maukinak Trail Diary

Somewhere between Bending Lake and Three Mile Lake July, three years ago. I'm sitting on the deep moss beside the trail. My son sits on the wanigan eating an orange — no, more like *attacking* the orange, hands sticky with juice, big smile on his face. He is fourteen. It's not as if he isn't used to this, by now comfortable enough with hardship. As long as he has his orange and a handful of gorp, he's happier than a bull moose waist-deep in a lily pond. It's good to have his company; too many days paddling alone on this venture and I miss my family.

This portage was in dire need of servicing, probably used more as a winter snowmobile track between the two lakes. The two of us hauled the fully loaded canoe by ropes, strung out like a human dog team — over bog grass, through muck that sucked at our boots, swatting mosquitoes when we had a free hand, sweat pouring off our faces and down our backs, hands burning — until we both collapsed laughing. It's like that often: you laugh so hard when that last thread of strength is fraying and you realize it's a lot better than crying. Easier, in fact, and instead of feeling deflated, you get back up and push even harder. Laughing never gets in the way.

Then the bog ended and we stopped pulling, reorganized our load and trudged on, packs on our backs, leaving the canoe behind for the next trip. We picked a spot on the trail that might afford a soft, dry perch, a bit of shade and much needed respite.

Chris finishes his orange and wipes his hands on his pants. The *eh-eh-eh-eh-eh* staccato call of a pileated woodpecker from a nearby pine chicot rises above the drone of mosquitoes. Summer song.

Dashwa Lake October, three falls ago. *Dashwa* means "shield of the tortoise" in Ojibwe, but all the painted turtles have already burrowed deep into the loon shit at the bottom of the lake. V's of geese are a regular sky pattern now, and the tamaracks are ablaze with orange as if on fire. The water in the coffee pot was frozen this morning. There's a patina of ice on the overturned canoe but the sky is indigo, with no clouds, and the sun stretches its golden fingers to touch the waiting earth. The fire crackles into life and the coffee pot is perched on the grate. "Is the coffee ready yet?" A voice from the interior. "Soon," I say. Andrea waits patiently for her morning coffee.

I go over the maps of the day and plan a route, check my notes, calculate distances. The cold slows our progress; it takes longer to leave the comfort of the fire. Shorter days, too, make a big difference in how far we go each day. But we aren't in a hurry; there's so much to investigate, to feel the vibrancy of place. In the fall, smells are richer, more poignant, more penetrating. Sounds are clearer, more expressive. Loons have been gathering for the past two months, socializing, reveling in the anticipation of change, on each lake calling out a different haunting melody.

Eye and Ear River Two days later. I've paddled some creeks that are more like rivers and some rivers that are mere creeks, with barely the width to hold a canoe. It's not surprising that the Eye and Ear Rivers, flowing south into the Seine, at this time of the season run shallow and slow — creeks by any other comparison. On a fine day such as this, with the temperature straining to reach five degrees Celsius, working the canoe down the rapids is a pleasant enough job.

Andrea and I walk the bald rocks along the shore while the roped canoe slips along on the current of its own accord. It's like taking an eager dog for a walk, the canoe tugging at the line as if impatient to get somewhere else. White pines tower above the sloped bedrock shores, the ground beneath littered with freshly fallen needles, crisp and tan but soft enough to lie down on. We eat lunch, a little chilled after we've stopped working the canoe down the rapids, then lie on a bed of pine needles and moss and watch the clouds push each other across the sky.

Turtle River evening.

Author's son, Chris, taking a much needed orange break.

Erratic boulder on Dibble Lake.

Sometimes it's just easier to haul the load by rope over the grass.

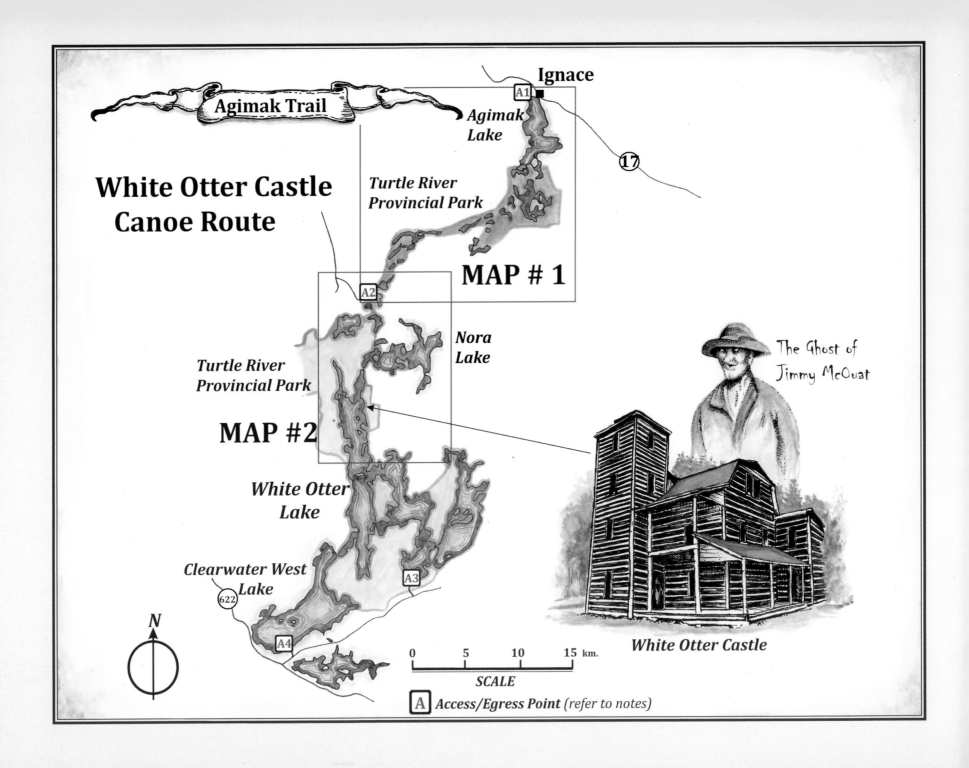

White Otter Castle Canoe Route

Agimak Trail

Ignace

A1

Agimak Lake

17

Turtle River Provincial Park

MAP # 1

Nora Lake

Turtle River Provincial Park

MAP #2

A2

White Otter Lake

Clearwater West Lake

622

A3

A4

The Ghost of Jimmy McOuat

White Otter Castle

N

0   5   10   15 km.

SCALE

A Access/Egress Point *(refer to notes)*

Chapter 7

Part 4
Agimak Trail

Topographic Map Locations
1:100,000 scale (provincial series)
White Otter Lake 52-G/4
1:50,000 scale
52-F/1 – 52-C/16 – 52-B/13

Agimak (pronounced *ogimok*) is Ojibwe for "ash tree," and *agim* means "snowshoe." Black ash growing along the low edges of marshy bays had many uses for the Anishinabe people, aside from making snowshoes (*agimikewin*). Its leaves and bark have medicinal properties, and they are still used as a laxative, diuretic, purgative and stimulant. The bark, when boiled as a tea, was used to bring down fevers, and young leaves could ease the pain of gout and arthritis. In Russia it was used to stimulate blood circulation in the extremities, both applied as a poultice and drunk as a tea. Besides snowshoe frames, the Anishinabeg used it to make paddles and they cut strips of ash bark to make baskets.

The Agimak Trail canoe route from Ignace to White Otter Lake became known following the town's birth as a stop on the Canadian Pacific Railway in 1879. Archeological digs have unearthed pottery fragments and stone tools that predate European activity by thousands of years. At the turn of the 20th century, the Ontario Department of Lands and Forests (now the Ministry of Natural Resources and Forestry) sent fire rangers to man observation towers and to clear portage routes, followed close behind by surveyors, claim-stakers and settlers. One notable individual from this time was Jimmy McOuat (pronounced "ma-koo-it"), and the story behind the man is what makes this route all the more interesting.

James Alexander McOuat was born in the Ottawa Valley in 1855. By 1877 he was homesteading in the Rainy River District, but he gambled and lost everything during the gold rush, then built a shack on White Otter Lake in 1903. Jimmy had been scolded as a lad that he'd "never do any good and [would] die in a shack." Taking those words to heart, he set about building a log castle, just to prove everyone wrong.

Though he was not a big man, McOuat made up for it in determination and grit. Red pine logs measuring up to 37 feet and weighing nearly a ton were hauled to the site using a winch and raised with a block and tackle. He worked alone. Lumber for flooring and roof boards was cut with a whipsaw; beautiful dovetail joints were hand-hewn for each corner joint. The main building was 24 by 28 feet and the kitchen 14 by 20; this was doubled for the second storey, on top of which he built a 40-foot tower! Windows and hardware were portaged and hauled over 15 portages after they arrived by train in Ignace.

Jimmy finished the castle in 1914. Now he just needed a wife to join him. A mail-order bride was forthcoming, but when Jimmy refused to meet her parents, the wedding was called off. McOuat drowned four years later, out front of his castle, while netting fish. His body was recovered the next spring and buried by the shore.

Agimak Trail Diary

Summer 2013 My son, Chris, and I decide to break the rules and pitch our camp right next to the Castle, probably in Jimmy's old potato garden. I need to be close enough to feel whether Jimmy's energy is still potent, maybe conjure up his ghost. The Castle has undergone a million-dollar rebuild, which I'm sure has expunged some of McOuat's energy from the cabin. Better to let things go back to the earth perhaps, let Jimmy's ghost rest in peace.

We tour the castle, every room, inspect the construction and imagine the work that went into the building of it — Jimmy all alone, for a pittance. Then a dozen volunteers came along with an inordinate amount of cash to spruce it up. The cabin's windows are missing; in the gloom they look like vacant eye sockets. I stand outside, hoping to see Jimmy's ghost float by. Nothing — he's gone. We sit beside his grave with tin cups of wine (a gift from the girl in the floatplane) and toast Jimmy. We congratulate him on his workmanship, but mostly for his strength of purpose. I tell him that we have many things in common, that I've spent 20 years building my own castle in a most unlikely and difficult place. I know exactly what he went through. And I know that he loved, more than anything else, the land on which he built his castle.

White Otter Castle Canoe Route

Maps 1, 2

Classification experienced novice

Distance 40 km (25 mi)

Duration 5 to 6 days (round trip)

Portages 15, totaling 5,272 m (3.3 mi), 13% of distance

Season mid-May to mid-October

Preferred craft lightweight Kevlar or Innegra canoe

Campsites all established, with firepits

Access north beach in Ignace or on Moosehide Road (short trips)

Water Characteristics & General Hazards

+ Heading south, it is quite possible to run into headwinds, especially on the bigger lakes.

Features

+ A very pretty route within White Otter Provincial Park.
+ Native pictographs can be found at Devil's Gap Lake and south of the Gap, as well as several on White Otter Lake.
+ The real draw is Jimmy McOuat's log castle on White Otter Lake, and the intriguing story attached to it.

White Otter Castle

WWII POW camp

Glacial erratic or sacred monument?
Photo credit: Dennis Smyk

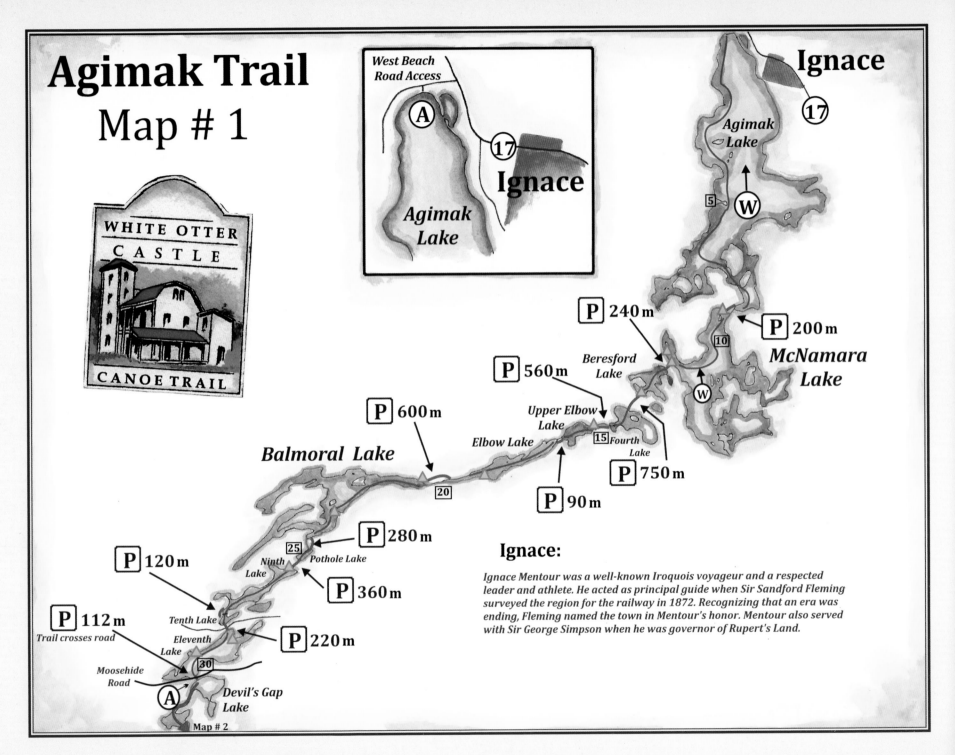

Agimak Trail
Map # 1

West Beach Road Access

(A)

(17) **Ignace**

Agimak Lake

Ignace

(17)

Agimak Lake

WHITE OTTER
CASTLE
CANOE TRAIL

(W)

[5]

[P] 240 m

[P] 200 m

Beresford Lake

[P] 560 m

McNamara Lake

[P] 600 m

Upper Elbow Lake

[10]

(W)

Balmoral Lake

Elbow Lake

[15] *Fourth Lake*

[P] 750 m

[20]

[P] 90 m

[P] 280 m

[25]

Ninth Lake

Pothole Lake

[P] 120 m

[P] 360 m

Ignace:

Ignace Mentour was a well-known Iroquois voyageur and a respected leader and athlete. He acted as principal guide when Sir Sandford Fleming surveyed the region for the railway in 1872. Recognizing that an era was ending, Fleming named the town in Mentour's honor. Mentour also served with Sir George Simpson when he was governor of Rupert's Land.

[P] 112 m

Tenth Lake

Trail crosses road

Eleventh Lake

[P] 220 m

Moosehide Road

[30]

(A)

Devil's Gap Lake

Map # 2

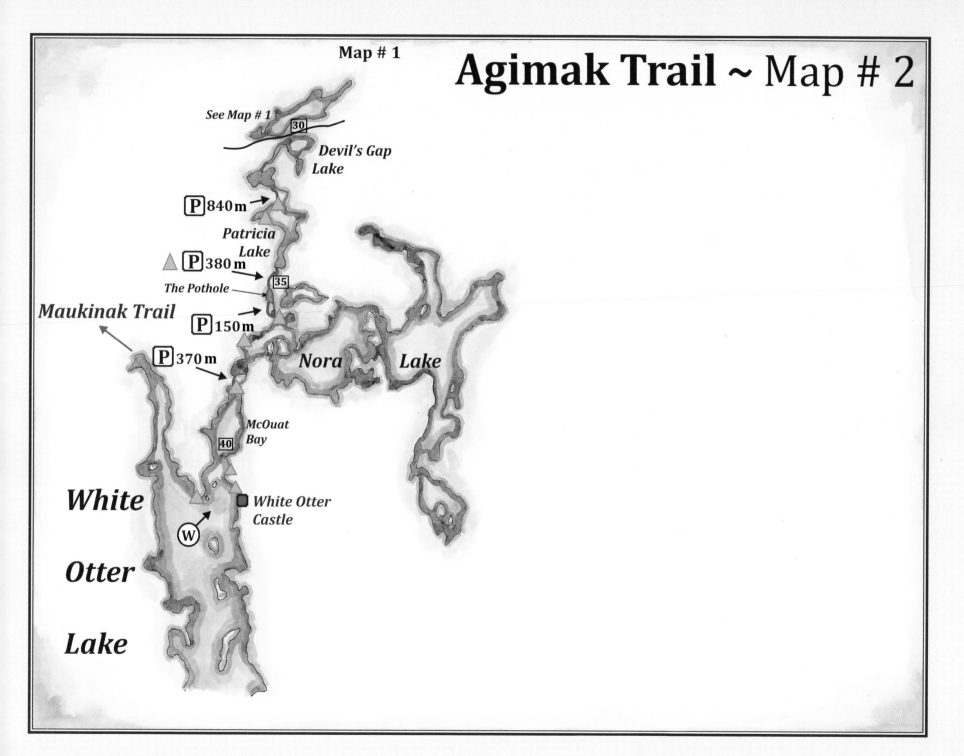

Map # 1

Agimak Trail ~ Map # 2

See Map # 1

30

Devil's Gap Lake

P 840m

Patricia Lake

△ P 380m

35

The Pothole

Maukinak Trail

P 150m

P 370m

Nora Lake

McOuat Bay

40

White

Otter

Lake

W

White Otter Castle

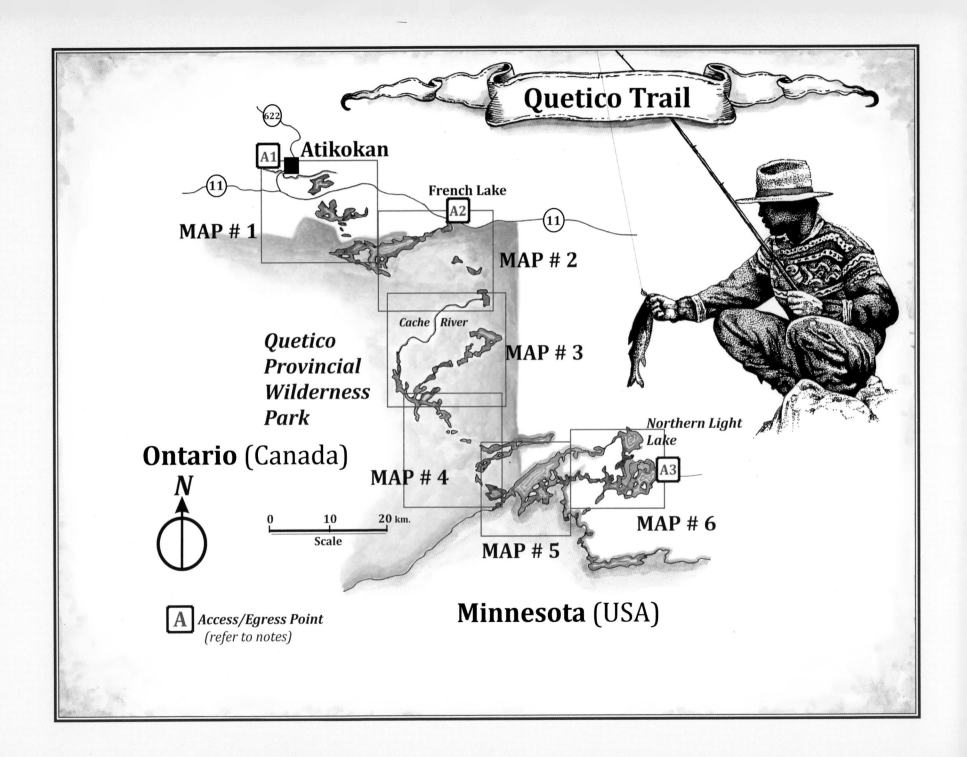

Chapter 8

Part 5
Quetico Trail

Topographic Map Locations
1:100,000 scale (provincial series)
Marmion Lake 52-B/NW – Agnes Lake 52-B/SW – Northern Light Lake 52-B/SE
1:50,000 scale
52-B/11 – 52-B/14 – 52-B/13 – 52-B/6

The name *Quetico* and its origin are something of a mystery. Locals may claim that it originated with a nonexistent timber company, and First Nations think it is derived from the name of a benevolent spirit that resides in places of great beauty.[5] The most plausible explanation is that it comes from an early French reference to *la quête de la côte*, meaning "search for the coast," during a time when early explorers were obsessed with finding the far coast of Canada. (Of course, to the local Anishinabeg, the Great Ocean was Lake Winnipeg.)

Quetico Provincial Park is a wilderness park established in 1913, the same year that Vilhjalmur Stefansson's contentious arctic expedition set out and a wild November storm sank 34 ships on the Great Lakes. Bracketed to the south by the Boundary Waters Canoe Area (part of the larger Superior National Forest), it created a sizeable, somewhat protected paradise for wilderness canoeing (logging stopped in 1971). Creation of the park instigated a conflict with Lac La Croix First Nation, whose reserve was within the new park's boundary. The Province of Ontario arbitrarily cancelled the band's right to the reserve and relocated it outside the park. The grievances were not addressed until 1991, when the band received an official apology and permission to operate motorboats on their traditional waters for the purpose of guiding (to be phased out).

There was no road access to the park until 1954. Once the nearby town of Atikokan became accessible, local tourist operators took advantage of the park's fame and branded Atikokan the "Canoeing Capital of Canada" (some other canoeing destinations, such as Algonquin Park and Temagami, might have argued that assertion). The 1960s and '70s saw Quetico positioned as the "ultimate"

---

5 Father Frederic Baraga's Ojibwe dictionary has no words beginning with the letter Q. Frederic Baraga, *A Dictionary of the Otchipwe Language, Explained in English* (Cincinnati: Jos. A. Hermann, 1853).

wilderness experience — and with good reason. While other canoeing destinations were struggling with clearcutting forestry operations, Quetico seemed to hold its own, surviving the onslaught of mechanized logging.

During the design phase for Path of the Paddle, the Park authorities did not want the trail to pass along commonly used routes. From my perspective, that was good enough reason to select a route along the east corridor of the park: the Cache River and on to Northern Light Lake by way of the border route. The Quetico Trail leaves Nym Lake at the southwest end to connect to Batchewaung Lake and then Pickerel Lake. It then goes from Pine Portage to Deux Rivières, Sturgeon Lake, the Maligne River and Keats Lake, then rejoins again at Kawnipi Lake. (This particular route was not favored by the former superintendent of Quetico Park.) The portages along the Cache River route had not been maintained for some time, as I discovered. It was

like finding a pot of gold in a closet full of old, worn-out clothes. This is a gem of a route — not for the timid, but with all the bells and whistles that come with the world-famous park.

This trail is divided into two sections: the Atikokan River route and the Quetico route. The Trans Canada Trail opted to bypass the Atikokan River in favor of a ski trail from Nym Lake back to the town. To me this didn't make any sense, because it disconnects the water trail and introduces a seasonal trail that nobody can use in the summertime. As well, the Ministry of Natural Resources was reluctant to establish new portage trails to connect the park with the river. As a day excursion, the Atikokan River is just plain fun, surprisingly pristine and not that difficult to access. Quetico . . . well, it takes the best features of Temagami, Algonquin, Killarney and Wabikimi and crams them into one 4,758-square-kilometer wilderness park.

The Quetico Trail leaves Nym Lake at the southwest end to connect to Batchewaung Lake, to Pickerel Lake and Pine Portage; Deux Rivieres to Sturgeon Lake to Maligne River, Keates Lake then rejoins again at Kawnipi. This particular route was not favoured by the former Quetico Park Superintendent.

Atikokan River Route
Map 1 and Detail Maps

Classification intermediate

Distance 15 km (9 mi) to park, 20 km (12 mi) to midtown

Duration 1 to 2 days

Portages 10 from Hwy 11 to Atikokan, totaling 1,470 m (0.9 mi)

Season early May to late June

Preferred craft durable, lightweight Kevlar, ABS or Innegra canoe

Campsites plateau has several undeveloped sites

Access Hwy 11 at Nym Lake

Egress Bunnell Park or midtown Atikokan

Water Characteristics and General Hazards

- The Atikokan is a typical small Ontario Shield river, which means it drains rather quickly after the spring run.
- Rapids are not technical but do become rocky by early summer. Aside from the various rapids, the river runs at a gentle pace. If you run it in the summer, rapids can be lined or waded through.
- During high water, the approach to Atikokan Falls (see map) is in strong current. When approaching landings, make sure the stern is in tight.

Features

- A very pleasant early-season day trip, with enough rapid-play to excite the enthusiast.
- No development, except for the railway line that runs beside the river.
- A very pretty river with an overburden of jack pine, black spruce and poplar.
- Keep an eye out for whitetail deer, painted turtles, kingfishers, blue herons and a wide variety of ducks.

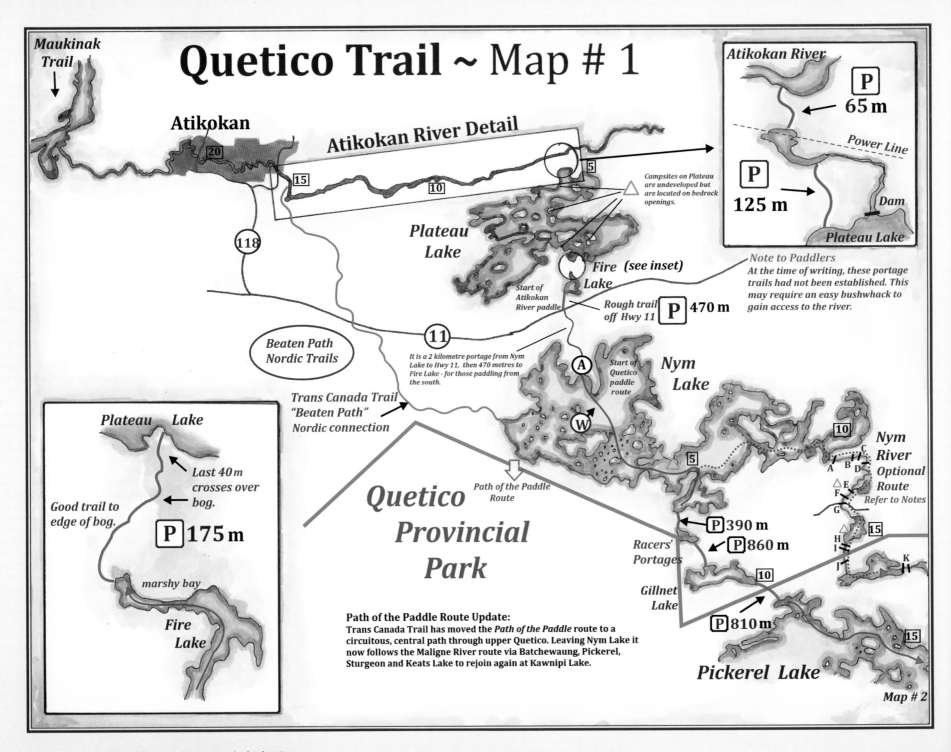

Quetico Trail ~ Map # 1

Maukinak Trail

Atikokan

Atikokan River Detail

Plateau Lake

Campsites on Plateau are undeveloped but are located on bedrock openings.

Atikokan River (inset)

P 65 m

Power Line

P 125 m

Dam

Plateau Lake

Fire Lake (see inset)

Start of Atikokan River paddle

Note to Paddlers
At the time of writing, these portage trails had not been established. This may require an easy bushwhack to gain access to the river.

Rough trail off Hwy 11   P 470 m

Beaten Path Nordic Trails

It is a 2 kilometre portage from Nym Lake to Hwy 11, then 470 metres to Fire Lake - for those paddling from the south.

Nym Lake

A

W

Start of Quetico paddle route

Trans Canada Trail "Beaten Path" Nordic connection

Path of the Paddle Route

Quetico Provincial Park

10

Nym River Optional Route
Refer to Notes

A B C D E F G H I J K

15

P 390 m
P 860 m

Racers' Portages

15

Gillnet Lake

10

P 810 m

Pickerel Lake

15

Map # 2

Plateau Lake (inset)

Last 40 m crosses over bog.

Good trail to edge of bog.

P 175 m

marshy bay

Fire Lake

Path of the Paddle Route Update:
Trans Canada Trail has moved the *Path of the Paddle* route to a circuitous, central path through upper Quetico. Leaving Nym Lake it now follows the Maligne River route via Batchewaung, Pickerel, Sturgeon and Keats Lake to rejoin again at Kawnipi Lake.

20
15
118
10
5
11
5

NYM RIVER DETAIL
From Map # 1
Paddler's Note:

Nym River is by far one of the most interesting small river treks along the Path of the Paddle route. Quetico Park officials wanted this eliminated from the selected trail because it would add another access route into the park that they would have to manage. Since few people have ventured this way, it makes for a bit of a challenge well worth the effort. It rates high on the wildlife viewing scale. If you compare the distances of the three "Racers Portages" at 2,060 metres, the five portages along Nym River (635 metres) makes for less work. Granted, there are several obstructions requiring liftovers and lining, but in all, my choice would be the river less travelled. Here is what you'll encounter on your way downstream:

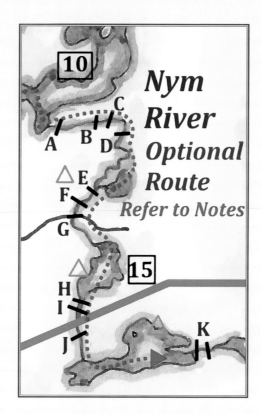

A. Portage 85 metres just beyond old rock berm.

B. Possible to run the top and line bottom for 100 metres (variable conditions apply).

C. Old bridge, liftover 4 metres but watch out for submerged spikes!

D. Portage 145 metres, left side (trail needed work), then pass through rocky shallows.

E. Deep water past small lake and potential campsite.

F. Portage 80 metres on left side (beaver dam).

G. Portage 130 metres, right side along trail over road.

H. Run or line 35 metres; rocky at bottom pool (variable conditions apply).

I. Wade or pull over on right side for 10 metres.

J. Just past beaver dam – run swifts on right or wade (variable conditions apply).

K. Portage 145 metres (may require bushwhacking); followed by swifts.

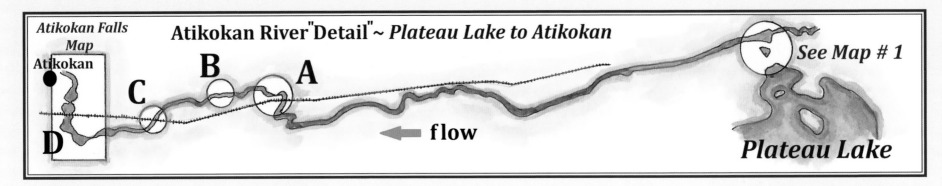

Atikokan River "Detail" ~ Plateau Lake to Atikokan

Atikokan Falls Map

Atikokan

B

C

A

D

← flow

See Map # 1

Plateau Lake

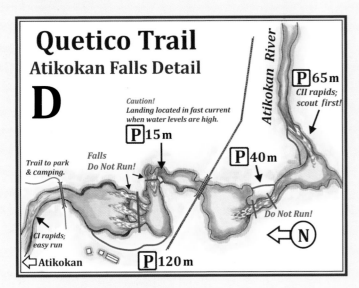

Quetico Trail
Atikokan Falls Detail

D

Atikokan River

P 65 m
CII rapids; scout first!

Caution! Landing located in fast current when water levels are high.

P 15 m

P 40 m

Falls Do Not Run!

Trail to park & camping.

Do Not Run!

CI rapids; easy run

← Atikokan

P 120 m

N →

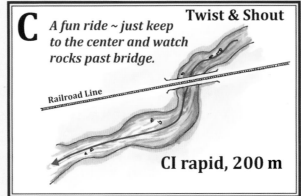

C

A fun ride ~ just keep to the center and watch rocks past bridge.

Twist & Shout

Railroad Line

CI rapid, 200 m

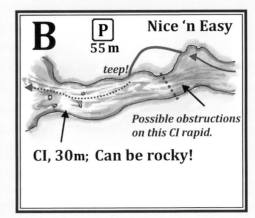

B

P 55 m

Nice 'n Easy

teep!

Possible obstructions on this CI rapid.

CI, 30m; Can be rocky!

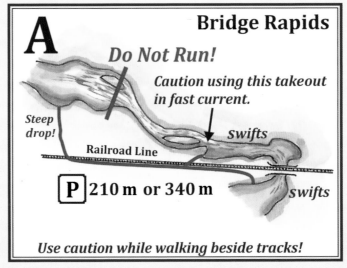

A

Bridge Rapids

Do Not Run!

Caution using this takeout in fast current.

Steep drop!

Railroad Line

swifts

P 210 m or 340 m

swifts

Use caution while walking beside tracks!

Cache Bay morning.

Quetico Route
Maps 2, 3, 4, 5, 6

Classification intermediate

Distance 167 km (104 mi)

Duration 8 to 10 days

Portages 29, totaling 11,490 m (7 mi), 7% of distance

Season mid-May to mid-October

Preferred craft lightweight Kevlar; expedition Kevlar or Innegra if you run the Cache River

Campsites most sites established, with firepits

Access Nym Lake; French Lake for shorter trips

Egress Northern Light Lake

Water Characteristics and General Hazards
- This route takes advantage of prevailing winds, so chances are you will have the wind behind you.
- Several large lakes (Pickerel, Saganaga, Northern Light) may be difficult if there is a south wind.
- Cache River can be run throughout the season, but the rapids get rockier as the season progresses. The skill required to miss them needs to be in top form.

Features
- Aside from the acclaimed beauty, majestic cliffs, pine-studded shorelines, great fishing and grandiose waterfalls, there are also historic and prehistoric elements.
- Aboriginal activity dates back almost 9,000 years. There are more than 20 recorded pictograph sites in the park, several of which are located along the Path of the Paddle. Scout the central islands on McKenzie and Kawnipi Lakes and think of the shaman standing in a canoe applying his red ochre paint, not to mention the magic that made that paint adhere for thousands of years.
- Historically speaking, Quetico was part of the Dawson Trail, from Thunder Bay to the Red River Settlement (Winnipeg) in Manitoba. Highway 11 up to French Lake follows the old path, continuing on through Pickerel and a series of lakes and portages, west to Lake of the Woods.

Wild iris along the Falls Chain.

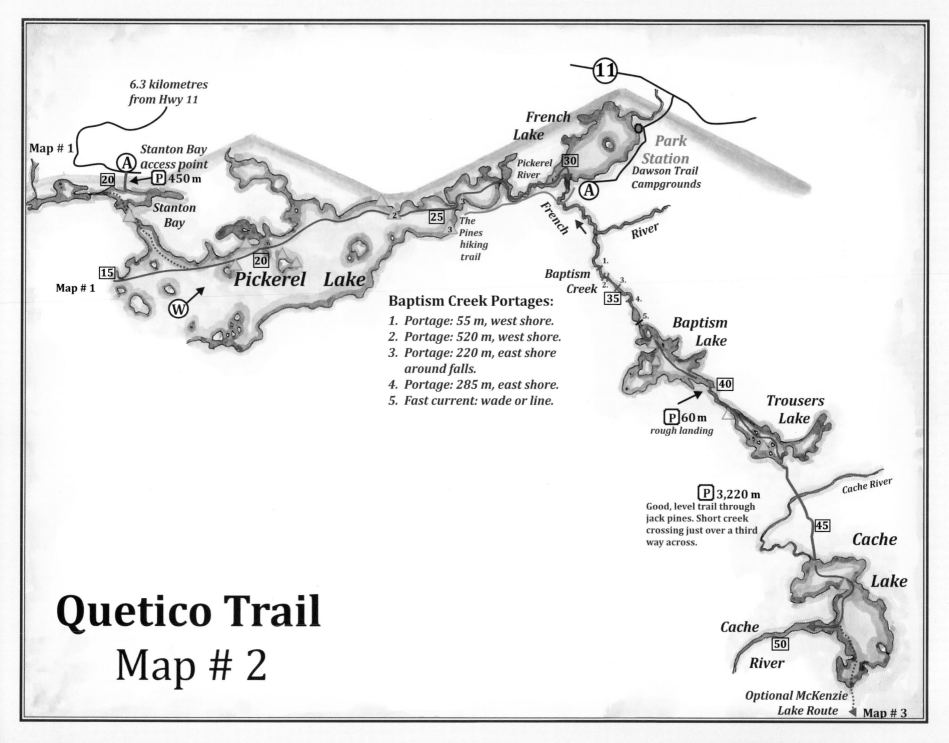

6.3 kilometres from Hwy 11

Map # 1

Stanton Bay access point

Ⓐ

20

Ⓟ 450 m

Stanton Bay

Map # 1

15

20

Ⓦ

Pickerel Lake

French Lake

Pickerel River

30

Park Station

Dawson Trail Campgrounds

Ⓐ

25

2

3

3

The Pines hiking trail

French

River

Baptism Creek Portages:

1. Portage: 55 m, west shore.
2. Portage: 520 m, west shore.
3. Portage: 220 m, east shore around falls.
4. Portage: 285 m, east shore.
5. Fast current: wade or line.

Baptism Creek

1.

2.

3.

35

4.

5.

Baptism Lake

40

Ⓟ 60 m
rough landing

Trousers Lake

Ⓟ 3,220 m
Good, level trail through jack pines. Short creek crossing just over a third way across.

Cache River

45

Cache

Lake

Cache

River

50

Optional McKenzie Lake Route

Map # 3

Quetico Trail
Map # 2

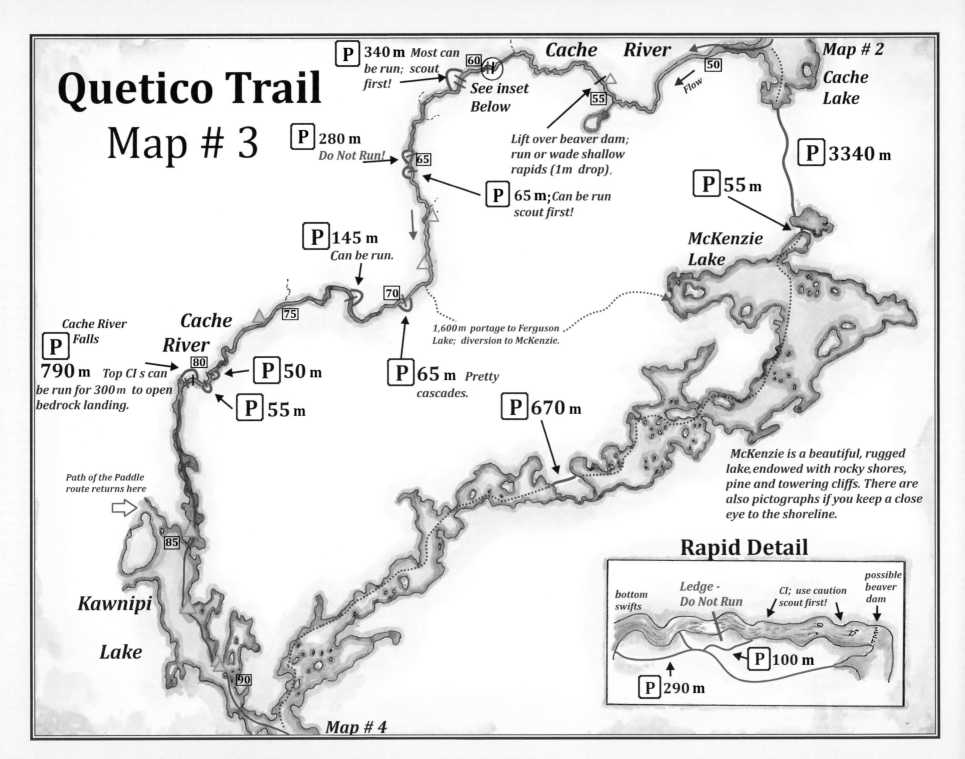

Quetico Trail
Map # 3

P 340 m *Most can be run; scout first!*

60

See inset Below

Cache River

55

50

Flow

Map # 2

Cache Lake

Lift over beaver dam; run or wade shallow rapids (1m drop).

P 280 m *Do Not Run!*

65

P 65 m; *Can be run scout first!*

P 3340 m

P 55 m

McKenzie Lake

P 145 m *Can be run.*

70

75

1,600 m portage to Ferguson Lake; diversion to McKenzie.

Cache River Falls

P 790 m *Top CI s can be run for 300 m to open bedrock landing.*

Cache River

80

P 50 m

P 55 m

P 65 m *Pretty cascades.*

P 670 m

McKenzie is a beautiful, rugged lake, endowed with rocky shores, pine and towering cliffs. There are also pictographs if you keep a close eye to the shoreline.

Path of the Paddle route returns here

85

Kawnipi Lake

90

Map # 4

Rapid Detail

bottom swifts

Ledge - Do Not Run

CI; use caution scout first!

possible beaver dam

P 100 m

P 290 m

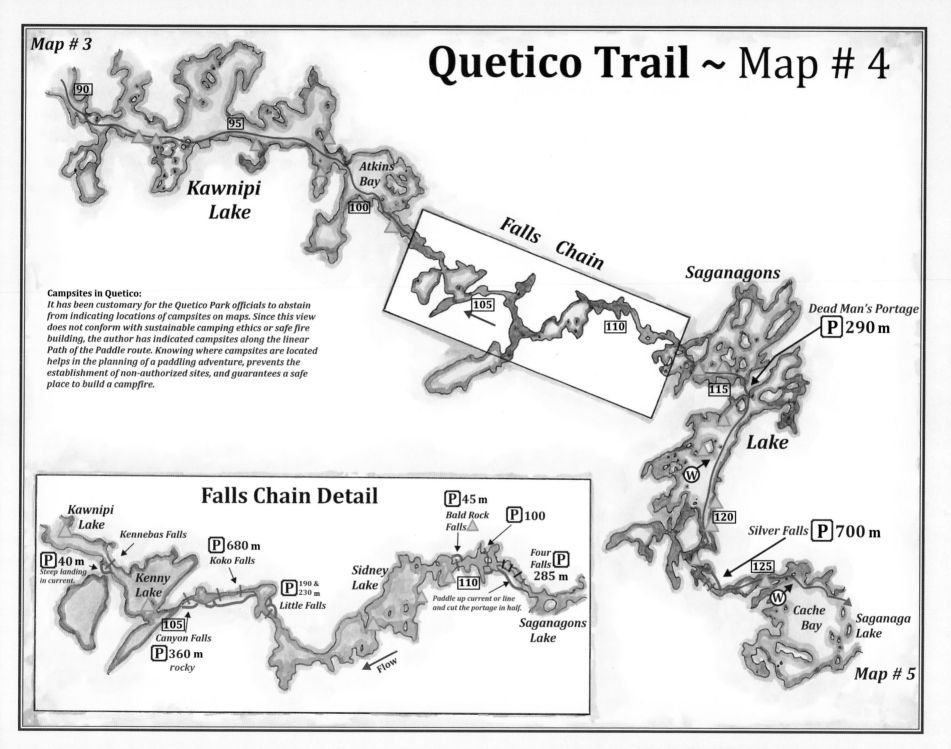

Map # 3

Quetico Trail ~ Map # 4

90

95

Atkins Bay

100

Kawnipi Lake

Campsites in Quetico:
It has been customary for the Quetico Park officials to abstain from indicating locations of campsites on maps. Since this view does not conform with sustainable camping ethics or safe fire building, the author has indicated campsites along the linear Path of the Paddle route. Knowing where campsites are located helps in the planning of a paddling adventure, prevents the establishment of non-authorized sites, and guarantees a safe place to build a campfire.

Falls   Chain

105

110

Saganagons

Dead Man's Portage
P 290 m

115

Lake

120

Silver Falls P 700 m

125

W

Cache Bay

Saganaga Lake

Map # 5

Falls Chain Detail

Kawnipi Lake

Kennebas Falls

P 40 m
Steep landing in current.

Kenny Lake

P 680 m
Koko Falls

105
Canyon Falls
P 360 m
rocky

P 190 & 230 m
Little Falls

P 45 m
Bald Rock Falls

P 100

Sidney Lake

Four Falls P 285 m

110
Paddle up current or line and cut the portage in half.

Saganagons Lake

Flow

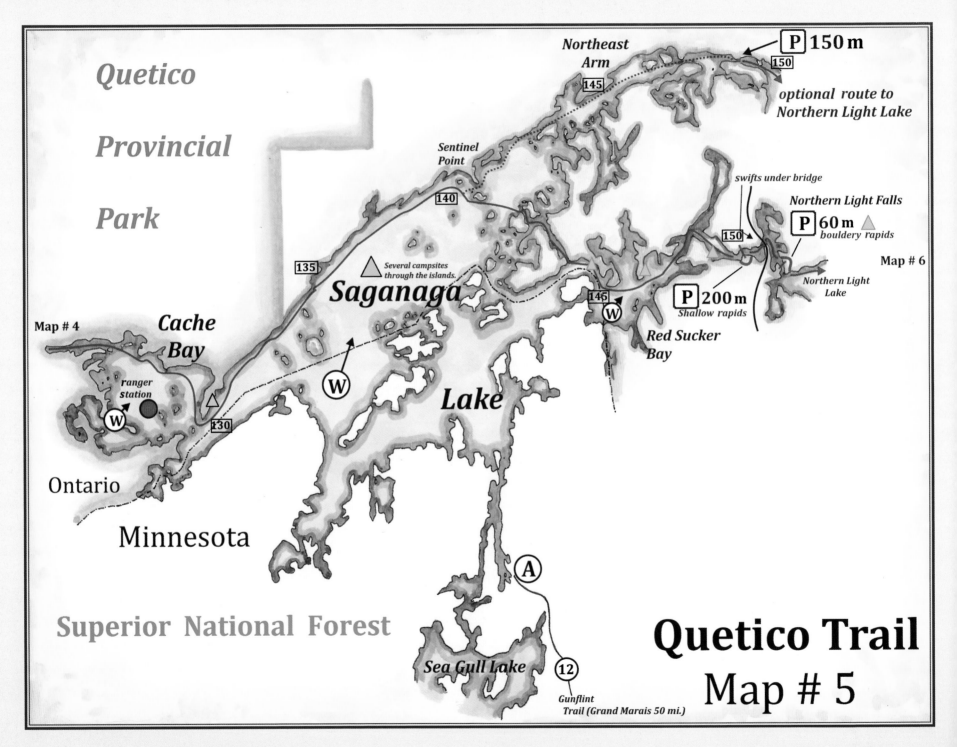

Quetico

Provincial

Park

Northeast Arm

P 150 m
150

optional route to Northern Light Lake

145

Sentinel Point

140

swifts under bridge

Northern Light Falls

P 60 m ▲ bouldery rapids

150

Map # 6

135

Several campsites through the islands.

Saganaga

Map # 4

Cache Bay

P 200 m
Shallow rapids

145
Ⓦ

Northern Light Lake

Red Sucker Bay

ranger station

Ⓦ

130

Lake

Ⓦ

Ontario

Minnesota

Superior National Forest

Ⓐ

Quetico Trail

Map # 5

Sea Gull Lake

⑫

Gunflint Trail (Grand Marais 50 mi.)

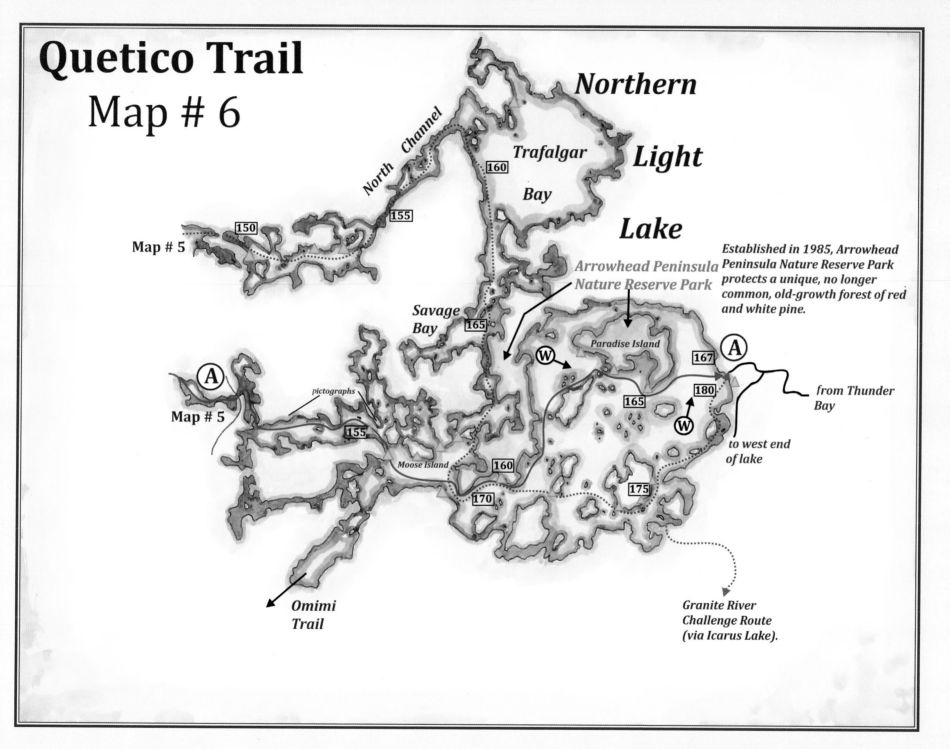

Quetico Trail
Map # 6

Northern

Light

Lake

North Channel

Trafalgar
Bay

[160]

[155]

[150]

Map # 5

Savage
Bay

[165]

Arrowhead Peninsula
Nature Reserve Park

*Established in 1985, Arrowhead
Peninsula Nature Reserve Park
protects a unique, no longer
common, old-growth forest of red
and white pine.*

Paradise Island

(W)

(A)

[167]

from Thunder
Bay

(A)

Map # 5

pictographs

[155]

[180]

[165]

(W)

to west end
of lake

Moose Island

[160]

[170]

[175]

Omimi
Trail

*Granite River
Challenge Route
(via Icarus Lake).*

Quetico Trail Journal

Odds are, if you spend a lot of time on the trail, pushing the season for six months, you'll have an opportunity to experience the best and the worst of weather. Paddling and portaging through the years have taken a toll on my joints, the knees first to go, when the cartilage disappeared. Six years ago I was recovering from a knee replacement the previous winter and was anxious to continue the fieldwork for Path of the Paddle. Swift Canoe had donated an expedition Kevlar boat, which took a lot of the strain off the mending leg, but I was in no way ready for what was to unfold over the next several days.

Trousers Lake, Quetico July, six years ago. I've spent some time at French Lake getting a feel for the territory, camping, talking with a couple of park rangers, hiking out to the Pines on Pickerel Lake. It's one of those hot, muggy summer episodes that mosquitoes revel in. Thunderstorms threaten in the late afternoons, and lying in a stuffy tent, sweating and listening to the hum of mosquitoes, keeps you awake all night.

Leaving the "civilized" Dawson Trail campground, I've made good time down Baptism Creek, measuring portages and taking notes, and I've found a decent enough campsite on the west shore of Trousers Lake. I've done everything as I usually do: cooked a one-pot meal (this time on a camp stove, as it's far too hot for a campfire); set up my tent a way back from the open bedrock shore, a good spot nestled against a copse of young jack pine; perched my ass on a camp chair out on the point, where the breeze keeps the bugs to an acceptable social interface; and wrote in my journal while sipping on a drop of Irish whiskey in a tin cup. Feeling satisfied with the day's accomplishments, I go to bed at dusk and fall fast asleep on top of my sleeping bag.

It's the sound of my canoe rolling across the campsite that wakes

We used to call them "push storms" — like mini tornadoes but without the funnel — devastating and dangerous to be anywhere near. I have had several close encounters over the years, at the outer edges, racing them to shore to take cover, but until the Trousers Lake storm, I'd never been right in the middle of one. Called "micro bursts," the sudden downdraft and wind shear work much like the opposite of a tornado, but they can whip up winds of more than 270 kph (170 mph) and have the same effect as a tornado. The following day I headed south to the 3,200 m (2 mi) portage to Cache Lake and found that hundreds of jack pine had blown down over the trail, piled high and tangled like pick-up sticks. It took the whole day to move my gear across the portage.

me hours later. *I haven't secured it!* I pulled it up almost to my tent but failed to use one of the painters to snag it to a tree. Now it's heading toward the lake, pushed by an incredible force of wind — *tornado!* I grab the canoe, drag it up into the bush and wedge it between two trees, tying it off securely, then run over to save my tent before it flies off like a kite to the next lake. It's flattened, but I manage to stand on it and pin it down while holding on to a rope I tethered to a nearby tree. No need for a flashlight, as there's no break in the lightning show — a surreal explosion of phosphorescent brightness, everything moving around me, over me, tree tops bent to the ground, some crashing somewhere close by, rain driving sideways. It takes all my strength to hold on to the rope, and I'm damned if I'm going to lose my tent! The sound is deafening as it reaches a crescendo; I crouch low, waiting to be swept away.

And then it stops. Just like that. A low rumble farther down the lake, trees above me trembling, shaking off the rain. Everything soaked. I re-pitch my tent; by some fluke of luck, it's still dry inside.

Saganagons Lake, Quetico A few days later. They say that your chance of being struck by lightning is about one in 6,500. I suspect that the more time you spend outdoors under certain environmental conditions, the more that statistic decreases drastically — probably why a lot of hardcore golfers get struck by lightning every year. I don't play golf but I do spend an inordinate amount of time on the trail, sometimes pushing the boundaries to get to wherever I'm going.

I put ashore as an electrical storm begins, pitch my rain tarp in a copse of small trees — the thing to do during a thunderstorm — and wait for it to pass. I wait until the lightning flashes cease and go down to the shore to fill my coffee pot. Next thing I know I'm sitting on the ground, disoriented, ears buzzing like a chainsaw and shaking like a trembling aspen in a gale. For a few seconds I can't hear and my breathing is labored, heart racing, and I want to throw up. I manage to light my camp stove and make tea, then sit there for at least three hours before thinking about paddling on. When I do, I go only about a kilometer before pulling in to make camp for the night. I've heard rumors that sex is better after being hit by lightning; I can't wait to get home to see if it's true.

Afternoon calm on Kawnipi Lake.

Falls Chain – a highlight along the Quetico Trail.

Cache Falls

Paddling the Saganaga island archipelago.

Cache River — intimate and wild.

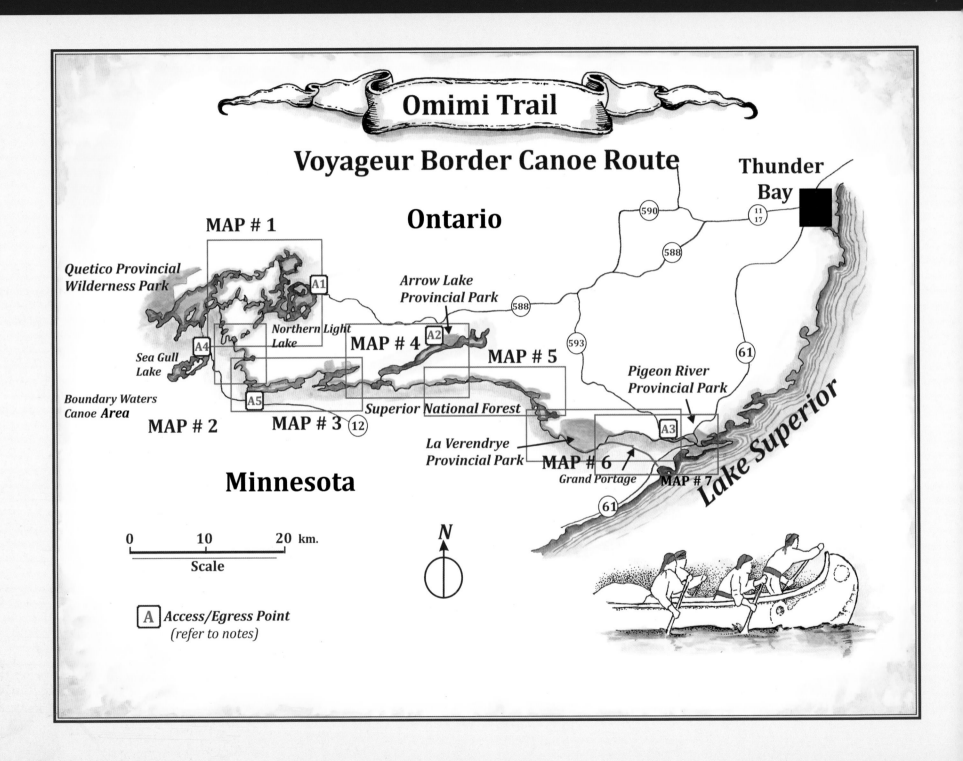

Omimi Trail

Voyageur Border Canoe Route

Ontario

Thunder Bay

590

588

11 17

588

593

61

MAP # 1

Quetico Provincial Wilderness Park

A1

Arrow Lake Provincial Park

A2

MAP # 4

Northern Light Lake

A4

Sea Gull Lake

A5

MAP # 2

MAP # 3

12

Superior National Forest

Boundary Waters Canoe Area

MAP # 5

Pigeon River Provincial Park

La Verendrye Provincial Park

A3

MAP # 6

Grand Portage

MAP # 7

Lake Superior

Minnesota

61

0   10   20 km.
Scale

N

A *Access/Egress Point*
(refer to notes)

Chapter 9

Part 6
Omimi Trail

Topographic Map Locations
1:100,000 scale (provincial series)
Northern Light Lake 52-B/SE – Thunder Bay 52-A/SW

The Boundary Waters–Voyageur Waterway is a chain of lakes and river channels that marks the boundary between Minnesota and Ontario. It drains in two directions, as it sits along the divide between the Hudson Bay and Atlantic drainage systems, through undeveloped wilderness shaped by glaciation and water. The Thunder Bay region, along its lower reaches, contains outstanding and unique geological features more than a billion years old.

The Omimi Trail follows the eastern half of the Canadian Heritage Waterway, which was designated in 1986 for its natural and cultural value. La Verendrye Provincial Park, a waterway park, also traces its path along the entire stretch of the Omimi Trail on the Ontario side. This is a non-operating park; both its waterway park and heritage classifications afford no protection, nor does it benefit from periodic maintenance. Conversely, on the American side of the Omimi Trail, the Boundary Waters Canoe Area (BWCA) Wilderness and Superior National Forest are maintained — Minnesota takes great pride in preserving this important tourist and cultural attraction.

During the 18th and 19th centuries, the main travel route between Montreal and the new settlement of Red River (Winnipeg) was what is now called the Voyageur Waterway. The Omimi Trail leaves North Fowl Lake at the northeast corner, following North Fowl Lake Road to Pit Road, then onto Highway 593 to join up with the trail at Pigeon River Provincial Park. This leaves out the Gunflint Lake and Pigeon River part of the Voyageur Waterway. The original route was a reliable, albeit difficult canoe trail that made trade with and exploration of the west possible. Mining, logging, railway construction and wildfires have all left their signatures along the route, but it offers accessible urban wilderness recreation that supports local industry today. The region is rich in archeological sites (124 recorded), including Paleo-Indian stone quarries that date back 10,000 years and more recent pictographs, dolmen stones and petroforms. Even the portages used today are remnants of a past era of survival, trade and exploration.

Omimi (or *omiimii*) is the Ojibwe word for "passenger pigeon," a bird that was once prolific along the Pigeon River corridor. The Pigeon River originates in Mountain Lake and is one of the larger rivers that flow into the north shore of Lake Superior. The upper stretch is navigable, while the lower reaches descend through a series of tumultuous cascades, rapids and waterfalls. High Falls, at 37 m (120 ft), is the highest waterfall in Minnesota. Grand Portage bypasses the lower river — for good reason.

Voyageur Border Canoe Route
Maps 1, 2, 3, 4, 5, 6, 7

Classification intermediate

Distance 130 km (81 mi) with Canadian takeout; 145 km (90 mi) with Grand Portage (US) takeout

Duration 7 to 9 days; add 1 extra day for Grand Portage

Portages 23, totaling 14,670 m (9 mi), 11% of distance; 18,370 m (11 mi), 13% of distance via Grand Portage route

Season mid-May to mid-October

Preferred craft lightweight expedition Kevlar or Innegra canoe

Campsites most established campsites are on American side

Access Northern Light Lake

Egress 1 km past Partridge Falls (Canadian side); Grand Portage National Monument, Grand Portage, MN

Water Characteristics and General Hazards

- Wind conditions on Northern Light Lake may present problems.
- Pine and Granite Rivers become quite shallow in the summer but are still passable and not difficult to line or portage. Rapids are mostly Class I and Class II, easy to run when water levels are high.
- Because of fire damage, the possibility of "sweepers" or "strainers" (trees that get jammed in the rapids) may present a hazard. Scout all fast water if you decide to head north to descend the Pine and Granite Rivers.
- Pigeon River also becomes shallow but passable, with a reasonably strong current — hard work if you decide to travel upstream on the Path of the Paddle route.

Features

- The trail is home to 400 plant species, of which 13 are rare. Plant species found on the cliffs of North and South Fowl Lakes are throwbacks to another time that are more typically found in subarctic, arctic and western mountain regions.
- Micro-fossils two billion years old — the oldest in North America — are found along Gunflint and North Lakes.
- Historic sites include a fur-trading post on the Pigeon River at Fort Charlotte (Grand Portage). This was the North West Company's major depot and the site of the annual rendezvous, when 600 to 800 men from the northern and Montreal fur brigades met for revelry and to exchange goods.
- The trail is closely linked with many of Canada's early explorers, such as Claude-Jean Allouez (1666), Daniel Greysolon Dulhut (1678), Zacharie de La Noue (1722), Pierre de La Vérendrye (1731), Alexander Henry (1775), Simon Fraser, Alexander Mackenzie and David Thompson (1783). In 1801 the Montreal-based North West Company moved its operations north to British territory on the Kaministiquia River, after border disputes with the United States.
- Remnants of old corduroy roads, marine railways and excavations can be seen along several of the portages.
- The route has a higher-than-average tally of portages. Trails are generally in good

shape on the American side (part of the Superior National Forest trail initiative), including trails such as Long Portage that join up with the Minnesota system. The portage from South Fowl Lake to the Pigeon River was in poor shape when assessed in 2014.

◆ Although the route forms an international boundary, there is no development and no border stations, just phenomenal scenery.

◆ Thunder Bay's diabase-capped mesas give the trail a mountainous feel. There are several superb vantage points along the way.

The Omimi Trail leaves North Fowl Lake at the northeast corner, following the North Fowl Lake Road to Pit Road, then on to Hwy # 593 to join up with the trail at Pigeon River Provincial Park. This leaves out the Gunflint Lake & Pigeon River route along the Voyageur Canoe Route.

The only indication of an international boundary are the occasional sign and cairn.

Omimi Trail ~ Map # 1

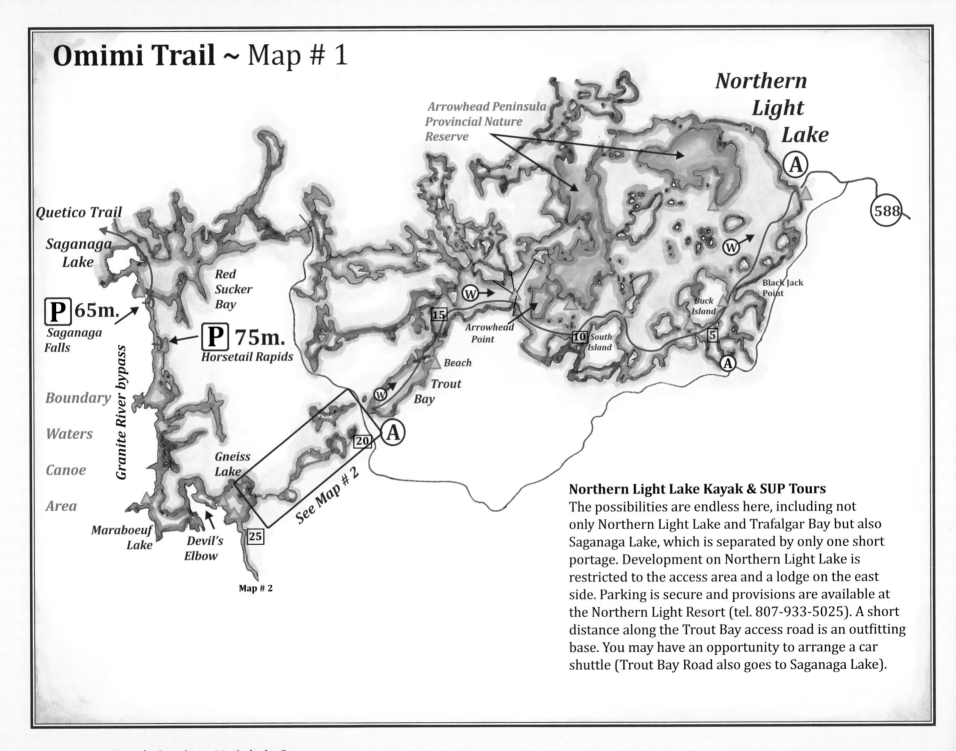

Northern Light Lake

Arrowhead Peninsula Provincial Nature Reserve

588

Black Jack Point

Buck Island

Quetico Trail

Saganaga Lake

Red Sucker Bay

P 65m.

Saganaga Falls

P 75m.

Horsetail Rapids

Granite River bypass

Boundary

Waters

Canoe

Area

Arrowhead Point

15

10 South Island

5

Beach

Trout Bay

A

20

Gneiss Lake

See Map # 2

Maraboeuf Lake

Devil's Elbow

25

Map # 2

Northern Light Lake Kayak & SUP Tours

The possibilities are endless here, including not only Northern Light Lake and Trafalgar Bay but also Saganaga Lake, which is separated by only one short portage. Development on Northern Light Lake is restricted to the access area and a lodge on the east side. Parking is secure and provisions are available at the Northern Light Resort (tel. 807-933-5025). A short distance along the Trout Bay access road is an outfitting base. You may have an opportunity to arrange a car shuttle (Trout Bay Road also goes to Saganaga Lake).

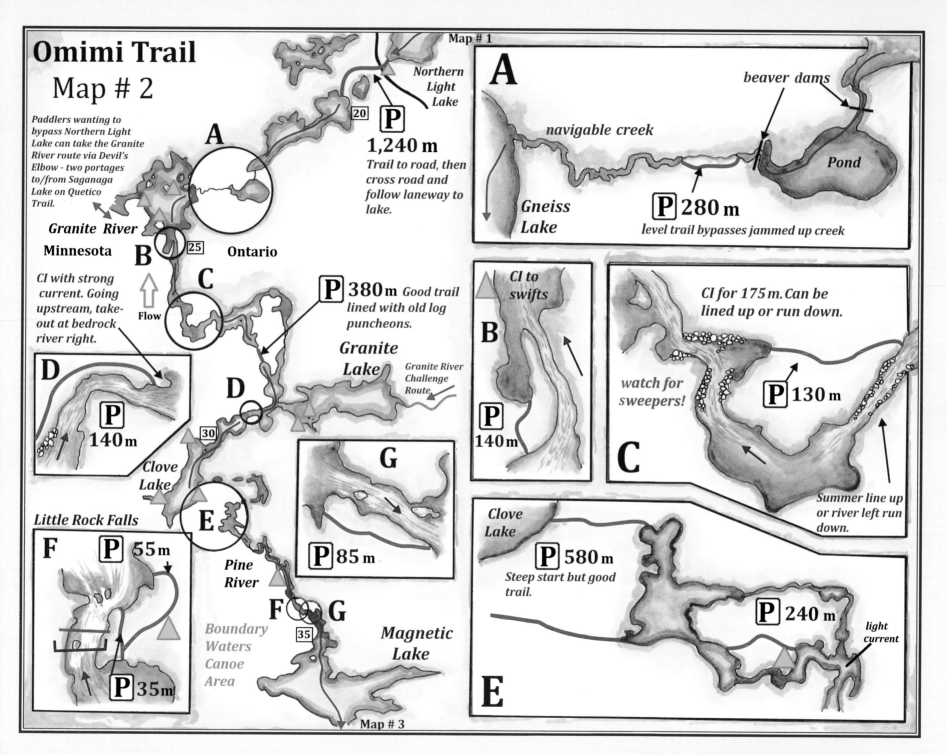

Omimi Trail
Map # 2

Map # 1

Paddlers wanting to bypass Northern Light Lake can take the Granite River route via Devil's Elbow - two portages to/from Saganaga Lake on Quetico Trail.

Northern Light Lake

A

20

P 1,240 m
Trail to road, then cross road and follow laneway to lake.

Granite River

Minnesota

B

25

Ontario

CI with strong current. Going upstream, take-out at bedrock river right.

Flow

C

P 380 m *Good trail lined with old log puncheons.*

Granite Lake

Granite River Challenge Route

D

P 140 m

D

30

Clove Lake

Little Rock Falls

E

G

P 85 m

F

P 55 m

Pine River

F

G

35

P 35 m

Boundary Waters Canoe Area

Magnetic Lake

Map # 3

A

beaver dams

navigable creek

Pond

P 280 m

level trail bypasses jammed up creek

Gneiss Lake

CI to swifts

B

P 140 m

CI for 175 m. Can be lined up or run down.

watch for sweepers!

P 130 m

C

Summer line up or river left run down.

Clove Lake

P 580 m
Steep start but good trail.

P 240 m

light current

E

Omimi Trail ~ Map # 3

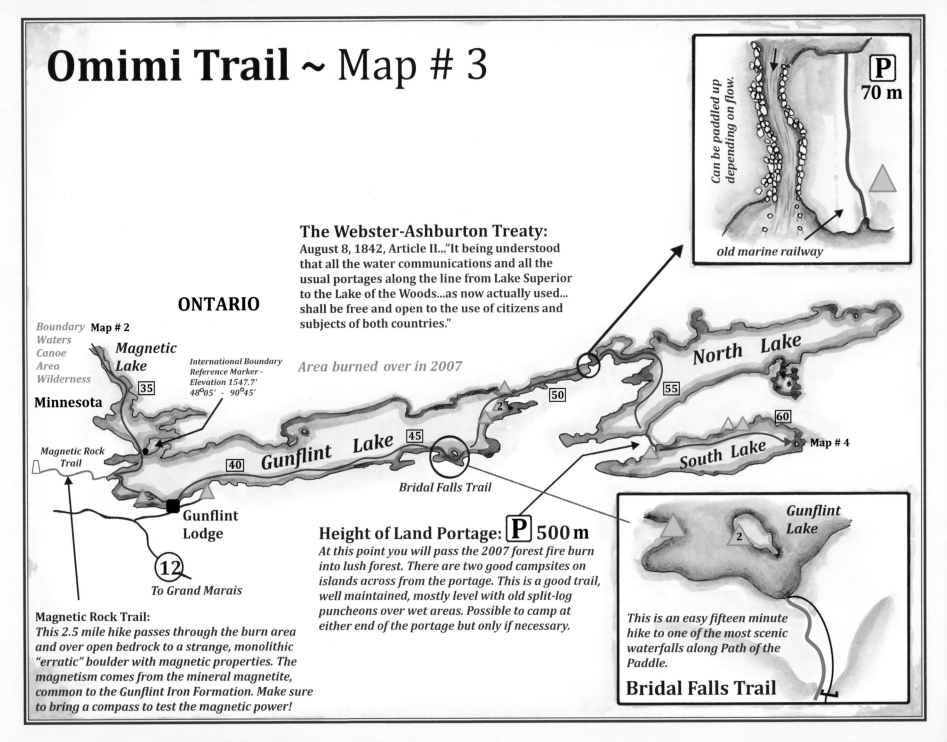

P 70 m

Can be paddled up depending on flow.

old marine railway

The Webster-Ashburton Treaty:
August 8, 1842, Article II..."It being understood that all the water communications and all the usual portages along the line from Lake Superior to the Lake of the Woods...as now actually used... shall be free and open to the use of citizens and subjects of both countries."

ONTARIO

Boundary Waters Canoe Area Wilderness

Map # 2

Magnetic Lake

International Boundary Reference Marker - Elevation 1547.7' 48°05' - 90°45'

Minnesota

35

Area burned over in 2007

North Lake

55

50

2

60

Magnetic Rock Trail

Gunflint Lake

45

40

Bridal Falls Trail

South Lake

Map # 4

Gunflint Lodge

(12)

To Grand Marais

Height of Land Portage: **P** 500 m
At this point you will pass the 2007 forest fire burn into lush forest. There are two good campsites on islands across from the portage. This is a good trail, well maintained, mostly level with old split-log puncheons over wet areas. Possible to camp at either end of the portage but only if necessary.

Magnetic Rock Trail:
This 2.5 mile hike passes through the burn area and over open bedrock to a strange, monolithic "erratic" boulder with magnetic properties. The magnetism comes from the mineral magnetite, common to the Gunflint Iron Formation. Make sure to bring a compass to test the magnetic power!

Gunflint Lake

2

This is an easy fifteen minute hike to one of the most scenic waterfalls along Path of the Paddle.

Bridal Falls Trail

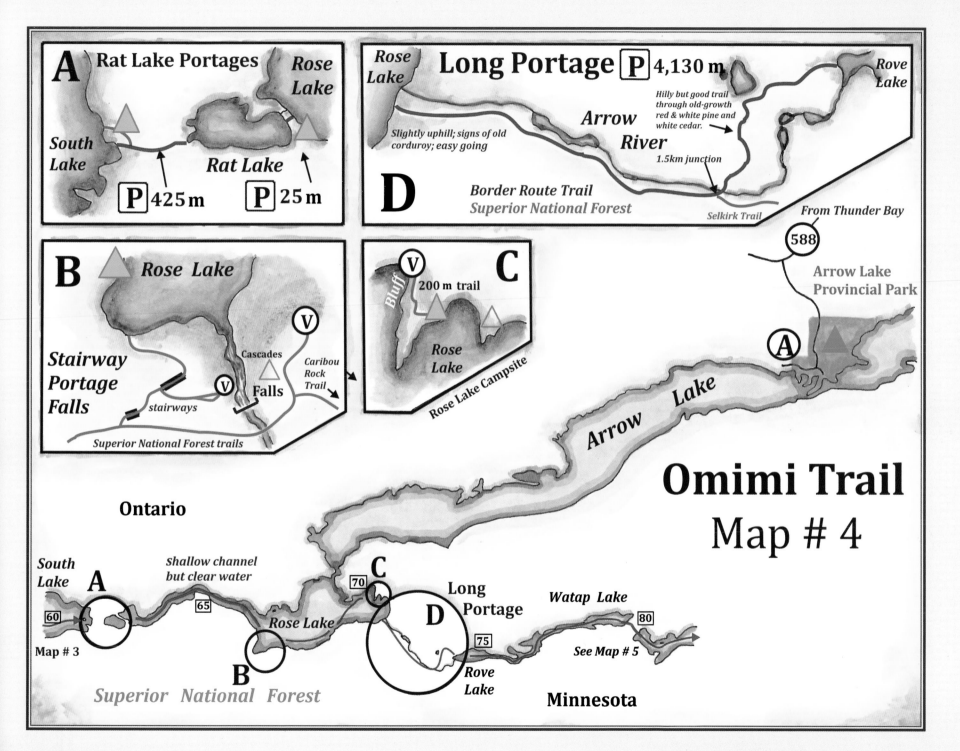

A Rat Lake Portages

Rose Lake

South Lake

Rat Lake

P 425 m   P 25 m

D Long Portage P 4,130 m

Rose Lake

Rove Lake

Arrow River

Hilly but good trail through old-growth red & white pine and white cedar.

Slightly uphill; signs of old corduroy; easy going

1.5km junction

Border Route Trail
Superior National Forest

Selkirk Trail

From Thunder Bay

588

Arrow Lake Provincial Park

Ⓐ

B

Rose Lake

Stairway Portage Falls

Cascades

V

Caribou Rock Trail

V

Falls

stairways

Superior National Forest trails

C

V

Bluff

200 m trail

Rose Lake

Rose Lake Campsite

Arrow Lake

Omimi Trail

Map # 4

Ontario

South Lake

Shallow channel but clear water

A

60

65

Map # 3

B

Rose Lake

70 C

D

Long Portage

Watap Lake

80

75

See Map # 5

Rove Lake

Minnesota

Superior National Forest

Omimi Trail ~ Map # 5

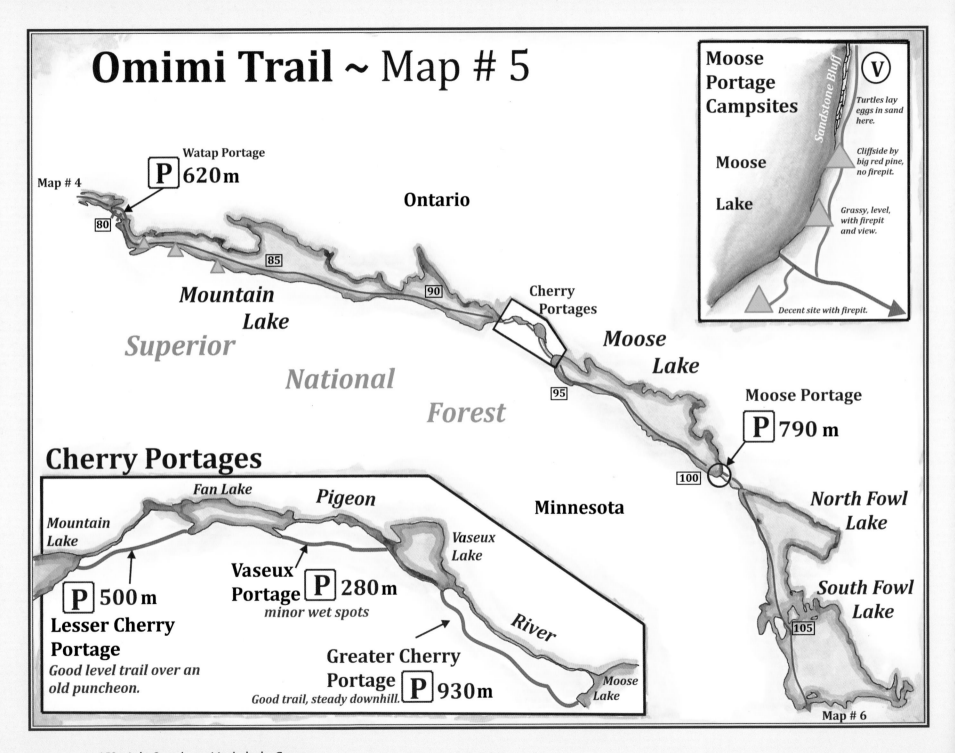

Watap Portage

P 620 m

Map # 4

80

Ontario

85

90

Mountain Lake

Superior

National

Forest

Cherry Portages

95

Moose Lake

Moose Portage

P 790 m

100

Minnesota

North Fowl Lake

South Fowl Lake

105

Cherry Portages

Fan Lake

Pigeon

Mountain Lake

P 500 m

Lesser Cherry Portage
Good level trail over an old puncheon.

Vaseux Portage P 280 m
minor wet spots

Vaseux Lake

River

Greater Cherry Portage P 930 m
Good trail, steady downhill.

Moose Lake

Map # 6

Moose Portage Campsites

V

Sandstone Bluff

Turtles lay eggs in sand here.

Moose Lake

Cliffside by big red pine, no firepit.

Grassy, level, with firepit and view.

Decent site with firepit.

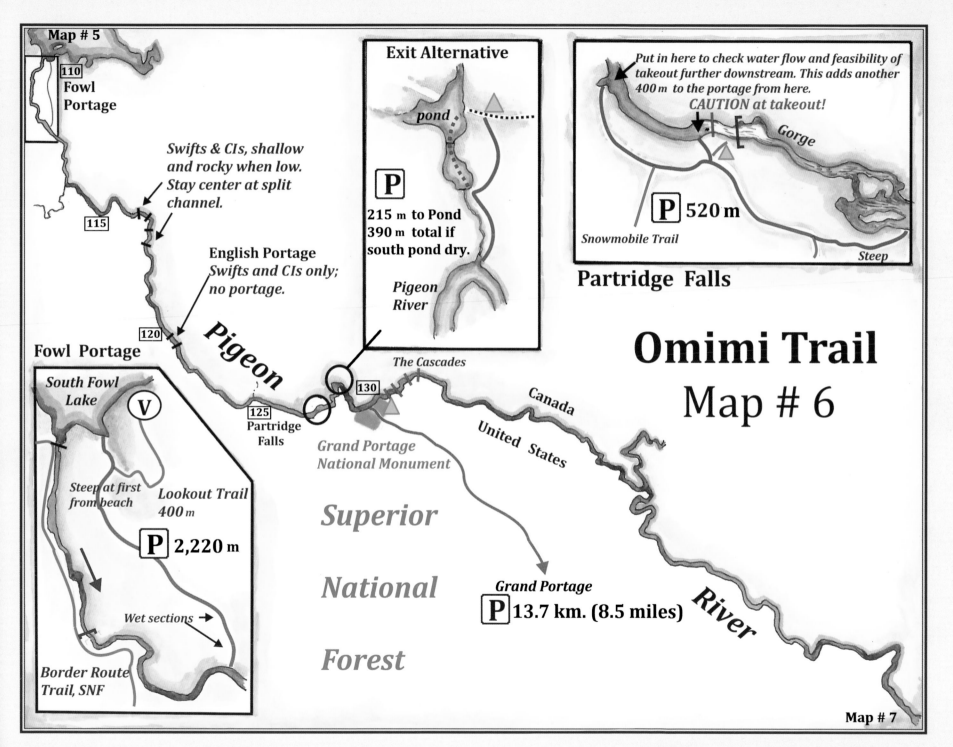

Map # 5

110 Fowl Portage

Swifts & CIs, shallow and rocky when low. Stay center at split channel.

115

English Portage
Swifts and CIs only; no portage.

Fowl Portage

South Fowl Lake

V

Steep at first from beach

Lookout Trail 400 m

P 2,220 m

Wet sections →

Border Route Trail, SNF

120

Pigeon

125 Partridge Falls

Exit Alternative

pond

P

215 m to Pond
390 m total if south pond dry.

Pigeon River

130

The Cascades

Grand Portage National Monument

Canada

United States

Superior

National

Forest

Grand Portage

P 13.7 km. (8.5 miles)

Put in here to check water flow and feasibility of takeout further downstream. This adds another 400 m to the portage from here.
CAUTION at takeout!

Gorge

P 520 m

Snowmobile Trail

Steep

Partridge Falls

Omimi Trail
Map # 6

River

Map # 7

Omimi Trail ~ Map # 7

Path of the Paddle Note:

The all-Canadian water trail was originally meant to end here and connect with a newly built land trail from Pigeon River Provincial Park. Because of time constraints and lack of funds to upgrade this access/egress point and build new overland trails from Thunder Bay, the Trans Canada Trail opted to include the Animikii-Superior route, and the road system from North Fowl Lake, essentially leaving out the lower Pigeon River entirely. This 13 km bush road is currently suitable only for 4-wheel-drive vehicles, but driving is a possible option for those who do not want to lug their gear 13.7 km over Grand Portage.

593

For information about the trails at Pigeon River Provincial Park see Animikii Trail.

61

bush road

Ontario

Minnesota

Optional Canadian Egress Point for Pick-Ups only.

(A)

See Map # 6 for portage information.

Grand Portage [P] **13.7 km. 8.5 miles**

Pigeon River Provincial Park

Pigeon River

No Connection

(A)

old Hwy 61

Grand Portage National Monument

Pigeon Point

61

Animikii Trail

(A)

Grand Portage

Grand Portage Bay

Grand Portage:

Today's trail is part of the Grand Portage National Monument. It is divided into 2 distinct sections, for hikers who don't want to walk the entire length of the trail in one direction. The eastern part passes through valleys and gaps, neatly bypassing the high rocky ridges; the western section takes advantage of ridge crests in order to avoid steep slopes, bogs and swamps. There is a parking area at old Highway 61 where hikers can choose which part of history they want to explore.

Lake Superior

Omimi Trail Diary

Summer, 2013 Knocked my mountain bike and rack off the top of the car this afternoon while driving down an overgrown bush road. Forgot the bike was there. Totaled it.

A few days later Andrea and I head across Gunflint Lake to talk with the folks at Gunflint Lodge, on the American side. So far, traveling upstream on the Granite and Pine Rivers, we've seen nothing to indicate an International border — BWCA on one side, La Verendrye on the other. The 2006 wildfire has left its mark, the "scorched earth" protocol of a fire-dependent ecosystem.

We approach the dock and are immediately greeted by a well-dressed young man. "Welcome to Gunflint Lodge," he says. Is he going to valet our canoe? "Staying for lunch, are we?" His hand makes a sweeping gesture toward the main entrance and I think he may have bowed slightly. Andrea and I discuss the state of our dress and the obvious smoky aroma. "I'm sure they're used to paddlers," Andrea comments, certainly more concerned than I am — I can already taste the cold beer.

Gunflint Lodge is an iconic landmark in Minnesota that has been operating as a resort and outfitting base since 1925 (and by the Kerfoot-Spunner family since 1929). It is now a full-fledged four-season resort with a five-star gourmet restaurant and beer served in ice-chilled glasses. The outfitting base has the capacity to handle more than 200 campers, who are mostly bound for the BWCA and Quetico. An occasional party of pre-camp staff descends the Pigeon and the Grand Portage as a "challenge warm-up" for the season. [Since our visit they've also added a zip-line and tree-canopy tour. In 2016 the lodge was sold for more than $6 million to John and Mindy Fredrikson.]

For us a stopover at Gunflint Lodge is a pleasant diversion. How often do you get to enjoy a five-star gourmet lunch midway along a wilderness canoe trail? Not often enough, in my book. Chatting with the Kerfoots, I learn a lot about the Gunflint Trail — the lake and the route we've just come from. They're excited to hear that a new guidebook for the river is imminent.

From Gunflint on we see no other canoeing party, nor do we see any other human animals until we get picked up a few days later off the lower Pigeon. We do see numerous bald eagles, tundra swans, nesting loons, vultures and herons. Side explorations take us to incredible waterfalls and scenic outlooks, ancient stone tent rings and awe-inspiring forests. The back-and-forth travel along the international boundary seems odd, the portages often marked with rock cairns and brass markers. One minute we're carrying our gear through the United States, the next through Ontario, with no indication except the boundary indicators and occasional sign.

Bear with me . . . literally There's a forestry road that skirts the Pigeon River on the Canadian side for about 14 km. It comes within 350 meters of the river almost directly across from the Grand Portage entrance on the American side. This would be a perfect takeout point for Path of the Paddle. Discussions with the Ontario Ministry of Natural Resources head office in Thunder Bay seemed favorable for upgrading the road. The Trans Canada Trail people began discussing an overland connection from Pigeon River Provincial Park to meet up with the Omimi Trail. This would effectively close the gap across Northwest Ontario. But none of this materialized; the OMNR waffled, talks broke down regarding who would build the land-trail connection, and the bush track remained a four-wheel-drive road. In May 2011, before all this transpired, I needed to investigate whether or not the road was worthy of discussion:

I drive my car along the lightly rutted track for about two kilometers, until it starts getting a bit sketchy. I take down my bike from the roof rack and start pedaling the rest of the 12 kilometers, hoping to find a good takeout point on the Pigeon. My bike has been a handy companion on several mapping excursions under 25 kilometers. I leave the bike at the endpoint, then drive my car to the starting point with the canoe, finish up before dark and then pedal back to my car.

I'm making good time and the road is in pretty fair shape. What's disconcerting is the piles of fresh bear scat I've being deftly maneuvering around since leaving my car. I've had plenty of bear experiences, particularly with black bears, and in most instances a bear will prefer to mind his own business, so long as you mind yours. But sometimes they are unpredictable. The one standing on his hind legs, nose in the air, blocking my way on the trail, doesn't seem to want to move along and let me through.

Alder and willow bushes hem us in, so the road is more like a one-way tunnel with nowhere else to go. I stop pedaling but don't get off my bike until he starts walking toward me. He seems to have some purpose. His head sways back and forth and the distance between us begins to shrink quickly. He has a bit of an attitude, as young male bears often do. My car is at least five kilometers away, and I know better than to try to out-pedal the bear.

I have no bear spray or "bangers" with me — I usually carry them only in polar bear or grizzly country. I do have my bike. Picking it up, I wave it over my head, yelling a war whoop as I run straight at the bear. He's so surprised that he does a backward somersault, shits himself and then runs off down the road and into the bush.

As I carry on to the end of the road and the shores of the Pigeon River, I pass four more black bears. All of them keep their distance. Word gets around, I suppose.

Route research often required many miles by mountain bike.

Granite River

THE GRAND PORTAGE
OLD US 61   4.0M   7.7K
FUR TRADE HQTS.   8.5M   13.6K

Andrea at the Trailhead of the Grand Portage.

Bluff lookout over South Fowl Lake

Bridal Falls — Gunflint Lake

Mesa formation along the Voyageur route.

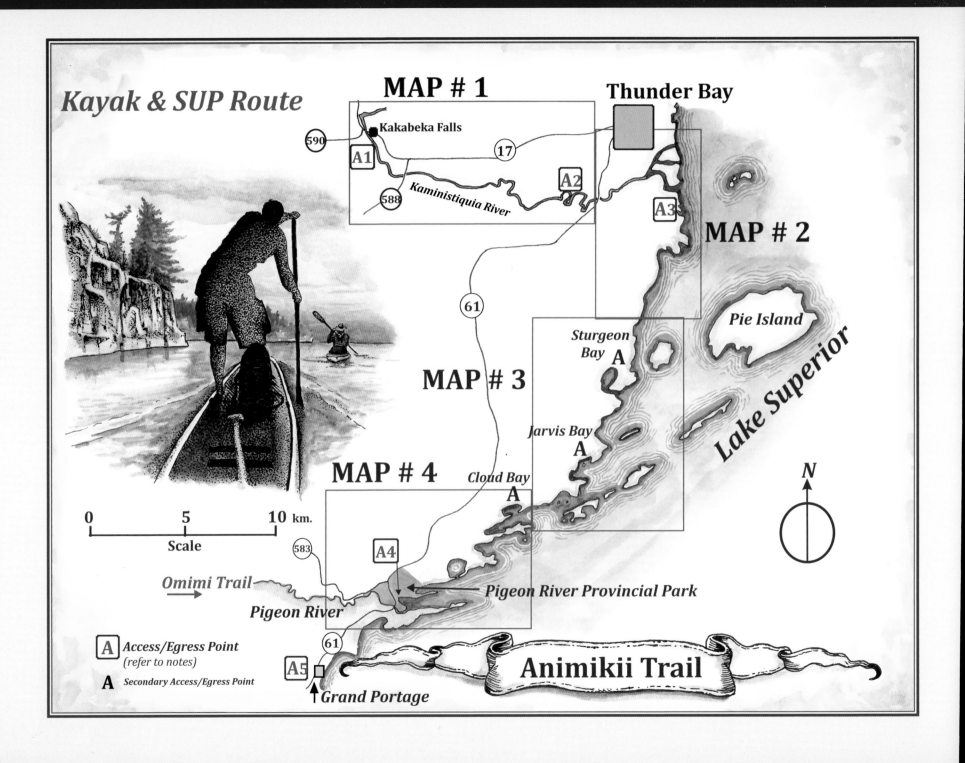

Kayak & SUP Route

MAP # 1

MAP # 2

MAP # 3

MAP # 4

Thunder Bay

590

Kakabeka Falls

A1

17

588

Kaministiquia River

A2

A3

61

Sturgeon Bay A

Pie Island

Jarvis Bay A

Lake Superior

Cloud Bay A

583

A4

Omimi Trail

Pigeon River

Pigeon River Provincial Park

61

A5

↑ *Grand Portage*

Animikii Trail

A *Access/Egress Point* (refer to notes)

A *Secondary Access/Egress Point*

0   5   10 km.
Scale

N

Chapter 10

Part 7
Animikii Trail

> **Topographic Map Locations**
> **1:100,000 scale (provincial series)**
> Thunder Bay 52-A/SW

*A*nimikii, the Thunder Bird, resides in Mount McKay, which is visible from all points in the city of Thunder Bay. Thunder Bay was aptly named by the Fort William Anishinabeg for the summer storms that roll in across *gitchigami*, the "big sea," evoking the restless spirit of Animikii.

Path of the Paddle would not be complete without a grand tour along the spectacular coast of Lake Superior. First-time paddlers will find the first few strokes out onto the uninterrupted waters of Superior rather daunting. It evokes a slightly uneasy impression, not unlike traveling over the arctic tundra for the first time, a feeling of insignificance generated by the scale of things. Stories abound — shipwrecks number in the hundreds — the water is cold (though it's warming every year because of climate change), and the coastline is austere and ancient. It's all beautiful beyond any comparison: the vastness of the crystal-clear waters seething against billion-year-old ramparts of Mother Earth, the turtle's back. Superior is just that — superior — in all ways. It's strangely gentle at times, which can be deceiving, because at other times it can be vicious, demonic.

Superior demands respect. There are places along the shore that will not harbor a boat during a strong wind, riffles turn into two-meter swells in short order, and the irregular coastline means long crossings. Play it smart and Superior will divulge its many secrets.

The Animikii Trail is divided into two very different tours: the Kaministiquia River and the Superior coast. Both are unique, rife with history and character, and both surprisingly challenging.

Kaministiquia River
Map 1

Gaa-ministigweeyaa is Ojibwe for "river with islands," referring to the two large islands, McKellar and Mission, at the mouth of the river. Known by most as "the Kam," it is, like its counterpart to the south, Pigeon River, steeped in history.

After getting turfed from the Grand Portage route west, the North West Company was hard pressed to find an alternative route on the Canadian side of the border. There really wasn't another easier route, but in 1799 Simon McTavish, chief founding partner of the NWC, approved the route up the Kam, which had been used by explorer Jacques de Noyen in 1688. The grueling "Mountain Portage" around Kakabeka Falls — made famous by the Frances Hopkins painting *Red River Expedition* — was

soon bypassed by a rough corduroy road. From there the river was fast and shallow, with several tough portages to get to the east side of what is now Quetico (French and Pickerel Lakes) and then down the Maligne River to Lac la Croix, Lake of the Woods and down the Winnipeg River to the Red River Settlement. The canoe-portage route was later modified by building of the Dawson Trail.

Kakabeka, or *gakaabikaa*, meaning "waterfall over a cliff," has been nicknamed the "Niagara of the North." It plunges 47 meters (154 feet) through an unstable, eroding gorge that contains billion-year-old fossils. Kakabeka Falls is immortalized in the Ojibwe legend of Green Mantle, which is well worth looking up on the Internet.[6]

---

6 One source is http://www.thunderbaynet.com/history.html.

Classification	intermediate
Distance	27 km (17 mi) to Old Fort William; 35 km (22 mi) to Thunder Bay city center
Duration	4 to 6 hours
Portages	Kakabeka Falls, 1,450 m (0.9 mi), 5% of total distance
Season	late April to October (variable water levels)
Preferred craft	durable canoe or kayak playboat, inflatable SUP
Campsites	Kakabeka Falls Provincial Park, Fort William Historical Park
Access	Kakabeka Falls Provincial Park
Egress	Old Fort William

Kakabeka Falls

Water Characteristics and General Hazards

- The Kakabeka Generating Station has been supplying Thunder Bay with power since 1906 with a peak output of 25 megawatts — enough to service 16,000 homes. It still operates with its original equipment; water is sluiced in from Ecarte Rapids, just upstream from the falls. As with any other generating station, water levels below the outflow can change at certain times of the day. Paddlers can easily check the conditions from several vantage points.
- The Kam is a fast, shallow, meandering river that demands tight maneuvering through many rock-garden Class I rapids.
- There is only one technical Class I–II rapid (Shaganash), which drops through a series of shallow ledges. This can be waded through in the summer or run carefully.
- Paddlers can start this trip at Stanley and bypass the long portage at the Falls.

Features

- Once you've lugged your boat or SUP over the Mountain Portage, the Kam River is just plain fun. Aside from the rapid play, the river has a rural charm all the way to Fort William — a thoroughly enjoyable cruise for an afternoon.
- Calm sections are "grazing" points for Canada geese and the occasional swan.

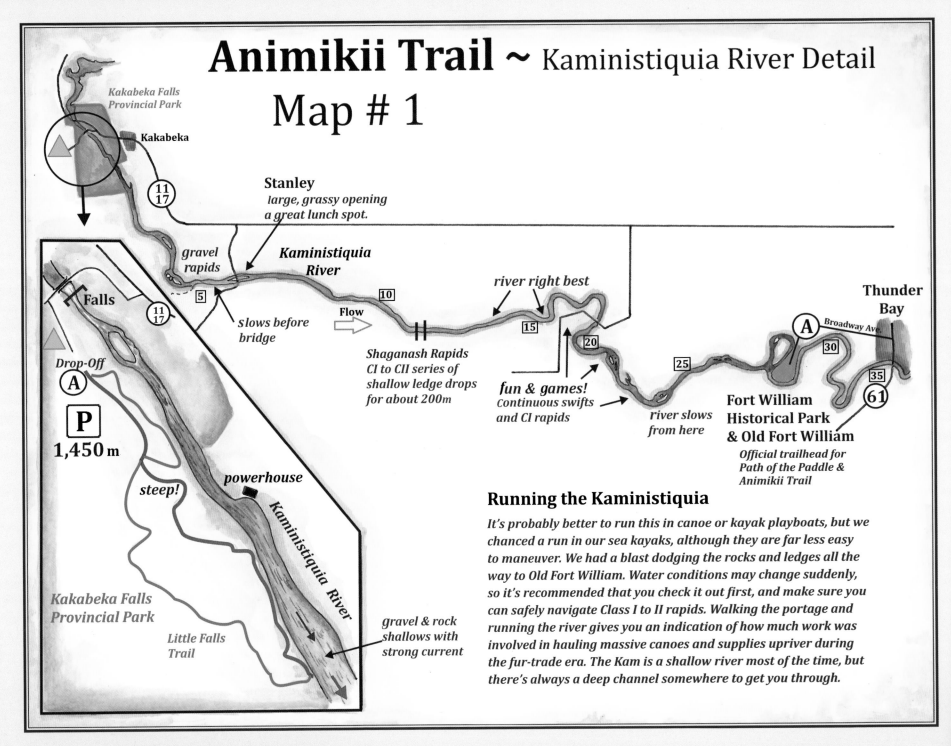

Animikii Trail ~ Kaministiquia River Detail
Map # 1

Kakabeka Falls Provincial Park

Kakabeka

11 17

Stanley
large, grassy opening a great lunch spot.

gravel rapids

Kaministiquia River

5

slows before bridge

Falls

11 17

Drop-Off

A

P

1,450 m

steep!

powerhouse

Kakabeka Falls Provincial Park

Little Falls Trail

Kaministiquia River

Flow

10

Shaganash Rapids
CI to CII series of shallow ledge drops for about 200m

river right best

15

20

fun & games!
Continuous swifts and CI rapids

river slows from here

25

gravel & rock shallows with strong current

Thunder Bay

A Broadway Ave.

30

35

61

Fort William Historical Park & Old Fort William

Official trailhead for Path of the Paddle & Animikii Trail

Running the Kaministiquia

It's probably better to run this in canoe or kayak playboats, but we chanced a run in our sea kayaks, although they are far less easy to maneuver. We had a blast dodging the rocks and ledges all the way to Old Fort William. Water conditions may change suddenly, so it's recommended that you check it out first, and make sure you can safely navigate Class I to II rapids. Walking the portage and running the river gives you an indication of how much work was involved in hauling massive canoes and supplies upriver during the fur-trade era. The Kam is a shallow river most of the time, but there's always a deep channel somewhere to get you through.

Kaministiquia River Diary

Summer 2016 Andrea, Alexa and I, with the help of a friend from T-Bay, lug our kayaks down to the bottom of Mountain Portage at Kakabeka. All we have are our touring kayaks, as we plan to head out onto Superior the next day — not the ideal craft for maneuvering through the rock gardens that lie ahead. Alexa has never paddled a kayak before, but at 16 she has proved herself a competent whitewater paddler and is just coming off a six-week canoe trip with Camp Keewaydin. There's nothing to worry about.

The Kam, as it turns out, is a lot similar to other rivers we have been on: shallow, meandering, sometimes more rock than water by late summer, but we can always find a channel to get us through. I can't help thinking about the men who plied their way upstream in their "north canoes," heavily laden with 30 or more packs — wading, lining, cursing, singing, probably thinking about their noonday dram of rum and stick of jerked venison. And here we are in our techno gear and unwieldy, out-of-place sea kayaks cruising merrily downstream, trying to digest all those Finnish pancakes we ate at the Hoito in Thunder Bay.

"It was here [Kakabeka Falls], for the first time, that we had an opportunity of witnessing what all travellers on this route had so justly admired, that light spirit with which the voyageurs perform their hard tasks. The mode which they adopt for carrying their load [of two ninety-pound pieces each] is by means of a leather strap of about three inches in width [tump-line], which they fasten round the load, leaving a loop which passes round the forehead. When all is ready, away they run, and return until there is no more to carry, never resting on the road, but rarely slackening their pace into a walk".

John Palliser
(British North American Expedition, 1857)

Lake Superior
Maps 2, 3, 4 and Pigeon River Provincial Park

Animikii Trail

There was a time when you might have called it Lake *Soup*-erior because of all the industrial effluent being dumped into the lake from a number of sources. Thunder Bay was no exception. The section of coast from the Kaministiquia outlet south to Pie and Flatland Islands has been branded an "area of concern," focusing on water-quality impacts from industrial and urban development. Over the years, industrialization, dredging, waste disposal, channelization and the release of a number of pollutants have had a deleterious effect on the quality and state of fish habitat and populations. Some improvements have been made to mitigate effluent discharge, along with the introduction of alternative industrial processes, but environmental challenges still remain.

Lake Superior is the largest freshwater lake in the world and is peopled by the Ojibwe on all sides. To the Ojibwe people historically it is the center of the world and what remains from the Great Flood. Geologically, ancient granites dominate the north shore and tectonic forces have deposited rich veins of copper, iron, gold and nickel. The hard diabase landforms were formed by injected magma, creating flat-topped mesas along the coast, atop Pie Island and, more

Rest stop along the coast.

famously, along the Sleeping Giant Peninsula, which is noticeable on the horizon as you cruise down the coast. There are more than 80 species of fish, but overfishing and environmental impacts, including climate change, have been a factor in the decline of

fish populations and their related habitat.

Not all these things are visible to the naked eye. What remains static is the water, the sky and the spectacular coast, and — not to be ignored — the ghosts of voyageurs, explorers, surveyors and provocateurs.

Classification experienced intermediate

Distance 59 km (37 mi) from Chippewa Park to Pigeon River Park; 78 km (48 mi) from Chippewa Park to Grand Portage National Monument

Duration 3 to 4 days to Pigeon River; 4 to 5 days to Grand Portage. Side excursions and wind conditions may add more time.

Portages 1 (350 m), along boardwalk at Pigeon River

Season May through October; June through September suggested because of weather, water temperatures and wind

Preferred craft touring kayak; expedition canoe with spray skirt; touring SUP

Campsites few established campsites but several cobblestone beaches

Access Chippewa Park

Egress Pigeon River Park or Grand Portage National Monument

Water Characteristics and General Hazards

- Check on weather and wind conditions. If north or east winds prevail, travel south; if south or west winds prevail, then travel north.
- Solo paddlers must be adept at self-rescue and properly outfitted with rescue gear.
- Waves tend to be ocean-type swells, which are easily handled. Once they start capping, it is time to get off the lake.
- Depending on the weather, some sections of the shoreline are not hospitable.

Features

- Extraordinary scenery.
- Crystalline water, with exceptional clarity for viewing underwater rock features.
- Opportunity to explore Pie and Flatland Islands.
- Traveling the coast of Superior gives you a feel for the environment and the conditions once experienced by the early explorers.

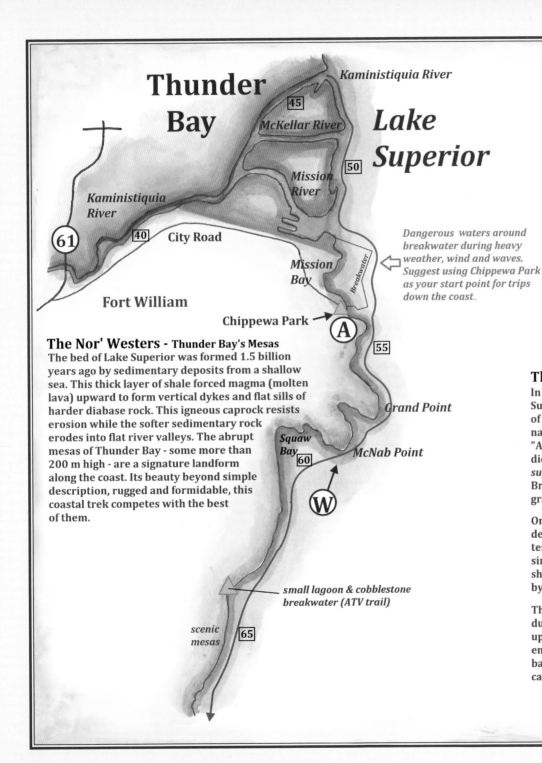

Animikii Trail
Map # 2

Thunder Bay

Kaministiquia River

45

McKellar River

Lake Superior

50

Mission River

Kaministiquia River

61 40 City Road

Breakwater

Mission Bay

Dangerous waters around breakwater during heavy weather, wind and waves. Suggest using Chippewa Park as your start point for trips down the coast.

Fort William

Chippewa Park → A

55

The Nor' Westers - Thunder Bay's Mesas
The bed of Lake Superior was formed 1.5 billion years ago by sedimentary deposits from a shallow sea. This thick layer of shale forced magma (molten lava) upward to form vertical dykes and flat sills of harder diabase rock. This igneous caprock resists erosion while the softer sedimentary rock erodes into flat river valleys. The abrupt mesas of Thunder Bay - some more than 200 m high - are a signature landform along the coast. Its beauty beyond simple description, rugged and formidable, this coastal trek competes with the best of them.

Grand Point

Squaw Bay
60

McNab Point

W

small lagoon & cobblestone breakwater (ATV trail)

scenic mesas 65

The Largest Lake in North America
In "The Song of Hiawatha" Henry Wadsworth Longfellow calls Lake Superior "Gitche Gumee." Gordon Lightfoot, in his song "The Wreck of the *Edmund Fitzgerald*," also mispronounces the lake's Ojibwe name, which is actually Anishinaabe (or Ojibwe) Gichigami - "Anishinabe's Great Sea." (Father Frederick Baraga's 1878 Ojibwe dictionary got it right.) The first French explorers called it *le lac superieur* (the upper lake), since it lies above Lake Huron. The British soon anglicized the name to Superior, because it is the grandest of all the Great Lakes.

Only Great Slave Lake is deeper than Lake Superior; the average depth is 147 m (483 ft). The water surface is slow to react to temperature change, ranging from 0 to 13 degrees C (4.5 degrees F) since 1979. Though Samuel de Champlain reported ice along the shore in June 1608, it is predicted that Lake Superior will be ice-free by 2040.

The cold waters of the lake present an increased risk of hypothermia during a capsize. Tradition has it that "Lake Superior seldom gives up her dead," an idea immortalized in Lightfoot's song. It's true enough - the unusually low water temperature inhibits the growth of bacteria that feed on a decaying corpse, producing the gases that cause it to rise to the surface.

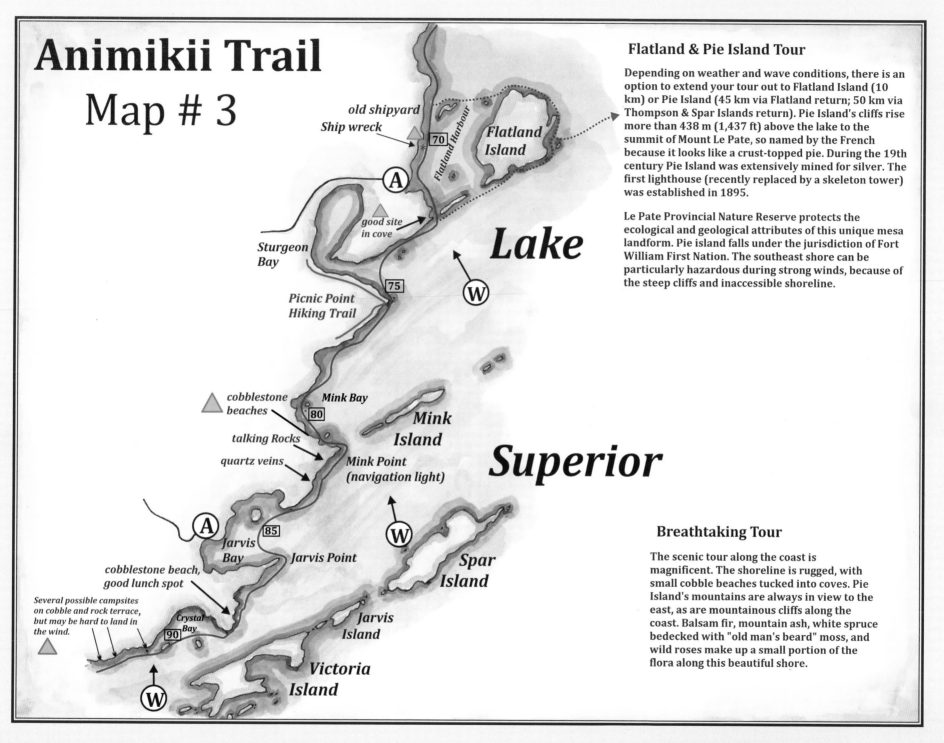

Animikii Trail
Map # 3

old shipyard
Ship wreck

Flatland Harbour

Flatland Island

Ⓐ

70

good site in cove

Sturgeon Bay

75

Ⓦ

Picnic Point Hiking Trail

Lake

Superior

cobblestone beaches

Mink Bay

80

talking Rocks

quartz veins

Mink Point (navigation light)

Mink Island

Ⓦ

Ⓐ

85

Jarvis Bay

Jarvis Point

Spar Island

Ⓦ

cobblestone beach, good lunch spot

Several possible campsites on cobble and rock terrace, but may be hard to land in the wind.

Crystal Bay

90

Jarvis Island

Victoria Island

Ⓦ

Flatland & Pie Island Tour

Depending on weather and wave conditions, there is an option to extend your tour out to Flatland Island (10 km) or Pie Island (45 km via Flatland return; 50 km via Thompson & Spar Islands return). Pie Island's cliffs rise more than 438 m (1,437 ft) above the lake to the summit of Mount Le Pate, so named by the French because it looks like a crust-topped pie. During the 19th century Pie Island was extensively mined for silver. The first lighthouse (recently replaced by a skeleton tower) was established in 1895.

Le Pate Provincial Nature Reserve protects the ecological and geological attributes of this unique mesa landform. Pie island falls under the jurisdiction of Fort William First Nation. The southeast shore can be particularly hazardous during strong winds, because of the steep cliffs and inaccessible shoreline.

Breathtaking Tour

The scenic tour along the coast is magnificent. The shoreline is rugged, with small cobble beaches tucked into coves. Pie Island's mountains are always in view to the east, as are mountainous cliffs along the coast. Balsam fir, mountain ash, white spruce bedecked with "old man's beard" moss, and wild roses make up a small portion of the flora along this beautiful shore.

Animikii Trail ~ Map # 4

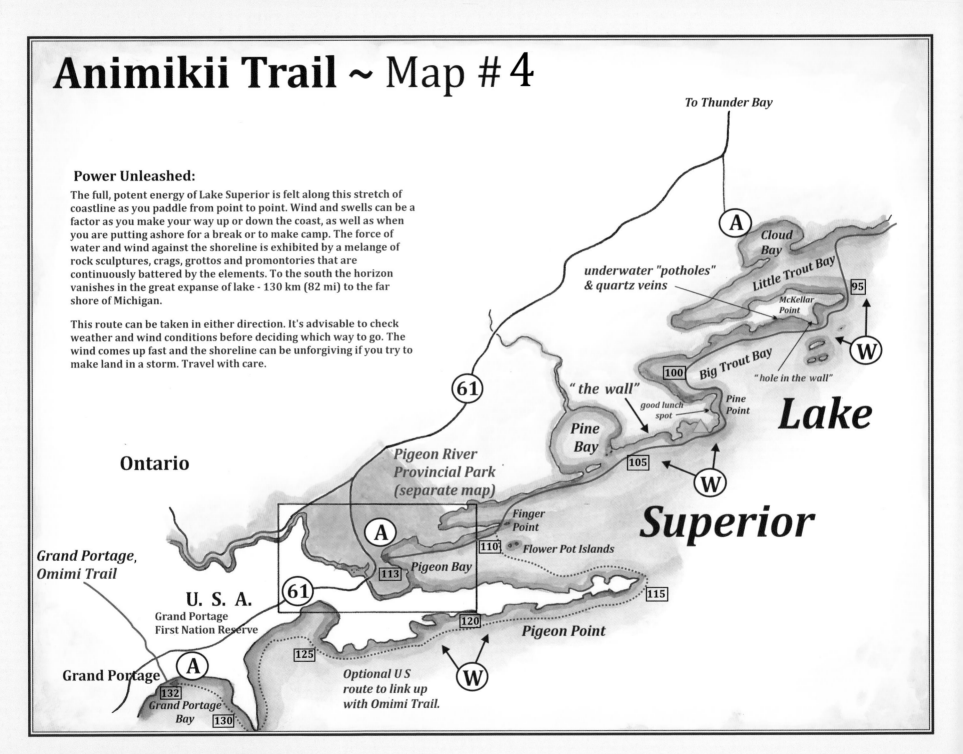

Power Unleashed:

The full, potent energy of Lake Superior is felt along this stretch of coastline as you paddle from point to point. Wind and swells can be a factor as you make your way up or down the coast, as well as when you are putting ashore for a break or to make camp. The force of water and wind against the shoreline is exhibited by a melange of rock sculptures, crags, grottos and promontories that are continuously battered by the elements. To the south the horizon vanishes in the great expanse of lake - 130 km (82 mi) to the far shore of Michigan.

This route can be taken in either direction. It's advisable to check weather and wind conditions before deciding which way to go. The wind comes up fast and the shoreline can be unforgiving if you try to make land in a storm. Travel with care.

To Thunder Bay

Cloud Bay

Little Trout Bay

underwater "potholes" & quartz veins

McKellar Point

95

100 Big Trout Bay

"the wall"

good lunch spot

Pine Point

"hole in the wall"

Lake

Pine Bay

105

Superior

Ontario

Pigeon River Provincial Park (separate map)

Finger Point

Flower Pot Islands

110

113 Pigeon Bay

115

120

Pigeon Point

Grand Portage, Omimi Trail

U. S. A.

Grand Portage First Nation Reserve

61

125

Grand Portage

A

132

Grand Portage Bay

130

Optional U S route to link up with Omimi Trail.

Pigeon River Provincial Park

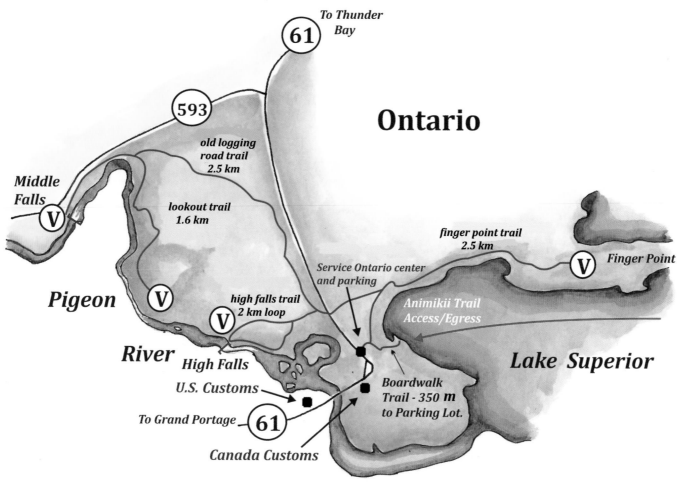

To Thunder Bay

61

593

Ontario

old logging road trail 2.5 km

Middle Falls

(V)

lookout trail 1.6 km

finger point trail 2.5 km

(V) **Finger Point**

Service Ontario center and parking

Pigeon

(V)

high falls trail 2 km loop

(V)

Animikii Trail Access/Egress

Lake Superior

River

High Falls

U.S. Customs

Boardwalk Trail - 350 m to Parking Lot.

To Grand Portage

61

Canada Customs

Minnesota (U.S.A.)

Lake Superior Diary

August last year Opportunities to paddle Lake Superior don't come very often. I've been on Superior on other occasions: along the east coast to Agawa Rock and beyond, looking for caribou in Pukaskwa, and I've spent the winter on a beach at Michipicoten. All memorable, sometimes dangerously fun experiences. I have great respect for cold water and unabashed appreciation for elements beyond my control; I manage to comfortably accept my station in the abstract realm of life.

We stop at a cove late in the afternoon, Flatland Island a tarnished steel haze in the background. A good place to camp. It isn't a campsite but has great potential, and we spend some time clearing away low branches and scrub until we have plenty of room for tents. I'm surprised that it hasn't been developed already, as the cove and the beach — not cobbles but sand, which makes it more suitable for landing — is a fine place to stop before heading south around the point if there's a strong wind blowing.

But something tells me that this was a choice campsite sometime in the past. Curious always (it's in my nature), I scuff along the shore at the back of the beach, where the turf is flat, hoping to find some clues. There it is: an old firepit on a raised shelf tucked behind the ridge, a perfect spot for a fire while camped up behind the beach. The firepit rocks are crusted with lichen, shrubs poking their way through the old ash. There's a story here, maybe several.

A strong south gale would force the canots du maître to pull into this cove. Here they would camp until before dawn, when they would strike out again, headed for the post at Grand Portage. Maybe Archibald McDonald stopped here, bound for Red River to fill his new post as deputy governor. He was fond of the rabaska, or canot du maître: "I never heard of such a canoe wrecked, or upset, or swamped . . . they swam like ducks." I can picture three or four rabaskas tipped over on their sides along the beach, men splayed out underneath, smoking pipes, mending clothing, nursing their allowance of rum, a greasy black pot perched over this very firepit I crouch beside. That would have been two hundred years ago.

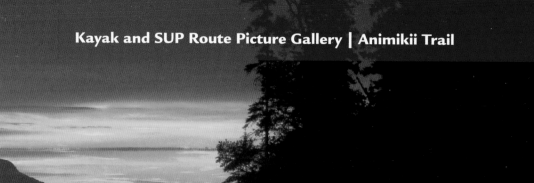

Sunrise over Flatland Island, Lake Superior.

Shipwreck in Flatland Harbour.

Afterword

If you were going to define Canada, historically and geographically, using only one place across the country, it would be *le petit nord* — the Path of the Paddle heartland. Tectonic forces billions of years ago kicked off a sequence of events that carried on through the millennia, building mountains, carving valleys, the rugged land eventually scoured and scraped by massive ice sheets, worn down by time. The narration here is anything but boring, the landscape anything but lackluster.

The human history is one of brutal territorial and environmental conflicts, greed and the drive for prosperity. Success was rooted in the colonial idea that Canada was an endless cornucopia of resources, be they furs, gold and other minerals, forests or even water. They were all usurped with little regard for aboriginal culture, ecological propriety or responsible management. Traders cheated the First Nations, beavers were trapped almost into extinction, forests were clearcut, mercury and other contaminants were dumped into the rivers and lakes, and mining left the land littered with refuse from camps and abandoned operations. The city of Winnipeg continues to draw its clean water from under the noses of the Shoal Lake First Nations, who are obliged to import bottled water. The Whitedog and Grassy Narrows reserves are still trying to deal with the aftereffects of mercury poisoning.

To sugar-coat the historical events and to ignore the atrocities inflicted on human populations and natural resources would, in my opinion, omit a large part of the Canadian story. The fur trade was fierce, the lifestyle raw and dangerous; it was attractive to young recruits in the same way that young men clamor for military action today. Explorers, surveyors and prospectors braved extreme weather, isolation and bitter rivals. They opened the door for the corporations that took what they wanted, at a time in Canadian history when there was no such thing as an environmental assessment, transparency or sustainable resource management.

Luckily, things are changing, slowly but in a positive direction. Corporations are now more accountable; a good example is the 10-megawatt generating station at Valerie Falls, outside Atikokan, built in 1994. Once operated with coal, in 2012 it became North America's first 100% biomass-fueled power plant, generating renewable power. Economic development initiatives now include the protection of green spaces, trails and water resources.

Seven years ago I had never paddled any of these routes. The closest I came was a mapping project in Woodland Caribou Provincial Park, north of Kenora, when I was working on my Manitoba guidebook. Now, after numerous mapping excursions and research expeditions, I can make an informed comparison between *le petit nord* and other wild places I have been. The undeveloped nature and wildness of the Path of the Paddle corridor was surprising, particularly along the international border, the Omimi Trail and the Voyageur Route. The scenery was breathtaking, the geology fascinating, the human history captivating. Each route played out a different story; each river and lake was an opportunity to explore, connect and revitalize. Truly this is the very heart of this country.

Hap Wilson
— Rosseau, December 2016

Resources

Manitoba
Whiteshell Provincial Park, Falcon Lake
District
(204) 349-2201
http://www.gov.mb.ca/sd/parks/popular_
parks/eastern/whiteshell_info.html

Path of the Paddle trailhead
accommodation:
Jessica Lake Lodge, Rennie, MB
1-866-635-9555

Royal Canadian Mounted Police, Falcon
Lake detachment
(204) 349-2588

Ontario
Shoal Lake 40 First Nation
Shoal Lake, ON
(807) 733-2315

Dryden area canoe routes (with GPS
coordinates):
Garth Gillis, Canoehead Canoe Routes
https://www.etsy.com/ca/shop/
CanoeHeadCanoeRoutes

Ontario Ministry of Natural Resources,
Dryden District Office
(807) 227-2601

Quetico Provincial Park
(807) 597-4602
Trip planning information: (807) 597-2735
www.ontarioparks.com/english/quet

Friends of Quetico
PO Box 29127
Thunder Bay, ON P7B 6B9

John B. Ridley Research Library
Quetico Park
(807) 929-2571, ext. 224

Kenora Tourism
1-800-535-4549
www.tourism@kenora.ca

Pigeon River Provincial Park (includes
Kakabeka and La Verendrye Parks)
Kakabeka Falls, ON P0T 1W0
(807) 473-9231

Ontario travel information:
Service Ontario, Pigeon River
(May–October)
(807) 964-2094

Turtle River–White Otter Lake Provincial Park
Ontario Ministry of Natural Resources,
Ignace Area Office
PO Box 448, Ignace, ON P0T 1T0
(807) 934-2233

Friends of White Otter Castle
PO Box 2096
Atikokan, ON P0T 1C0

Archeological and White Otter Castle
information:
Dennis Smyk
PO Box 989
Ignace, ON P0T 1T0

United States
Superior National Forest
8901 Grand Avenue Place
Duluth, MN 55808
(218) 626-4300
www.fs.fed.us/r9/forests/superior/

Boundary Waters Canoe Area Wilderness
Reservation Center
PO Box 462
Ballston Spa, NY 12020
Toll-free: 1-877-550-6777
International: (518) 885-9964
www.bwca.com

Suggested Reading

Morse, Eric W. *Fur Trade Canoe Routes of Canada, Then and Now*, 2nd ed. (Ottawa: Parks Canada, 1979).

Nelson, Lori J. *The Explorers' Guide to Lake of the Woods* (Kenora: Lake of the Woods Museum, 2000).

Ray, Arthur J. *Indians in the Fur Trade: Their Role as Trappers, Hunters and Middlemen in the Lands Southwest of Hudson Bay, 1660–1870* (Toronto: University of Toronto Press, 1974).

Robertson, Heather, and Melinda McCracken. *Magical, Mysterious Lake of the Woods* (Winnipeg: Heartland Publishing, 2003).

Acknowledgments

A book of this nature cannot be written without the assistance of other individuals. I thank my editors, Gillian Watts, Michael Worek and designer, Hartley Millson, for their faith in my work and for having patience when I drifted past several deadlines. I thank the Trans Canada Trail organization for its support during the first two years, which allowed me to carry out the initial trail reconnaissance.

Thanks also to these individuals: Garth Gillis, the canoe guru from Dryden, the go-to guy for local knowledge; Dennis Smyk, historian and archeologist; Nicole Kennedy-Orr for the donated bottle of wine at White Otter Castle; shuttle drivers Paul Cordes, Calla Sampson and John Darahy and the taxi driver from Atikokan; Cuyler Cotton for his sage advice. There are certainly others whose names I have forgotten, whose help was much appreciated at spontaneous moments — hitchhiking with full gear, for example, and getting picked up in the pouring rain. And thanks to the many people I chanced to talk with along this journey who graciously enlightened me and shared their stories so willingly.

Most of all I wish to thank my family. To my son, Chris, and daughter, Alexa, thank you for joining me on this journey. I do apologize for dragging you through some terrible conditions, which you faced undaunted and with stoicism and perhaps emerged stronger for your efforts. And to the love of my life, my wife, Andrea, who can look beautiful despite the sun blisters, muskeg-impregnated clothing, bug bites, sweat and sometimes tears. Love really does endure all things.

Index